Teacher's 2

CCC Collaborative Literacy

Being a Reader™

GRADE
2

Center for the
Collaborative
Classroom™

First edition published 2016.

Being a Reader, CCC Collaborative Literacy, CCC ClassView, and CCC Handwriting are trademarks of Center for the Collaborative Classroom.

Developmental Reading Assessment (DRA) is a registered trademark and is copyrighted by Pearson Education, Inc. All rights reserved. *Fountas & Pinnell Benchmark Assessment System* is copyright © Irene C. Fountas & Gay Su Pinnell and Heinemann. All rights reserved. *Fountas & Pinnell Text Level Gradient* is a trademark and is copyrighted by Irene C. Fountas & Gay Su Pinnell and Heinemann. All rights reserved. *Lexile Framework for Reading* is a registered trademark and is copyrighted by MetaMetrics, Inc. All rights reserved. *Running Records Assessments* are copyright © Teachers College Reading and Writing Project. All rights reserved.

Front cover illustration by Jing Jing Tsong, copyright © Center for the Collaborative Classroom
Cover background illustration by Michael Wertz, copyright © Center for the Collaborative Classroom

Center for the Collaborative Classroom
1250 53rd Street, Suite 3
Emeryville, CA 94608-2965
(800) 666-7270; fax: (510) 464-3670
collaborativeclassroom.org

ISBN 978-1-61003-813-3

Printed in the United States of America

1 2 3 4 5 6 7 8 9 10 RRD 24 23 22 21 20 19 18 17 16 15

CONTENTS

(continues)

CONTENTS *(continued)*

Appendices

Week 13 OVERVIEW

Whole-class Instruction

Word Study

This week the students learn about consonant-*l-e* syllables. They read and sort words by syllable as a class. In spelling, the students use the independent spelling practice procedure during Independent Work in preparation for an optional spelling memory test later in the week.

Independent Work Check-in

This week we suggest you teach the "Conferring" check-in lesson in Appendix B, "Independent Work Resources." Depending on the needs of your students, you may decide to teach a different check-in lesson.

Small-group Reading Instruction and Independent Work Rotations

Small-group Reading

This week you will continue to teach Small-group Reading lessons at the small-group reading table while the students work independently in the reading, writing, and word work areas.

Independent Work

The students may have assigned work from Small-group Reading to do during Independent Work. The following are materials you might incorporate into independent work areas this week:

Word Work:

- "Week 12, Day 2 Sort" (see "Independent Work Connection" on page 286)

Week 13

RESOURCES

Extension
- "Connect Spelling to Writing"

Assessment Resource Book
- Week 13 assessment

Word Study Notebook
- Word Sorts
- Spelling Practice

 ## Online Resources

Visit the CCC Learning Hub (ccclearninghub.org) to find your online resources for this week.

Whiteboard Activities
- WA1–WA3

Assessment Form
- "Class Assessment Record" sheet (CA1)

Reproducible
- "Week 13, Day 3 Sort" (BLM1)

⏱ DO AHEAD

Word Study

✓ Prior to Day 1, familiarize yourself with the Day 1 Spelling Words.

✓ Prior to Day 2, familiarize yourself with the Day 2 Practice Words.

✓ Prior to Day 3, familiarize yourself with the Day 3 Sort Words.

✓ Prior to Day 3, visit the CCC Learning Hub (ccclearninghub.org) to access and print "Week 13, Day 3 Sort" (BLM1). Make several copies to place in the word work area before the lesson.

✓ Prior to Day 4, visit the CCC Learning Hub (ccclearninghub.org) to access and print the "Class Assessment Record" sheet (CA1); see page 87 of the *Assessment Resource Book*.

Independent Work Check-in

✓ Familiarize yourself with the "Conferring" check-in lesson (or another check-in lesson of your choice) in Appendix B, "Independent Work Resources." Collect and prepare any necessary materials. For more information about the check-in lessons, see Appendix B, "Independent Work Resources."

📅 SUGGESTED WEEKLY SCHEDULE

Monday	Tuesday	Wednesday	Thursday	Friday
Word Study (20)	Word Study (20)		Word Study (20)	Word Study (20)
Independent Work Rotations/Small-group Reading (60)	Independent Work Rotations/Small-group Reading (60)	Independent Work Check-in (35)	Independent Work Rotations/Small-group Reading (60)	Independent Work Rotations/Small-group Reading (60)
80 minutes	80 minutes	35 minutes	80 minutes	80 minutes

Day 1 Spelling Words		Day 2 Practice Words		Day 3 Sort Words	
beach	sand	bubble	pebble	apple	rumble
earth	sea	bundle	rattle	bubble	settle
hill	stream	eagle	saddle	dribble	simple
lake	water	handle	simple	handle	struggle
		little	stumble	marble	stumble
		marble	tumble	mumble	tremble
		needle	turtle	rattle	turtle
				riddle	wiggle

Academic Focus

- Students learn consonant-*l*-*e* syllables.
- Students read words with the consonant-*l*-*e* spelling and sort them.
- Students learn the procedure for spelling tests.

Social Development Focus

- Students follow classroom procedures.
- Students work in a responsible way.
- Students listen respectfully to the thinking of others and share their own.

Day 1 Word Study
Guided Spelling

Materials

- Class set of wipe-off boards, dry-erase markers, and tissues or cloth
- Posted "Spelling Practice Steps" chart from Week 12
- *Word Study Notebook* page 52 (in student toolboxes)
- Pencils

In this lesson, the students:

- Spell words from the Week 12 sort
- Take responsibility for their learning

ABOUT SPELLING TESTS

Beginning in this week, the lessons that make up the Word Study week are sequenced differently than earlier lessons to accommodate a spelling test on Day 4. The spelling words, which are selected from the previous week's sort, are introduced on Day 1. Then the students practice the words in independent word work during the week. The students will have repeated exposure to the words over two weeks, in the previous week's sort and again in the Day 1 spelling list, before they encounter the words on the spelling test. Having multiple opportunities to work with a set of words is more effective than memorizing a list of words during a single week.

Memorizing words for spelling tests does not automatically transfer to student writing. Over many repetitions, Guided Spelling alerts students to both regular and irregular spellings. Understanding the ways sounds can be spelled allows students to make more appropriate choices in their independent writing.

1 Get Ready to Spell

Have the students pick up their independent work toolboxes and return to their seats. Ask them to put their toolboxes on the floor next to their chairs. Review that in Guided Spelling, you will help the students use what they know about words to help them spell some of the words from last week's sort. Remind the students that practicing spelling with words from the sort will help them spell words when they are writing on their own.

Review that last week the students sorted words into alphabetical order. The words they sorted have many of the different vowel spellings they have learned. Tell the students that when they spell the words this week, they will have to think carefully about which vowel spelling to use for some words.

2 Guide the Students' Spelling

Distribute the wipe-off boards, markers, and tissues or cloths. Review that in Guided Spelling, you will say a word, use it in a sentence, and ask questions to help the students think about how to spell the word.

> beach   "The beach can be a nice place to visit in the summer."

Say *beach*. Use *beach* in a sentence. Have the students say *beach*. Then ask:

Q *What vowel sound do you hear in* beach? *(/ē/)*

Q *What is the name of that sound? (long e)*

Q *Are there different ways to spell the long e sound? (yes)*

Tell the students that in *beach*, long e is spelled *e-a*. Also explain that the sound /ch/ after a long vowel sound is usually spelled *c-h*. In the word *beach*, /ch/ is spelled *c-h*. Have the students write *beach*.

Write *beach* where everyone can see it, and have the students check their writing and erase and correct mistakes.

> water   "The water from the drinking fountain is cold."

Say *water*. Use *water* in a sentence. Have the students say *water*.

Tell the students that *water* is a high-frequency word. Remind the students that high-frequency words are words that are challenging to spell and that appear often in their reading. If *water* is not displayed on the word wall, you may wish to write it for the students.

Have the students write *water*.

Write *water* where everyone can see it, and have the students check their writing and erase and correct mistakes.

| lake | "Ducks live on the lake in the park." |

Say *lake*. Use *lake* in a sentence. Have the students say *lake*. Then ask:

Q *What vowel sound do you hear in* lake? *(long* a)

Q *Is there more than one way to spell the long* a *sound? (yes)*

Tell the students that *lake* uses the final *e* spelling for the long *a* sound and that the sound /k/ is spelled *k*.

Have the students write *lake*. When most students are finished, call for their attention. Write *lake* where everyone can see it, and have the students check their writing and erase and correct mistakes.

| sea | "Some boats sail on the sea." |

Say *sea*. Use *sea* in a sentence. Have the students say *sea*.

Point out that *sea* is a *homophone*—a word that sounds the same as another word but has a different spelling and meaning.

> **You might say:**
>
> "Two words sound the same: *see* as in 'the color I see' and *sea* as in 'the salty sea.' I know that these words are spelled differently, and the sentence tells me that I want to spell *sea* as in 'ocean.' I know that what I do with my eyes is spelled *s-e-e*. So *sea* meaning 'ocean' must be spelled *s-e-a*. When you hear a homophone, you have to figure out the meaning from the sentence and then decide which spelling to use."

Have the students write *sea*. When most students are finished, call for their attention.

Write *sea* where everyone can see it, and have the students check their writing and erase and correct mistakes.

Repeat the procedure for the words *stream, sand, earth,* and *hill*.

stream	"A stream is a small river."
sand	"There is a sandbox in the playground."
earth	"The earth in the garden is good for growing plants."
hill	"A hill is much smaller than a mountain."

3 Review Spelling Steps

Direct the students' attention to the "Spelling Practice Steps" chart. Review that last week the students learned and practiced these steps. Explain that the students will review the steps and then use the steps to practice the spelling words the first time they go to independent word work this week.

Point to, read, and remind the students of each step.

> ## Spelling Practice Steps
>
> 1. Look at the word, say it, and spell it.
>
> 2. Cover the word, say it, and spell it.
>
> 3. Uncover and check.
>
> 4. Cover the word and write it.
>
> 5. Uncover, check, and correct.
>
> If you get stuck, go back to Step 1 and start again.

Have the students take their *Word Study Notebooks* from their independent work toolboxes, and turn to page 50. Point out that these are the same spelling steps from the chart. Then have the students read the spelling practice words on page 52.

4 Discuss Independent Spelling Practice

Tell the students that they will have a spelling test on Friday (or whichever day this week you will teach the Day 4 lesson). On that day you will read the words and they will spell them from memory. It is important for them to practice during the week so that they remember how to spell the words. Ask:

Q *How will you make sure you do the spelling work this week?*

> **Students might say:**
>
> "I will do it first thing when I go to independent work."
>
> "I will put a sticky note in my *Word Study Notebook* to remind me."

Tell the students that you will check in with them to see how their independent spelling practice is going.

Teacher Note

You may wish to post the *Word Study Notebook* page number for this week's spelling practice in the word work area for the students to refer to during Independent Work.

Word Study
Introduce Consonant-*l*-e

Materials

- "Week 13, Day 2 Words" (WA1)

Teacher Note

This week the students are guided to read consonant-*l*-e words one syllable at a time. This will help them recognize and read consonant-*l*-e syllables quickly and automatically in unfamiliar words.

Teacher Note

If necessary, model by saying the word *copycat* and then repeating the word as you clap on each syllable: *cop-y-cat.*

In this lesson, the students:

- Read words with consonant-*l*-e syllables
- Take responsibility for their learning

1 Gather and Review Independent Work

Gather the class with partners sitting together, facing you. Review that the students did Guided Spelling yesterday and that they will practice spelling the words during the week. Ask:

Q *If you have already practiced your spelling during independent word work, how did it go?*

Have a few volunteers share. Ask and briefly discuss:

Q *If you have not done your spelling practice, how will you make sure you do it the next time you go to independent word work?*

2 Review Syllables

Review that the students have been learning strategies that will help them read and spell longer words. Remind the students that some words have more than one *syllable*, or part.

Tell the students that you will say a word and they will clap on and say each syllable. Have the students say and clap on the syllables using the following words: *underneath, bright, freeze, shower, traded, buzzing, flowerpot,* and *cube.*

Have the students say *cartoon.* Then ask:

Q *How many syllables do you hear in* cartoon? *(two)*

Write *cartoon* where everyone can see it, and draw a dot between *car* and *toon,* just below the word. Tell the students that the dot helps them see the syllables in the word. Have them read the syllables and then read the word.

Repeat this procedure for the words *landed* (land.ed), *jumping* (jump.ing), and *pencil* (pen.cil).

Tell the students that noticing the syllables in words can help them read and spell longer words.

3 | Introduce Consonant-*l*-e Syllables

Tell the students that today they will read words with more than one syllable. Have them clap on and say the syllables in the following words: *candle*, *middle*, and *puddle*.

 Q *What sounds the same in all the words you just heard? Turn to your partner.*

After a few moments, signal for the students' attention and have a few volunteers share their thinking with the class. If necessary, point out that all the words end with /dəl/.

Write the words *candle*, *middle*, and *puddle* where everyone can see them, draw a dot before the *dle* in each word, and explain that in these words, /dəl/ is spelled *d-l-e*. Explain that *-dle* is a consonant-*l*-e syllable. The first letter is the consonant *d* and the next two letters are *l-e*. Have the students read *candle*, first by syllables and then as a whole word.

Point to the words *middle* and *puddle*. Explain that when there is a double consonant in a word (as in *middle*), the students only say the consonant sound once when they read the whole word.

Explain that there are other consonant-*l*-e syllables. Write *tumble* and *pebble* where everyone can see them. Draw a dot before *ble* in each word and point out that in these words the consonant-*l*-e syllable is *-ble*. The first letter is the consonant *b* and the next two letters are *l-e*.

Use the same procedure for words ending with *-gle*, *-ple*, and *-tle*, using the following words: *giggle*, *jungle*, *apple*, *purple*, *bottle*, and *gentle*.

Tell the students that it is helpful to recognize consonant-*l*-e syllables because they will see many words ending with consonant-*l*-e syllables in their reading.

4 | Discuss a Word-reading Strategy

Tell the students that words ending with consonant-*l*-e syllables can be challenging to read, and that noticing the consonant-*l*-e syllable at the end of a word can help readers see the first syllable and read the whole word.

Explain that you will show a word. The students will name the consonant-*l*-e syllable, read each syllable, and then read the whole word.

Display the "Week 13, Day 2 Words" activity (◗ WA1). Point to the first word, *turtle*. Ask the students to name the consonant-*l*-e syllable at the end of the word. Ask:

Q *Which consonant-l-e syllable is at the end of the word? (/təl/)*

Draw a dot before the consonant-*l-e* syllable, and have the students read each syllable before reading the whole word.

Repeat this procedure for the remaining words on the "Week 13, Day 2 Words" activity (WA1).

Suggested Vocabulary

bundle: group of things that are held or tied together, such as sticks

stumble: trip

tumble: fall down

🌐 ELL Vocabulary

English Language Learners may benefit from hearing additional vocabulary defined, including:

eagle: large bird

needle: small, thin, sharp metal tool used with thread to sew cloth

saddle: seat put on a horse for a rider to sit on

marble: small ball of glass that is used to play games

rattle: make sounds by shaking

WA1

turtle	pebble	needle	saddle
bundle	simple	bubble	marble
little	stumble	handle	rattle
eagle	tumble		

5 Reflect on Reading

Ask and briefly discuss:

Q *How does noticing the syllables in words help you with your reading?*

> **Students might say:**
>
> "It helps me sound out words faster."
>
> "It helps me read longer words."

Word Study
Whole-class Sort (Closed)

In this lesson, the students:

- Read and sort words with consonant-*l-e*
- Listen respectfully to the thinking of others and share their own
- Handle materials responsibly

1 Gather and Get Ready to Sort

Gather the class with partners sitting together, facing you. Review that in the last lesson the students read words with consonant-*l-e* syllables at the end. Explain that in this lesson, students will read words with consonant-*l-e* syllables at the end and sort them into categories.

2 Read the Sort Words

Display the "Week 13, Day 3 Sort" activity (WA2) and have the students read the words together as a class.

dribble	settle	apple	mumble
marble	turtle	handle	rattle
simple	rumble	struggle	wiggle
riddle	tremble	bubble	stumble

🌐 ELL Vocabulary

English Language Learners may benefit from hearing the following vocabulary defined:

dribble: fall in small drops

riddle: question with a funny answer

rumble: make a low, deep sound

tremble: shake

struggle: have a hard time doing something

mumble: speak so softly it is hard for others to hear the words

rattle: make sounds by shaking

3 Review Consonant-*l-e* Syllables

Use "Think, Pair, Share" to discuss:

Q *What do you remember about consonant-*l-e* syllables?* [pause] *Turn to your partner.*

Materials

- "Week 13, Day 3 Sort" (WA2)
- Copies of "Week 13, Day 3 Sort" (BLM1) in the word work area

Teacher Note

Check with the students to see whether they have completed their spelling work. Ask:

Q *If you haven't done the spelling practice, how will you make sure you complete it before the spelling test?*

After a few moments, signal for the students' attention and have a few pairs share their thinking with the class.

> **Students might say:**
>
> "They all end in *l-e*."
>
> "Consonant-*l-e* is one syllable."
>
> "Consonant-*l-e* is at the ends of words."

Remind the students that noticing the consonant-*l-e* syllable at the end of a word can help readers see the first syllable and read the whole word.

4 Introduce the Sort

Explain that the class will now sort the words by reading the words and listening for the consonant-*l-e* syllables.

Direct the students' attention to the "Week 13, Day 3 Sort" activity (WA2). Create categories by writing the following syllables as headings on the chart: *ble, dle, gle, ple,* and *tle.* Have the students read the syllables aloud.

5 Sort by Consonant-*l*-e Syllable

Point to the word *dribble* on the "Week 13, Day 3 Sort" activity (WA2). Draw a dot before the consonant-*l-e* syllable, just below the word (*drib.ble*), and have the students read each syllable and then read the word. Repeat the procedure with the remaining words.

Click the reset icon on the CCC toolbar to clear the dots from the "Week 13, Day 3 Sort" activity (WA2). Point to *dribble.* Ask:

Q *What syllable do you hear at the end of* dribble? *(ble)*

Drag and drop the word under the appropriate category heading. Repeat this procedure with the remaining words. Then have the students read the sorted words under each heading.

WA2

ble	dle	gle	ple	tle
dribble	riddle	struggle	simple	settle
marble	handle	wiggle	apple	turtle
rumble				rattle
tremble				
bubble				
mumble				
stumble				

Teacher Note

If the students need additional support reading the words, consider framing the word parts as the students read them.

Tell the students that you have put copies of the sort in the "Word Sorts" bin in the word work area. When they go to independent word work, they will sort the words again and record their sorts in their *Word Study Notebooks*. Point out that they need five columns for the sort, so they will have to use two facing pages in their notebooks.

6 Reflect on Reading

Encourage the students to notice words with consonant-*l-e* syllables in their reading.

Use "Think, Pair, Share" to discuss:

 Q *How does noticing the parts of longer words help you read the words?* [pause] *Turn to your partner.*

After a few moments, signal for the students' attention and have a few pairs share their thinking with the class. Tell the students that in the coming weeks, they will use what they know about syllables to help them read much longer words.

Teacher Note

Consider telling the students that they can do the sort in pairs if they wish. Ask and briefly discuss:

Q *How will you find someone to do the sort with if you want to work with a partner?*

Q *What can you say if someone asks you to be his or her partner and you do not want to do the sort at that time?*

In this lesson, the students:

- Learn the procedure for a spelling test
- Learn the purpose for spelling tests
- Take a spelling test
- Handle materials responsibly

1 Get Ready to Spell

Have the students stay in their seats today. Review that earlier this week, you guided the students as they wrote the spelling words. You asked them questions to help them spell the words correctly, and they thought carefully as they wrote the words. Review that the students also used the spelling practice steps during independent work time to help them remember the words. Ask and briefly discuss:

Q *How did you do with independent spelling practice this week?*

Materials

- Lined paper and a pencil for each student
- "Week 13, Day 4 Spelling Words" (WA3)
- "Class Assessment Record" sheet (CA1)

2 Discuss Spelling Tests

Explain that each week, after Guided Spelling and independent spelling practice, the students will write the spelling words from memory. Explain that when writers spell a word from memory, they use everything they know about the word to help them spell it correctly.

Tell the students that if they are not sure how to spell part of a word or are not sure they spelled a word correctly, they can ask themselves questions like the ones you ask during Guided Spelling. Explain that asking themselves questions will help them remember what they know about the word. Ask and briefly discuss:

Q *What questions can you ask yourself if you are not sure how to spell part of a word?*

Q *What questions can you ask yourself once you finish writing a word?*

> **Students might say:**
>
> "I can ask myself if there's more than one way to spell that part."
>
> "I can ask myself which way to spell the vowel sound."
>
> "Do I need to double the consonant?"
>
> "Does it look right?"

3 Introduce the Procedure for Spelling Tests

Distribute the paper and pencils to the students. Have them write their names at the top and number the first eight lines 1 to 8.

Explain the procedure for writing and checking the spelling words, using one of the words as an example.

> **You might say:**
>
> "The first spelling word is *beach*. I will say 'Number one: beach.' Then I will use the word *beach* in a sentence. I might say 'The waves crashed on the beach.' I'll say 'beach' again. Then you will write *beach* next to the number one on your paper. I will give you a minute or two to write before I tell you the next word. Remember to think carefully as you write the word. After you have written all eight words, I will display the words and you will check and correct your work."

Ask and briefly discuss:

Q *What questions do you have about the spelling test?*

4 Spelling Test

Begin the spelling test. Say "Number one: beach." Use *beach* in a sentence. Say *beach* again. Have the students write *beach*. Allow enough time for all the students to finish before moving on to the next word.

Repeat this procedure for the remaining spelling words.

1. beach   "The waves crashed on the beach."

2. water   "Fish live in the water."

3. lake   "Many fish live in the lake."

4. sea   "The ship sailed across the sea."

5. stream   "A small stream flows down the mountain."

6. sand   "Some kids love to play in the sand."

7. earth   "We dig in the earth to plant a garden."

8. hill   "It can be fun to roll down a hill."

5 Check and Correct the Words

After the students are finished writing the last word, display the "Week 13, Day 4 Spelling Words" activity (WA3). Explain that the students will check their work by looking at each word they wrote and comparing it to the corresponding word in the word list.

> **You might say:**
>
> "When it's time to check your spelling words, start by looking at word number one on the board. On this list, word number one is *beach*. Find number one on your paper and check to see if you spelled *beach* the same way it's spelled on the board. If you made a mistake, cross out *beach* on your paper and write the correct spelling of *beach* next to it. Check each word the same way."

Have the students check their work and correct mistakes. As they work, circulate and observe. Support struggling students by reminding them to look at each word on the board and ask themselves if they spelled the word the same way. When the students are finished checking and correcting their work, collect the papers.

Explain that spelling familiar words—using everything they know about words to spell the words correctly—helps writers know what to do when they spell words they have not written before.

 CLASS ASSESSMENT NOTE

Ask yourself:

- Do the students use the correct vowel spellings?

- Do the students omit letters?

- Are the students able to spell most words correctly?

Record your observations on the "Class Assessment Record" sheet (CA1); see page 87 of the *Assessment Resource Book.*

6 Reflect on Spelling

Have the students reflect on the spelling test. Ask and briefly discuss:

Q *How did you do with remembering how to spell the words?*

Q *How did the spelling practice during Independent Work help you on the test?*

Tell the students they will have more opportunities to practice spelling in the coming weeks.

EXTENSION

Connect Spelling to Writing

Review that one reason writers spell words correctly is to make sure readers can understand and enjoy their writing. Tell the students that after some spelling tests, you will ask them to think about how they might use the spelling words in their writing. Think aloud about how one of the words reminds you of something that happened to you.

> **You might say:**
>
> "When I read the word *sand*, it reminds me of the day we saw the movie about the desert. I had no idea that animals lived in a place that is so hot and dry. I could write about that."

Ask and discuss:

Q *Which of these words reminds you of something that happened to you? What is a story you could write about that? Turn to your partner.*

After a few moments, signal for the students' attention and have a few volunteers share their thinking with the class. Encourage the students to use the spelling words and other words from the week's sort in their writing.

Independent Work Connection

For next week's Independent Work, we suggest the following:

- If you have not done so already, place copies of "Week 13, Day 3 Sort" (BLM1) in the word work area.

Independent Work  OVERVIEW

This week the students continue to rotate to and work in all three independent work areas around the room while you teach Small-group Reading. We suggest continuing any procedures that have worked effectively in previous weeks.

Independent Work Check-in

This week you will continue to teach an Independent Work Check-in lesson on the day of the week you do not teach Small-group Reading. The purpose of these check-in lessons is to ensure that the students are able to maintain successful independent work rotations. The lessons provide the time for you to assess your students, conduct conferences, and introduce new materials and activities. For more information about the check-in lessons, see Appendix B, "Independent Work Resources."

This week we suggest you teach the "Conferring" check-in lesson in Appendix B, "Independent Work Resources." Depending on the needs of your students, you may decide to teach a different check-in lesson.

Week 14 OVERVIEW

Whole-class Instruction

Word Study

This week the students review suffixes and base words and read, discuss, and sort words with the suffixes -er and -est. On Day 3, the students build -er and -est words by syllable during "Build That Word." This week's spelling words are words with consonant-l-e syllables.

Independent Work Check-in

This week we suggest you teach the "Conferring" check-in lesson in Appendix B, "Independent Work Resources." Depending on the needs of your students, you may decide to teach a different check-in lesson.

Small-group Reading Instruction and Independent Work Rotations

Small-group Reading

This week, you will continue to teach Small-group Reading lessons at the small-group reading table while the students work independently in the reading, writing, and word work areas.

Independent Work

The students may have assigned work from Small-group Reading to do during Independent Work. The following are materials you might incorporate into independent work areas this week:

Word Work:

- "Week 13, Day 3 Sort" (see "Independent Work Connection" on page 304)

Week 14

RESOURCES

Extensions

- "Adding -*er* and -*est* to Base Words with Final *e*"
- "Adding -*er* and -*est* to Base Words that End with *y*"
- "Connect Spelling to Writing"

Assessment Resource Book

- Week 14 assessment

Word Study Notebook

- Spelling Practice

 ## Online Resources

Visit the CCC Learning Hub (ccclearninghub.org) to find your online resources for this week.

Whiteboard Activities

- WA1–WA4

Assessment Form

- "Class Assessment Record" sheet (CA1)

Reproducibles

- "Week 14, Day 2 Sort" (BLM1)
- "Week 14, Day 3 'Build That Word' Tiles" (BLM2)
- "Week 14, Day 3 'Build That Word' Sentences" (BLM3)

⏱ DO AHEAD

Word Study

✓ Prior to Day 1, familiarize yourself with the Day 1 Spelling Words.

✓ Prior to Day 2, familiarize yourself with the Day 2 Sort Words.

✓ Prior to Day 2, visit the CCC Learning Hub (ccclearninghub.org) to access and print "Week 14, Day 2 Sort" (BLM1). Make several copies to place in the word work area before the lesson.

✓ Prior to Day 3, visit the CCC Learning Hub (ccclearninghub.org) to access and print "Week 14, Day 3 'Build That Word' Tiles" (BLM2). Make half as many copies as you have pairs of students, since each sheet makes two sets of letter tiles. Cut each sheet in half.

✓ Prior to Day 4, visit the CCC Learning Hub (ccclearninghub.org) to access and print the "Class Assessment Record" sheet (CA1); see page 88 of the *Assessment Resource Book*.

✓ (Optional) If you plan to integrate "Build That Word" in the word work area, visit the CCC Learning Hub (ccclearninghub.org) to access and print "Week 14, Day 3 'Build That Word' Sentences" (BLM3). See "Independent Work Connections" on page 323.

Independent Work Check-in

✓ Familiarize yourself with the "Conferring" check-in lesson (or another check-in lesson of your choice) in Appendix B, "Independent Work Resources." Collect and prepare any necessary materials. For more information about the check-in lessons, see Appendix B, "Independent Work Resources."

📅 SUGGESTED WEEKLY SCHEDULE

Monday	Tuesday	Wednesday	Thursday	Friday
Word Study (20)	Word Study (20)		Word Study (20)	Word Study (20)
Independent Work Rotations/Small-group Reading (60)	Independent Work Rotations/Small-group Reading (60)	Independent Work Check-in (35)	Independent Work Rotations/Small-group Reading (60)	Independent Work Rotations/Small-group Reading (60)
80 minutes	**80 minutes**	**35 minutes**	**80 minutes**	**80 minutes**

Word Study

Day 1 Spelling Words		Day 2 Practice Words		Day 2 Sort Words	
apple	*Challenge Words*	darker	softer	deeper	smaller
handle	marble	darkest	softest	deepest	smart
rattle	turtle	deeper	sweeter	faster	smarter
riddle		deepest	sweetest	fastest	strong
rumble		louder	taller	longer	strongest
settle		loudest	tallest	longest	weak
simple		shorter	thicker	neat	weaker
struggle		shortest	thickest	neater	weakest

Academic Focus

- Students learn the suffixes -*er* and -*est*.
- Students read and sort words with -*er* and -*est*.
- Students build words.
- Students spell words with consonant-*l-e* syllables.

Social Development Focus

- Students work responsibly in pairs.
- Students listen respectfully to the thinking of others and share their own.

Day 1

Word Study
Guided Spelling

Materials

- Class set of wipe-off boards, dry-erase markers, and tissues or cloths
- *Word Study Notebook* page 53 (in student toolboxes)

In this lesson, the students:

- Review consonant-*l-e* syllables
- Spell words with consonant-*l-e* syllables
- Handle materials responsibly

1 Get Ready to Spell

Have the students pick up their independent work toolboxes and return to their seats. Ask them to put their toolboxes on the floor next to their chairs. Review that last week the students read and sorted two-syllable words that end in consonant-*l-e*. Explain that today the students will spell words ending with consonant-*l-e* syllables.

2 Review Consonant-*l-e* Syllables

Write the following words where everyone can see them: *riddle*, *mumble*, and *tremble*. Point to *riddle* and ask:

Q *What consonant-*l-e* syllable do you see in this word?* (dle)

Draw a dot between *rid* and *dle*, just below the word. Remind the students that when there is a double consonant in a word, they only say the consonant sound once when they read the whole word. Have the students read each syllable and then read the word.

Repeat the procedure for *mumble* and *tremble*.

3 Guide the Students' Spelling

Review that in Guided Spelling, you will help the students use what they know about words to help them spell some of the words from last week's sort. Remind the students that practicing spelling with words from the sort will help them spell words when they are writing on their own.

Distribute the wipe-off boards, markers, and cloth or tissues. Review that in Guided Spelling, you will say a word, use it in a sentence, and ask questions to help the students think about how to spell the word.

simple   "The recipe for the salad was very simple."

Say *simple*. Use *simple* in a sentence. Have the students say *simple*. Then ask:

Q *How many syllables are in* simple? *(two)*

Q *What is the first syllable in* simple? *(sim)*

Have the students write *sim*. Then ask:

Q *What is the second syllable in* simple? *(ple)*

Q *How is the consonant-*l-e* syllable spelled?* (p-l-e)

Have the students write *ple*.

Write *simple* where everyone can see it, and have the students check their writing and erase and correct mistakes.

Repeat the procedure with the words *struggle*, *apple*, *rattle*, *rumble*, *handle*, *settle*, and *riddle*.

struggle	"Sometimes I struggle to lift my book bag."
apple	"An apple is a good snack."
rattle	"The baby shook her rattle."
rumble	"I was so hungry I heard my tummy rumble."

Teacher Note

Do not erase any of the guided spelling words you write, as you will refer to them in the reflection at the end of the lesson.

handle	"We handle our classroom materials responsibly."
settle	"The children worked together to settle their argument."
riddle	"Once I heard a funny riddle."

If time permits, you may wish to challenge the students with the words *turtle* and *marble*, which have more challenging spellings in the first syllable.

turtle	"A turtle can hide its head inside its shell."

Say *turtle*. Use *turtle* in a sentence. Have the students say *turtle*. Then ask:

Q *What is the first syllable in* turtle? *(tur)*

Q *What is the vowel sound in* tur? *(/ûr/)*

Q *What are three ways to spell /ûr/?* (e-r, i-r, u-r)

Ask the students to think carefully about which spelling to use and have them write the letters *tur*. Have them say *turtle* again. Then ask:

Q *What is the second syllable in* turtle? *(tle)*

Have the students write the rest of *turtle*. When most students are finished, call for their attention and ask:

Q *Does* turtle *look right to you the way you spelled it? If not, do you want to change how you spelled it?*

Write *turtle* where everyone can see it, and have the students check their writing and erase and correct mistakes.

marble	"Joey's favorite marble has blue and green swirls."

Say *marble*. Use *marble* in a sentence. Then ask:

Q *What is the first syllable in* marble? *(mar)*

Q *What is the vowel sound in /mar/?* (/är/)

Q *What is one way to spell /är/?* (a-r)

Have the students write the letters *mar*. Have them say *marble* again. Then ask:

Q *What is the second syllable in* marble? *(ble)*

Have the students write the rest of *marble*.

Write *marble* where everyone can see it, and have the students check their writing and erase and correct mistakes.

4 Discuss and Reflect on Spelling Words

Direct the students' attention to the guided spelling words you have written. Ask:

 Q *What do you notice about these words? Turn to a person sitting next to you.*

Signal for the students' attention and have a few volunteers share their thinking with the class.

> **Students might say:**
>
> "They all end in *l-e*."
>
> "The *e* at the end is silent."

Explain that the students will have a spelling test on Friday (or whichever day this week you will teach the Day 4 lesson). Have the students take their *Word Study Notebooks* from their toolboxes and open to page 50. Read the spelling steps with the students. Then have the students turn to page 53 and remind them that they will practice spelling these words using the spelling steps. It is important for them to do their spelling practice when they go to independent word work so that they will remember how to spell the words.

Teacher Note

You may wish to post the *Word Study Notebook* page number for this week's spelling practice in the word work area for the students to refer to during Independent Work.

Word Study
Introduce the Suffixes *-er* and *-est*
Day 2

In this lesson, the students:

- Read and sort words with the suffixes *-er* and *-est*
- Listen respectfully to the thinking of others and share their own

1 Gather and Get Ready to Work

Gather the class with partners sitting together, facing you. Explain that in this lesson, partners will share what they know about some longer words. Ask and briefly discuss:

Q *What can you do to be respectful when you and your partner are talking?*

2 Discuss Words Ending with *-er* and *-est*

Write the word *quick* where everyone can see it and have the students read it aloud.

Materials

- "Week 14, Day 2 Words" (WA1)
- "Week 14, Day 2 Sort" (WA2)
- Copies of "Week 14, Day 2 Sort" (BLM1) in the word work area

Teacher Note

Check with the students to see whether they have completed their spelling work. Ask:

Q *If you haven't done the spelling practice, how will you make sure you complete it before the spelling test on [Friday]?*

Facilitation Tip

Continue to focus on **pacing class discussions** using techniques such as the following:

- Encourage just a few students to respond to each question even if others have their hands up.

- Use "Turn to Your Partner" if many students want to speak, and then call on just two or three students to share with the whole class.

- Restate the question if the discussion strays from the original topic.

- Use wait-time before calling on anyone to respond.

Write the word *quicker* under *quick*. Draw a dot between *quick* and *er*, just below the word, and remind the students that the dot can help them see and read syllables in a word. Have the students read *quicker*, first by syllables and then as a whole word. Then use "Think, Pair, Share" to discuss:

 Q *Which do you think is quicker, a shark or a cheetah? Why do you think that?* [pause] *Turn to your partner.*

After a few moments, signal for the students' attention and have a few volunteers share their thinking with the class.

> **Students might say:**
>
> "I think a shark is quicker because it is easier to go fast in the water."
>
> "I think a cheetah is quicker because I know it is the fastest animal on land."

Write *quickest* under *quicker*. Draw a dot between *quick* and *est* and have the students read *quickest*, first by syllables and then as a whole word. Then have the students discuss the following question, first in pairs and then as a class:

 Q *Does the quickest person always win a race? Why do you think that?* [pause] *Turn to your partner.*

Write the word *small* where everyone can see it. Read the word aloud. Have the students read it aloud.

Write the word *smaller* under *small*. Draw a dot between *small* and *er* and have the students read *smaller* aloud, first by syllables and then as a whole word. Then have the students discuss the following question, first in pairs and then as a class:

 Q *Which do you think is smaller, a puppy or a kitten? Why do you think that?* [pause] *Turn to your partner.*

Write the word *smallest* under *smaller*. Draw a dot between *small* and *est* and have the students read *smallest* aloud, first by syllables and then as a whole word. Then have the students discuss the following question, first in pairs and then as a class:

Q *Who is the smallest person in your family? Why do you think that? Turn to your partner.*

3 Review Base Words and Suffixes

Direct the students' attention to the words *quick*, *quicker*, and *quickest*. Ask:

Q *What is the same about these words?*

Have a few volunteers share. Underline *quick* in all three words and explain that *quick* is the *base word* in the words *quicker* and *quickest*. Then ask:

 Q *What makes* quicker *and* quickest *different from* quick? *Turn to your partner.*

After a few moments, signal for the students' attention and have a few volunteers share their thinking with the class.

> **Students might say:**
> "*Quicker* and *quickest* both have two syllables."
> "They have different endings."
> "They mean different things."

Circle *er* and *est* and explain that /ûr/, spelled *e-r*, and /ĕst/, spelled *e-s-t*, are both suffixes. Tell the students that a *suffix* is a letter or group of letters that is added to the end of a base word to make a new word. Explain that noticing a suffix at the end of a word can help readers read and understand the word.

4 Introduce the Suffixes -*er* and -*est*

Explain that the suffix -*er* means "more" and that when -*er* is added to the base word *quick*, it makes the word *quicker*, which means "more quick or faster." Draw a dot between the syllables *quick* and *er* and remind the students that the dot can help them see and read the syllables in a word. Have the students read *quicker*, first by syllables and then the whole word.

Explain that the suffix -*est* means "most" and that when -*est* is added to the base word *quick*, it makes the word *quickest*, which means "most quick or fastest." Draw a dot between *quick* and *est*. Have the students read *quickest*, first by syllables and then the whole word.

Repeat this procedure with *smaller* and *smallest*.

5 Read Words with the Suffixes -*er* and -*est*

Explain to the students that they will read more words with the suffixes -*er* and -*est*; you will show them a word and they will say the suffix and then read the word. Display the "Week 14, Day 2 Words" activity (WA1). Point to the word *darker*. Ask:

Q *Which suffix do you see?* (-er)

Draw a dot between *dark* and *er*. Have the students read the word, first by syllables and then as a whole word.

Teacher Note

The suffix -*er* is introduced to mean "a person who" in the vocabulary instruction of the *Making Meaning®* program from Center for the Collaborative Classroom. If you have taught the -*er* lesson in the *Vocabulary Teaching Guide*, you many want to point out that the ending -*er* has two different meanings. The "a person who" meaning of -*er* is taught in Week 16 of Word Study.

Repeat this procedure for the remaining words.

darker	tallest	deeper	thickest
deepest	shorter	softer	sweeter
sweetest	softest	shortest	loudest
taller	thicker	louder	darkest

6 Introduce the Sort

Display the "Week 14, Day 2 Sort" activity (WA2) and read the words with the students.

smart	weak	deeper	weakest
longest	smaller	weaker	smarter
faster	deepest	fastest	strongest
strong	longer	neat	neater

Ask:

Q *What are some words you can group together? What is the same about them? Turn to your partner.*

After a few moments, signal for the students' attention and have a few volunteers share their thinking with the class.

Tell the students that you have put copies of the sort in the "Word Sorts" bin in the word work area. When they go to independent word work, they will sort the words and record their sorts in their *Word Study Notebooks*.

7 Reflect on Working Together

Ask and briefly discuss:

Q *What did you do to be respectful when you were talking about the words with your partner today?*

Tell the students that in the next lesson they will use word parts to build words.

EXTENSIONS

Adding -er and -est to Base Words with Final e

Remind the students that they learned about the suffixes -er and -est.

Say cuter. Ask:

Q What is the base word in cuter? (cute)

Write the word cute where everyone can see it. Have the students read the word. Point out that cute has the final e spelling of the long u sound (/ū/). Ask:

Q What do you know about adding the endings i-n-g or e-d to words with the final e spelling? Turn to your partner.

After a few moments, signal for the students' attention and have a few volunteers share their thinking with the class. If necessary, remind the students that to add the endings -ing or -er to a word, they must first drop the final e. Explain that to add e-r to cuter, the students will also drop the final e before adding the ending. Erase the e and add er to cute. Have the students read cuter.

Tell the students that they will use the same strategy to add e-s-t to words with the final e spelling. Write cute where everyone can see it. Have the students read the word. Erase the final e in cute and then add est. Have the students read cutest. Repeat this procedure for nicer, nicest, riper, and ripest.

Adding -er and -est to Base Words that End with y

Remind the students that they learned about the suffixes -er and -est. Ask:

Q What do you remember about adding e-d to words that end with y?

If necessary, remind the students that to add e-d to words that end with y, they must first change the y to i.

Say funnier. Then ask:

Q What is the base word in funnier? (funny)

Write the word funny where everyone can see it. Have the students read the word. Point out that funny ends with y. Tell the students that to spell funnier, they must change y to i before adding e-r. Erase the final y in funny, write i, and then add er. Have the students read funnier.

Tell the students that they use this same strategy to add e-s-t to words ending with y.

Write funny where everyone can see it. Have the students read the word. Erase y in funny, write i, and then add est. Have the students read funniest. Repeat this procedure for the words sleepier, sleepiest, luckier, and luckiest.

Materials

- "Week 14, Day 3 'Build That Word'" (WA3)
- Copy of "Week 14, Day 3 'Build That Word' Tiles" (BLM2), halved, for each pair
- Scissors for each pair

Teacher Note

You can have the students move to sit with their partners or work with the person sitting next to them.

In this lesson, the students:

- Play "Build That Word"
- Handle materials responsibly
- Work responsibly with a partner

1 Review "Build That Word"

Have the students stay in their seats. Explain that today, the students will work with partners to build words. Each pair will have one "Build That Word" sheet to share as they do when they sort with partners.

Review that to play "Build That Word," the students will use letters to build words. Explain that each pair will get a copy of the "Build That Word" sheet and cut the letters apart. Ask and briefly discuss:

Q *What will you do to handle the materials responsibly?*

2 Play "Build That Word"

Display the "Week 14, Day 3 'Build That Word'" activity (◐ WA3). Explain that this week, you will read some sentences that have missing words. Pairs will decide which word fits in each sentence and build that word with tiles.

WA3

er	strong	tall	sweet	deep
est	dark	short	fast	loud

_____

Explain that the students will have to think carefully about the meanings of words in order to build them. You will read a clue with a missing word and partners will use the word parts they have to build the missing word. Model, using the following clue:

- "Joe is the only person who can reach the top shelf of the bookcase. He is the _____ person in his class." (*tallest*)

> **You might say:**
>
> "'Joe is the only person who can reach the top shelf of the bookcase. He is the _____ person in his class.' If no one else can reach the top shelf, that means no one in the class is as tall as Joe. I think that Joe must be the tallest person in his class. I'm going to build *tallest* and repeat the sentence to make sure *tallest* makes sense. [Drag *tall* and *est* together to make *tallest*.] 'Joe is the only person who can reach the top shelf of the bookcase. He is the *tallest* person in his class.'"

Distribute "Week 14, Day 3 'Build That Word' Tiles" (BLM2) and scissors and have the students cut the tiles apart.

Read the next clue aloud:

- "Mei can stand on the bottom at one end of the pool. She can't stand on the bottom at the other end. One end of the pool is _____ than the other." (*deeper*)

Ask:

Q *What word makes sense in this sentence? Turn to your partner.*

After a few moments, signal for the students' attention and have a volunteer share. Reread the clue, inserting the word *deeper* to confirm that it makes sense. Have the students build the word *deeper*.

Drag *deep* and *er* together to build *deeper* on the "Week 14, Day 3 'Build That Word'" activity (WA3). Have the students check and correct their work.

Repeat this procedure with the remaining clues. After the students have built the word, read the clue with the word inserted to check that it makes sense.

- Alvaro can hold 3 pounds of apples. Jess can hold 4 pounds. But I can hold 6 pounds! I am the _____. (*strongest*)

- Joshua can run _____ than some of the other boys on the team. (*faster*)

- When the lights went out, it got much _____. (*darker*)

- My tea has more sugar in it than yours. My tea is _____. (*sweeter*)

- That thunder yesterday was the _____ noise I have ever heard. (*loudest*)

- Makayla's story has five chapters. Ben's story has six chapters. Mine has three. It is the _____. (*shortest*)

3 Reflect on "Build That Word"

After playing "Build That Word," ask and briefly discuss:

Q *How did you and your partner do with sharing the work fairly during "Build That Word"?*

Explain that in the coming weeks, the students will play "Build That Word" to build more long words.

Day 4 | Word Study
Spelling Test

Materials

- Lined paper and a pencil for each student
- "Week 14, Day 4 Spelling Words" (WA4)
- "Class Assessment Record" sheet (CA1)

In this lesson, the students:

- Review the purpose for spelling tests
- Review the procedure for a spelling test
- Spell words with consonant-*l-e* syllables
- Handle materials responsibly

1 Get Ready to Spell

Have the students stay in their seats today. Review that earlier this week, you guided the students as they wrote the spelling words. You asked them questions to help them spell the words correctly, and they thought carefully as they wrote the words. Review that the students also have been using the spelling practice steps to practice writing spelling words during independent work time. Ask and briefly discuss:

Q *How did you do with your independent spelling practice this week?*

2 Discuss Spelling Tests

Review that each week, after Guided Spelling and independent spelling practice, the students will write the spelling words from memory. Remind the students that when writers spell a word from memory, they use everything they know about the word to help them spell it correctly.

Review that if the students are not sure how to spell part of a word or are not sure they spelled a word correctly, they can ask themselves questions like the ones you ask during Guided Spelling. Asking themselves questions will help them remember what they know about the word. Ask and briefly discuss:

Q *What questions can you ask yourself if you are not sure how to spell part of a word?*

Q *What questions can you ask yourself once you finish writing a word?*

Students might say:

"I can ask myself if there's more than one way to spell that part."

"I can ask myself which way to spell the vowel sound."

"Does it look right?"

3 Review the Procedure for Spelling Tests

Distribute the paper and pencils to the students. Have them write their names at the top and number the first eight lines 1 to 8.

Review the procedure for writing and checking the spelling words, using one of the words as an example.

You might say:

"The first spelling word is *simple*. I will say 'Number one: *simple*.' Then I will use the word *simple* in a sentence. I might say 'The game came with very simple instructions for how to play.' I'll say *simple* again. Then you will write *simple* next to the number one on your paper. I will give you a minute or two to write before I tell you the next word. Remember to think carefully as you write the word. After you have written all eight words, I will display the words and you will check and correct your work."

Ask and briefly discuss:

Q *What questions do you have about the spelling test?*

4 Spelling Test

Begin the spelling test. Say "Number one: simple." Use *simple* in a sentence. Say *simple* again. Have the students write *simple*. Allow enough time for all the students to finish before moving on to the next word.

Repeat this procedure for the remaining spelling words.

1. simple   "The game came with very simple instructions for how to play."

2. struggle   "It was a struggle to climb the stairs after playing all day."

3. apple   "I will pick an apple from the tree."

4. rattle   "That baby's rattle is very loud."

5. rumble   "We heard a loud rumble when the truck went by."

6. handle   "He held the spoon by its handle."

7. settle   "My mom sang a lullaby to settle the baby and help her sleep."

8. riddle   "No one in our class could solve the riddle."

5 Check and Correct the Words

After the students are finished writing the last word, display the "Week 14, Day 4 Spelling Words" activity (WA4). Review that the students will check their writing by looking at each word they wrote and comparing it to the corresponding word in the word list.

> **You might say:**
>
> "When it's time to check your spelling words, start by looking at word number one on the board. On this list, word number one is *simple*. Find number one on your paper and check to see if you spelled *simple* the same way it's spelled on the board. If you made a mistake, cross out *simple* on your paper and write the correct spelling of *simple* next to it. Check each word the same way."

Have the students check their work and correct mistakes. As they work, circulate and observe. Support struggling students by reminding them to look at each word in the list and ask themselves if they spelled the word the same way. When the students are finished checking and correcting their work, collect the papers.

Explain that spelling familiar words from memory—using everything they know about words to spell the words correctly—helps writers know what to do when they spell words they have not written before.

CLASS ASSESSMENT NOTE

Ask yourself:

- Do the students use the correct consonant-*l-e* spellings?
- Do the students omit letters?
- Are the students able to spell most words correctly?

Record your observations on the "Class Assessment Record" sheet (CA1); see page 88 of the *Assessment Resource Book*.

6 Reflect on Spelling

Have the students reflect on the spelling test. Ask and briefly discuss:

Q *How did you do with remembering how to spell the words?*

Q *How did the spelling practice during Independent Work help you?*

Tell the students they will have more opportunities to practice spelling in the coming weeks.

EXTENSION

Connect Spelling to Writing

Review that one reason writers spell words correctly is to make sure readers can understand and enjoy their writing. Think aloud about how one of the words reminds you of something that happened to you that you could write about.

> **You might say:**
>
> "When I read the word *rattle*, it reminds me of the time when my baby sister lost her rattle. She would not stop crying. We looked for it all over the house. Then suddenly it was quiet. All we could hear was the rattle. My baby sister had found it next to her and picked it up herself for the first time! We were all very excited. I could write a story about that."

Ask and discuss:

Q   *Which of these words reminds you of something that happened to you? What is a story you could write about that? Turn to your partner.*

After a few moments, signal for the students' attention and have a few volunteers share their thinking with the class. Encourage the students to use the spelling words and other words from the week's sort in their writing.

Independent Work Connections

For next week's Independent Work, we suggest the following:

- If you have not done so already, place additional copies of "Week 14, Day 2 Sort" (BLM1) in the word work area.

- Make additional copies of "Week 14, Day 3 'Build That Word' Tiles" (BLM2) as well as copies of "Week 14, Day 3 'Build That Word' Sentences" (BLM3) to place in the word work area.

OVERVIEW Independent Work

This week the students continue to rotate to and work in all three independent work areas around the room while you teach Small-group Reading. We suggest continuing any procedures that have worked effectively in previous weeks.

Independent Work Check-in

This week you will continue to teach an Independent Work Check-in lesson on the day of the week you do not teach Small-group Reading. The purpose of these check-in lessons is to ensure that the students are able to maintain successful independent work rotations. The lessons provide the time for you to assess your students, conduct conferences, and introduce new materials and activities. For more information about the check-in lessons, see Appendix B, "Independent Work Resources."

This week we suggest you teach the "Conferring" check-in lesson in Appendix B, "Independent Work Resources." Depending on the needs of your students, you may decide to teach a different check-in lesson.

Week 15 OVERVIEW

Whole-class Instruction

Word Study

This week the students read and discuss words with the suffix -ly. They sort words with the suffixes -er, -est, and -ly as a class and in pairs. The week's spelling words are words with the suffixes -er and -est.

Independent Work Check-in

This week we suggest you teach the "Introduce New Materials" check-in lesson in Appendix B, "Independent Work Resources." Depending on the needs of your students, you may decide to teach a different check-in lesson.

Small-group Reading Instruction and Independent Work Rotations

Small-group Reading

This week you will continue to teach Small-group Reading lessons at the small-group reading table while the students work independently in the reading, writing, and word work areas.

Independent Work

The students may have assigned work from Small-group Reading to do during Independent Work. The following are materials you might incorporate into independent work areas this week:

Word Work:

- "Week 14, Day 2 Sort" (see "Independent Work Connections" on page 323)
- "Week 14, Day 3 'Build That Word' Tiles" and "Week 14, Day 3 'Build That Word' Sentences" (see "Independent Work Connections" on page 323)

Week 15

RESOURCES

Extension
- "Connect Spelling to Writing"

Assessment Resource Book
- Week 15 assessment

Word Study Notebook
- Word Sorts
- Spelling Practice

 Online Resources

Visit the CCC Learning Hub (ccclearninghub.org) to find your online resources for this week.

Whiteboard Activities
- WA1–WA3

Assessment Form
- "Class Assessment Record" sheet (CA1)

Reproducibles
- "Week 15, Day 3 Sort" (BLM1)
- (Optional) "Week 15 High-frequency Words" (BLM2)

⏱ DO AHEAD

Word Study

✓ Prior to Day 1, decide how you will randomly assign partners to work together during the next several weeks.

✓ Prior to Day 1, familiarize yourself with the Day 1 Spelling Words.

✓ Prior to Day 2, familiarize yourself with the Day 2 Practice Words.

✓ Prior to Day 3, familiarize yourself with the Day 3 Sort Words.

✓ Prior to Day 3, visit the CCC Learning Hub (ccclearninghub.org) to access and print "Week 15, Day 3 Sort" (BLM1). Make enough copies for each pair of students to have one.

✓ Prior to Day 3, visit the CCC Learning Hub (ccclearninghub.org) to access and print the "Class Assessment Record" sheet (CA1); see page 89 of the *Assessment Resource Book*.

✓ (Optional) If you plan to integrate the new high-frequency words in the word work area, visit the CCC Learning Hub (ccclearninghub.org) to access and print "Week 15 High-frequency Words" (BLM2). See "Independent Work Connections" on page 338.

Independent Work Check-in

✓ Familiarize yourself with the "Introduce New Materials" check-in lesson (or another check-in lesson of your choice) in Appendix B, "Independent Work Resources." Collect and prepare any necessary materials. For more information about the check-in lessons, see Appendix B, "Independent Work Resources."

📅 SUGGESTED WEEKLY SCHEDULE

Monday	Tuesday	Wednesday	Thursday	Friday
Word Study (20)	Word Study (20)		Word Study (20)	Word Study (20)
Independent Work Rotations/Small-group Reading (60)	Independent Work Rotations/Small-group Reading (60)	Independent Work Check-in (35)	Independent Work Rotations/Small-group Reading (60)	Independent Work Rotations/Small-group Reading (60)
80 minutes	**80 minutes**	**35 minutes**	**80 minutes**	**80 minutes**

Word Study

Day 1 Spelling Words		Day 2 Practice Words		Day 3 Sort Words	
darker	fastest	bravely	only	brave	kind
deeper	loudest	brightly	quickly	bravely	kinder
deepest	smarter	clearly	reply	braver	kindest
faster	strongest	fairly	sadly	bravest	kindly
		friendly	safely	bright	slow
		kindly	slowly	brighter	slower
		neatly	softly	brightest	slowest
		nicely		brightly	slowly

Academic Focus

- Students spell words with the suffixes -er and -est.
- Students learn the suffix -ly.
- Students read and sort words with the suffix -ly.

Social Development Focus

- Students work in a responsible way.
- Students listen respectfully to the thinking of others and share their own.

Day 1

Word Study
Guided Spelling

Materials

- Wipe-off board, dry-erase marker, and tissue or cloth for each student

Teacher Note

The students may work in partnerships already established, or you may assign new partners for the Word Study lessons. The partners you assign today will work together for the next five weeks of Word Study.

In this lesson, the students:

- Begin working with new partners
- Review the suffixes -er and -est
- Spell words with the suffixes -er and -est
- Handle materials responsibly

1 Get Ready to Spell

Randomly assign partners and have the students sit at tables with partners together. Review that last week, the students sorted words with the suffixes -er and -est. Explain that today the students will spell words with the suffixes -er and -est.

2 Review the Suffixes -er and -est

Review that a *suffix* is a letter or group of letters that is added to the end of a base word to make a new word. Explain that noticing a suffix at the end of a word can help readers read and understand the word.

Write the words *louder* and *loudest* where everyone can see them. Read the words with the students; then ask and briefly discuss:

Q *What is the base word in these words?* (loud)

Then ask:

 Q *What is the loudest noise you have ever heard? Turn to your partner.*

After a few moments, signal for the students' attention and have a few volunteers share.

Review that the suffix *-er* means "more." When *e-r* is added to the base word *loud*, it makes the word *louder*, which means "more loud." Review that when *e-s-t* is added to the base word *loud*, it makes the word *loudest*, which means "most loud."

3 Guide the Students' Spelling

Distribute the wipe-off boards, markers, and tissues or cloths.

> faster   "Our cat is faster than our dog."

Say *faster*. Use *faster* in a sentence. Have the students say *faster*. Then ask:

Q *How many syllables are in* faster? (two)

Q *What is the base word in* faster? (fast)

Have the students write *fast*. Then ask:

Q *What is the suffix in* faster? (-er)

Have the students write the rest of *faster*.

Write *faster* where everyone can see it, and have the students check their writing and erase and correct mistakes.

> deepest   "Shay dove into the deepest part of the pool."

Say *deepest*. Use *deepest* in a sentence. Have the students say *deepest*. Then ask:

Q *How many syllables are in* deepest? (two)

Q *What is the base word in* deepest? (deep)

Q *What is the vowel sound in* deepest? (long e)

Q *How can you spell the long e sound in the middle of a word?* (e-e, e-a, e_e)

Tell the students to think carefully about which spelling of the long *e* sound to use.

Have the students write *deep*. When most students are finished, call for their attention, and ask:

Q *Does* deep *look right to you the way you spelled it? If not, do you want to change how you spelled /long e/?*

Then ask:

Q *What is the suffix in* deepest? *(-est)*

Have the students write the rest of *deepest*.

Write *deepest* where everyone can see it, and have the students check their writing and erase and correct mistakes.

Repeat the procedure with the words *loudest, deeper, fastest, darker, stronger,* and *smarter*.

loudest	"She was the loudest singer in the choir."
deeper	"It is safe to dive in the deeper end of the pool."
fastest	"The fastest way to travel is by plane."
darker	"It is darker at midnight than at noon."
strongest	"Felipe is the strongest swimmer on the team."
smarter	"Every time I learn something new, I feel smarter."

4 Discuss and Reflect on Spelling Words

Direct the students' attention to the guided spelling words. Ask:

 Q *What do you notice about these words? Turn to your partner.*

After a few moments, signal for the students' attention and have a few volunteers share their thinking with the class.

> **Students might say:**
>
> "They end with -er or -est."
>
> "They all have two syllables."

Remind the students that they will have a spelling test on Friday (or whichever day of the week you will teach the Day 4 lesson). Remind the students that in independent word work this week, they will practice the spelling words first before doing any other word work.

Ask and briefly discuss:

Q *How will you make sure that you do your spelling practice when you go to independent word work?*

In this lesson, the students:

- Read words with the suffix -*ly*
- Listen respectfully to the thinking of others and share their own

1 Gather and Review Base Words and Suffixes

Gather the class with partners sitting together, facing you. Remind the students that last week they read and spelled words with the suffixes -*er* and -*est*. Review that a *suffix* is a letter or group of letters that is added to the end of a base word to make a new word.

2 Introduce the Suffix -*ly*

Write the word *quickly* where everyone can see it. Underline *ly* and explain that *ly*, spelled *l-y*, is another suffix that the students will see often in their reading. Explain that the suffix -*ly* means "in a certain way." When *l-y* is added to the word *quick*, it makes the word *quickly*. If someone does something quickly, they do it in a quick or fast way.

Use *quickly* in a sentence. (For example, "We ran quickly back to the house when it started to rain.") Tell the students that noticing the suffix -*ly* at the end of a word can help readers read and understand the word.

Draw a dot between *quick* and *ly* and remind the students that the dot can help them see and read the syllables in a word. Have the students read *quickly*, first by syllables and then as a whole word.

Write the word *safely* where everyone can see it. Draw a dot between *safe* and *ly* and have the students read *safely*, first by syllables and then as a whole word. Ask:

Q *What do you do to cross the street safely?*

Have a few volunteers share their thinking with the class.

> **Students might say:**
>
> "I stop and look both ways before crossing."
>
> "I wait for the light to say it's safe to walk."

Point out that *safely* means "in a safe way."

3 Read the Words

Display the "Week 15, Day 2 Words" activity (WA1). Direct the students' attention to *nicely*. Draw a dot between *nice* and *ly* and have the students first read the syllables and then read the word.

Materials

- "Week 15, Day 2 Words" (WA1)

Teacher Note

The suffix -*ly* is introduced in the vocabulary instruction of the *Making Meaning*® program from Center for the Collaborative Classroom. If you have taught the -*ly* lesson in the *Vocabulary Teaching Guide*, you may want to briefly review -*ly* and then continue to Step 3.

Repeat this procedure for the next thirteen words.

nicely	brightly	neatly	safely
quickly	clearly	friendly	only
kindly	bravely	softly	reply
sadly	slowly	fairly	

When you get to *only* and *reply*, have the students read both words with you. Then ask:

Q *What do you notice about these words?*

> **Students might say:**
>
> "*Only* ends with *l-y*, but *l-y* doesn't mean 'in a certain way.'"
>
> "*Reply* ends with *l-y*, but *l-y* is part of the word."
>
> "Both words end with *l-y*, but *l-y* doesn't mean 'in a certain way.'"

Explain that the letters *l-y* at the end of a word are not always the suffix that means "in a certain way." Point out that noticing *l-y* at the end of a word can help the students read the word even when the letters are not a suffix.

4 Discuss a Spelling Strategy

Explain that words ending with the suffix -*ly* can be challenging to spell. Tell the students that if they are writing a word ending with *l-y* and are not sure how to spell the word, thinking about the base word can help them. Say *sadly*; then ask:

Q *What is the base word in* sadly? (sad)

Write *sad* where everyone can see it. Have the students read it aloud. Point out that *sad* ends with a consonant. Tell the students that to spell *sadly* they need only add *l-y*. Add *ly* to *sad*, and have the students read *sadly* aloud.

Repeat this procedure for *bravely*. Then tell the students that to add the suffix *l-y* to words that end with a consonant or final *e*, simply add *l-y*.

Say *happily*; then ask:

Q   *What is the base word in* happily? (*happy*)

After a few moments, signal for the students' attention and have a few volunteers share. Then write *happy* where everyone can see it, and have the students read it aloud. Point out that the base word *happy* ends with the letter *y*. Tell the students that to spell *happily*, they must change the *y* to an *i* and then add *l-y*. Erase the final *y* in *happy*, write an *i*, and then add *ly*. Have the students read *happily* aloud.

Teacher Note

If time permits, you may wish to model this again using additional words, such as *hungry* and *sleepy*.

5 Wrap Up

Encourage the students to use what they know about the suffix *-ly* to help them when they are reading and writing on their own. Tell them that next week, they will read and sort more words with suffixes.

Word Study
Pair Sort (Open)

Day 3

In this lesson, the students:

- Read and sort words with the suffixes *-er*, *-est*, and *-ly*
- Work responsibly with a partner
- Handle materials responsibly

1 Gather and Review the Suffix *-ly*

Have the students bring their pencils, pick up their independent work toolboxes, and gather with partners sitting together, facing you. Ask them to put their toolboxes on the floor next to them. Review that in the last lesson the students read words with the suffix *-ly* at the end. Remind them that a *suffix* is a letter or group of letters that is added to the end of a base word to make a new word. Tell the students that noticing a suffix at the end of a word can help readers see the first part of the word and read the whole word.

Materials

- "Week 15, Day 3 Sort" (WA2)
- Copy of "Week 15, Day 3 Sort" (BLM1) for each pair
- Scissors for each pair
- *Word Study Notebooks* (in student toolboxes)
- Pencils
- "Class Assessment Record" sheet (CA1)

Use "Think, Pair, Share" to discuss:

 Q *If you are treating someone kindly, what might you do or say?* [pause] *Turn to your partner.*

After a few moments, signal for the students' attention and have a few pairs share their thinking with the class. If necessary, explain that *kindly* means "in a kind way."

> **Students might say:**
>
> "I say something nice to the person."
>
> "I share with the person."
>
> "I say 'I'm sorry' when I make a mistake."

Review that the suffix *-ly* means "in a certain way."

2 Introduce the Sort

Explain that today partners will work together to do an open sort. Some of the words have the suffix *-ly* and some of them have other suffixes.

Use "Think, Pair, Share" to discuss:

 Q *What can be challenging about doing an open sort?* [pause] *Turn to your partner.*

After a few moments, signal for the students' attention and have a few volunteers share their thinking with the class.

> **Students might say:**
>
> "It can be hard to think of groups to sort into."
>
> "You and your partner might not agree on where a word should get sorted."

Tell the students that you will check in with them later to see how they did.

 Display the "Week 15, Day 3 Sort" activity (WA2). Have partners quietly read the words together.

brighter	kindly	slowest	bravely
slowly	brightest	slow	brave
kind	braver	bravest	slower
bright	kinder	kindest	brightly

When most pairs have finished reading, signal for the students' attention. Use "Think, Pair, Share" to discuss:

 Q *What are some words you could group together?* [pause] *Turn to your partner.*

Teacher Note

In this lesson, the students do not read all the sort words as a class. The purpose of this is to encourage the students to read the words carefully with their partners. Base words are included in the sort to provide extra support for students who find it challenging to read the polysyllabic words.

Teacher Note

If the students have difficulty generating ideas, prompt their thinking by reviewing the "Ways We Have Sorted" chart and sharing some of your own ideas.

After a few moments, signal for the students' attention and have a few pairs share their thinking with the class.

As volunteers share, ask follow-up questions such as:

Q *What is alike about [slowly and bravely]?*

Q *What other words could you group with [kinder and kindest]? Why does [kindly] go with [kinder and kindest]?*

Q *What did you notice about [brave and bright] that made you think of grouping them together?*

Tell the students that the words can be sorted in many different ways. Remind the students that if they start to sort one way and find it does not make sense, they may try sorting another way.

3 Sort in Pairs

 Distribute a copy of "Week 15, Day 3 Sort" (BLM1) and scissors to each pair. Have partners refer to the "Word Sort Steps" chart to cut apart and sort the words, and then record the sort in their *Word Study Notebooks*.

Circulate and observe as the students work, offering support as necessary.

 CLASS ASSESSMENT NOTE

Ask yourself:

- Are the students able to generate ideas and start sorting?
- Do their categories make sense?
- Are they able to name their categories?

Record your observations on the "Class Assessment Record" sheet (CA1); see page 89 of the *Assessment Resource Book*.

Support any pairs who struggle by asking questions such as:

Q *What is alike about these words? What other words might you group with them?*

Q *Why did you decide to group these words together?*

Q *How can you turn what you just told me into a name for the category?*

4 Reflect on Sorting

Ask:

Q *How did open sorting go today?*

After a few moments, signal for the students' attention, and have a few volunteers share their thinking with the class. Then share your observations about what went well during the open sort.

 Facilitation Tip

Continue to focus on **pacing class discussions** so they are lively and focused without dragging, losing the attention of your participants, or wandering off the topic. Class discussions should be long enough to allow time for thinking and short enough to sustain the students' attention. Good pacing requires careful observation of the class (not just the students who are responding) and the timely use of various pacing techniques.

Teacher Note

If your students need more support, you might use the "Week 15, Day 3 Sort" activity (WA2) to sort a few words as a class. Students may categorize by suffix, by base word, by vowel sound, by initial sounds/consonants, or they may find other ways to sort.

ELL Note

Check your English Language Learners' comprehension of the sort words and, if necessary, provide additional examples to clarify meaning.

Teacher Note

Have pairs who finish early find another way to sort the words. They do not need to record the second sort.

Materials

- Lined paper and a pencil for each student
- "Week 15, Day 4 Spelling Words" (WA3)

In this lesson, the students:

- Spell words with the suffixes *-er* and *-est*
- Handle materials responsibly

1 Get Ready to Spell

Have the students stay in their seats today. Review that earlier this week, you guided the students as they wrote the spelling words. Ask and briefly discuss:

Q *How did you do with your independent spelling practice this week?*

Review that if the students are not sure how to spell part of a word or are not sure they spelled a word correctly, they can ask themselves questions like the ones you ask during Guided Spelling. Asking themselves questions will help them remember what they know about the word. Ask and briefly discuss:

Q *What questions can you ask yourself if you are not sure how to spell part of a word?*

Q *What questions can you ask yourself once you finish writing a word?*

> **Students might say:**
>
> "I can ask myself how many syllables there are and spell the word one syllable at a time."
>
> "I can ask myself if there is more than one way to spell the vowel sound."
>
> "Does it look right?"

2 Review the Procedure for Spelling Tests

Distribute paper and pencils to the students. Have them write their names at the top and number the first eight lines 1 to 8.

Review the procedure for writing and checking the spelling words, using one of the words as an example.

> **You might say:**
>
> "The first spelling word is *faster*. I will say 'Number one: faster.' Then I will use the word *faster* in a sentence. I might say 'Cheetahs run faster than cats.' I'll say *faster* again. Then you will write *faster* next to the number one on your paper. I will give you a minute or two to write before I tell you the next word. Remember to think carefully as you write the word. After you have written all eight words, I will display the words and you will check and correct your work."

Ask and briefly discuss:

Q *What questions do you have about the spelling test?*

3 Spelling Test

Begin the spelling test. Say "Number one: faster." Use *faster* in a sentence. Say *faster* again. Have the students write *faster*. Allow enough time for all the students to finish before moving on to the next word.

Repeat this procedure for the remaining spelling words.

1.	faster	"Cheetahs run faster than cats."
2.	deepest	"The deepest part of the pool is under the diving board."
3.	loudest	"The loudest noise I have ever heard is thunder."
4.	deeper	"We walked deeper and deeper into the lake until the water finally reached our waists."
5.	fastest	"The fastest way to get there is to go down Main Street."
6.	darker	"We closed the shades to make the room darker."
7.	strongest	"My aunt is the strongest person I know."
8.	smarter	"Every time I learn something new, I feel smarter."

4 Check and Correct the Words

After the students are finished writing the last word, display the "Week 15, Day 4 Spelling Words" activity (◖ WA3). Explain that the students will check their work by looking at each word they wrote and comparing it to the corresponding word in the word list.

Have the students check their work and erase and correct mistakes. As they work, circulate and observe. Support struggling students by reminding them to look at each word in the word list and ask themselves if they spelled the word the same way. When the students are finished checking and correcting their work, collect the papers.

Explain that spelling familiar words from memory—using everything they know about words to spell the words correctly—helps writers know what to do when they spell words they have not written before.

5 Reflect on Spelling

Have the students reflect on the spelling test. Ask and briefly discuss:

Q *How did you do with remembering how to spell the words?*

Q *How did the spelling practice during Independent Work help you?*

Tell the students they will have more opportunities to practice spelling in the coming weeks.

EXTENSION

Connect Spelling to Writing

Review that one reason writers spell words correctly is to make sure readers can understand and enjoy their writing. Think aloud about how one of the words reminds you of something that happened to you.

> **You might say:**
>
> "When I read the word *loudest*, it reminds me of the time when my friends and I had a contest to see who could whistle the loudest. None of us could whistle very well so it was hard. Finally, after a lot of practice, my friend whistled so loud that her dog came running! We all laughed. I could write a story about that."

Ask:

Q *Which of these words reminds you of something that happened to you? What story you could write about that? Turn to your partner.*

After a few moments, signal for the students' attention and have a few volunteers share their thinking with the class. Encourage the students to use the spelling words and other words from the week's sort in their writing.

Independent Work Connections

For next week's Independent Work, we suggest the following:

- Make several copies of "Week 15, Day 3 Sort" (BLM1) to place in the word work area.

- Make several copies of "Week 15 High-frequency Words" (BLM2) and place them in the independent word work area. Your students can use these words to play any word games you have introduced, such as "Word Memory" and "Word Go Fish."

Independent Work | OVERVIEW

This week the students continue to rotate to and work in all three independent work areas around the room while you teach Small-group Reading. We suggest continuing any procedures that have worked effectively in previous weeks.

Independent Work Check-in

This week you will continue to teach an Independent Work Check-in lesson on the day of the week you do not teach Small-group Reading. The purpose of these check-in lessons is to ensure that the students are able to maintain successful independent work rotations. The lessons provide the time for you to assess your students, conduct conferences, and introduce new materials and activities. For more information about the check-in lessons, see Appendix B, "Independent Work Resources."

This week we suggest you teach the "Introduce New Materials" check-in lesson in Appendix B, "Independent Work Resources." Depending on the needs of your students, you may decide to teach a different check-in lesson.

Week 16 OVERVIEW

Whole-class Instruction

Word Study

This week the students discuss multiple meanings of the suffix *-er* and learn about the suffixes *-or* and *-ist*. They sort words as a class and in pairs. The week's spelling words are words with the suffix *-ly*.

Independent Work Check-in

This week we suggest you teach the "Share a Book" check-in lesson in Appendix B, "Independent Work Resources." Depending on the needs of your students, you may decide to teach a different check-in lesson.

Small-group Reading Instruction and Independent Work Rotations

Small-group Reading

This week you will continue to teach Small-group Reading lessons at the small-group reading table while the students work independently in the reading, writing, and word work areas.

Independent Work

The students may have assigned work from Small-group Reading to do during Independent Work. The following are materials you might incorporate into independent work areas this week:

Word Work:

- "Week 15, Day 3 Sort" (see "Independent Work Connections" on page 338)
- "Week 15 High-frequency Words" (see "Independent Work Connections" on page 338)

RESOURCES

Assessment Resource Book
- Week 16 assessment

Word Study Notebook
- Spelling Practice

 Online Resources

Visit the CCC Learning Hub (ccclearninghub.org) to find your online resources for this week.

Whiteboard Activities
- WA1–WA2

Assessment Form
- "Class Assessment Record" sheet (CA1)

Reproducible
- "Week 16, Day 3 Sort" (BLM1)

⏱ DO AHEAD

Word Study

✓ Prior to Day 1, familiarize yourself with the Day 1 Spelling Words.

✓ Prior to Day 3, familiarize yourself with the Day 3 Sort Words.

✓ Prior to Day 3, visit the CCC Learning Hub (ccclearninghub.org) to access and print "Week 16, Day 3 Sort" (BLM1). Make several copies to place in the word work area before the lesson.

✓ Prior to Day 4, visit the CCC Learning Hub (ccclearninghub.org) to access and print the "Class Assessment Record" sheet (CA1); see page 90 of the *Assessment Resource Book*.

Independent Work Check-in

✓ Familiarize yourself with the "Share a Book" check-in lesson (or another check-in lesson of your choice) in Appendix B, "Independent Work Resources." Collect and prepare any necessary materials. For more information about the check-in lessons, see Appendix B, "Independent Work Resources."

📅 SUGGESTED WEEKLY SCHEDULE

Monday	Tuesday	Wednesday	Thursday	Friday
Word Study (20)	Word Study (20)		Word Study (20)	Word Study (20)
Independent Work Rotations/Small-group Reading (60)	Independent Work Rotations/Small-group Reading (60)	Independent Work Check-in (35)	Independent Work Rotations/Small-group Reading (60)	Independent Work Rotations/Small-group Reading (60)
80 minutes	**80 minutes**	**35 minutes**	**80 minutes**	**80 minutes**

Word Study

Day 1 Spelling Words		Day 3 Sort Words	
bravely	*Challenge Words*	artist	largest
friendly	easily	brighter	lower
kindly	happily	clearest	player
neatly		darker	quicker
sadly		faster	sailor
safely		helper	slower
slowly		hunter	swimmer
softly		illustrator	teacher

Academic Focus

- Students spell words with the suffix *-ly*.
- Students learn the suffixes *-er*, *-ist*, and *-or*.
- Students read and sort words with the suffixes *-er*, *-ist*, and *-or*.

Social Development Focus

- Students work in a responsible way.
- Students listen respectfully to the thinking of others and share their own.

Day 1

Word Study
Guided Spelling

Materials

- Wipe-off board, dry-erase marker, and tissue or cloth for each student

In this lesson, the students:

- Review the suffix *-ly*
- Spell words with the suffix *-ly*
- Handle materials responsibly

1 Get Ready to Spell

Have the students stay at their seats. Explain that today the students will spell words with the suffix *-ly*.

2 Review the Suffix -ly

Review that a *suffix* is a letter or group of letters that is added to the end of a base word to make a new word. Explain that noticing a suffix at the end of a word can help readers read and understand the word.

Write the word *softly* where everyone can see it and have the students read the word. Ask and briefly discuss:

Q *What is the base word in* softly? *(soft)*

Q *If you touch something softly, how do you touch it?*

Explain that *soft* can also mean "quiet" and that *talking softly* means "talking in a quiet way."

Repeat the procedure with the word *slowly*.

3 Guide the Students' Spelling

Distribute the wipe-off boards, markers, and tissues or cloths. Explain that this week the students will spell words with the suffix *-ly*.

| kindly | "She always treats her pets kindly." |

Say *kindly*. Use *kindly* in a sentence. Have the students say *kindly*. Then ask:

Q *What is the base word in* kindly? *(kind)*

Have the students write *kind*. Then ask:

Q *What is the suffix in* kindly? *(-ly)*

Have the students write the rest of *kindly*.

Write *kindly* where everyone can see it, and have the students check their writing and erase and correct mistakes.

| sadly | "Wes sadly looked up at the scoreboard at the end of the game." |

Say *sadly*. Use *sadly* in a sentence. Then ask:

Q *What is the base word in* sadly? *(sad)*

Have the students write *sad*. Then ask:

Q *What is the suffix in* sadly? *(-ly)*

Have the students write the rest of *sadly*.

Write *sadly* where everyone can see it, and have the students check their writing and erase and correct mistakes.

Repeat the procedure with the words *bravely, friendly, slowly, neatly, softly*, and *safely*.

| bravely | "She took the training wheels off her bike and bravely rode down the sidewalk." |
| friendly | "We are friendly with new students in our class." |

Teacher Note

Do not erase any of the guided spelling words you write, as you will refer to them in the reflection at the end of the lesson.

Spelling Support

Continue to support the students in writing words with vowel sounds that can be spelled in more than one way by referring to the "Spelling-Sound Chart."

slowly	"A turtle moves slowly."
neatly	"We put our materials away neatly."
softly	"The mother sings softly to her baby."
safely	"The crossing guard helps us to safely cross the street."

You may wish to challenge your students with the words *happily* and *easily*. Guide the students as follows to change *y* to *i* before adding the suffix.

happily	"I will happily help you with your homework."

Say *happily*. Use *happily* in a sentence. Then ask:

Q *What is the base word in* happily? *(*happy*)*

Have the students write *happy*.

Write *happy* where everyone can see it, and have the students check their writing and erase and correct mistakes. Say *happily* again. Then ask and briefly discuss:

Q *What is the suffix in* happily? *(-ly)*

Remind the students that when the base word ends with *y*, they must change the *y* to *i* before adding *l-y*. Have the students erase *y*, write *i*, and then add the suffix to write *happily*. When most students are finished, write *happily* where everyone can see it, and have the students check their writing and erase and correct mistakes.

Repeat the procedure with the word *easily*.

easily	"With practice, you will soon be spelling easily."

4 Discuss and Reflect on Spelling Words

Direct the students' attention to the guided spelling words you have written. Ask:

 Q *What do you notice about these words? Turn to a person sitting next to you.*

After a few moments, signal for the students' attention and have a few volunteers share their thinking with the class.

> **Students might say:**
> "They end with *-ly*."
> "Most words have two syllables."

Explain that the students will have a spelling test on Friday (or whichever day of the week you will teach the Day 4 lesson). Remind them that it is important for them to practice these words in their *Word Study Notebooks* during the week so that they can do well on the test.

Teacher Note

You may wish to post the *Word Study Notebook* page number for this week's spelling practice in the word work area for the students to refer to during Independent Work.

In this lesson, the students:

- Read words with the suffixes -er, -ist, and -or

- Listen respectfully to the thinking of others and share their own

1 Gather and Review Suffixes

Gather the class with partners sitting together, facing you. Remind the students that in the last few weeks they have read and spelled words with the suffixes -er, -est, and -ly.

2 Introduce the Two Meanings of the Suffix -er

Write the word *small* where everyone can see it and have the students read it aloud.

Write the word *smaller* under *small* and have the students read it aloud. Review that the suffix -er means "more" and that when e-r is added to the base word *small*, it makes the word *smaller*, which means "more small, or littler." Tell the students that there is another meaning for -er.

Explain that the suffix -er can also mean "a person who." Write the word *farm* where everyone can see it, and have the students read it aloud.

Then write the word *farmer* under *farm* and have the students read it aloud. Draw a dot between the syllables *farm* and *er* and remind the students that the dot can help them see and read syllables in a word. Have the students read *farmer*, first by syllables and then as a whole word. Ask and briefly discuss:

Q *What does a farmer do?*

Write the word *teacher* where everyone can see it. Draw a dot between *teach* and *er* and have the students read *teacher*, first by syllables and then as a whole word.

Ask and briefly discuss:

Q *What does* teach *mean?*

Q *What does a teacher do?*

Repeat the procedure with the words *player* and *worker*.

Have the students brainstorm additional words that mean "a person who," and write the words where everyone can see them.

3 Discuss Multiple Meanings

Review that -er can mean either "more" or "a person who." Write the definitions of -er where everyone can see them.

Teacher Note

The suffix -er is introduced in the vocabulary instruction in the *Making Meaning*® program from Center for the Collaborative Classroom. If you have taught the -er lesson in the *Vocabulary Teaching Guide*, you may want to briefly review -er and then continue to Step 3.

Write the word *slower* where everyone can see it. Draw a dot between *slow* and *er* and have the students read *slower*, first by syllables and then as a whole word. Use *slower* in a sentence. Ask and briefly discuss:

Q *Which meaning does the ending -er have in* slower? *Why do you think that?*

Write the word *helper*. Have the students read *helper*, first by syllables and then as a whole word. Use *helper* in a sentence. Then ask:

Q *Which meaning does the ending -er have in* helper? *Why do you think that?*

Repeat the procedure with the words *reader*, *brighter*, *kinder*, and *swimmer*. Use the word *swimmer* to point out that for a base word with a short vowel sound, two consonants are needed when adding *e-r*, just as they are when adding *i-n-g* or *e-d*.

Use "Think, Pair, Share" to discuss:

 Q *How can you tell whether* -er *means "more" or "a person who"?* [pause] *Turn to your partner.*

After a few moments, signal for attention and have a few students share their thinking with the class.

> **Students might say:**
>
> "We can try each meaning of -*er* and decide which one makes sense."
>
> "If the base word means something you can do, -*er* means 'a person who.'"

Explain that when -*er* means "a person who," the base word is usually a *verb*—a word that shows action, and when -*er* means "more," the base word is usually an *adjective*—a word that describes a person, place, animal, or thing.

4 Introduce the Suffixes *-or* and *-ist*

Explain that the suffixes *-or* and *-ist* also mean "a person who." Write the word *sailor* where everyone can see it. Draw a dot between *sail* and *or* and remind the students that the dot can help them see and read the syllables in a word. Have the students read *sailor*, first by syllables and then as a whole word.

Explain that *sail* can mean "work on a ship or boat." Ask and briefly discuss:

Q *Would you want to be a sailor? Why or why not?*

Write *artist*. Draw a dot between *art* and *ist* and have the students read *artist*, first by syllables and then as a whole word. Ask and briefly discuss:

Q *What does an artist do?*

Teacher Note

For the words *artist* and *cartoonist*, you may wish to point out that the base words, *art* and *cartoon*, are nouns and not verbs.

Repeat the procedure with the words *visitor* and *cartoonist*.

5 Reflect on the Class Discussion

Ask and briefly discuss:

 Q *How did you do with talking and listening today? Turn to your partner.*

After a few moments, signal for the students' attention and have a few volunteers share their thinking with the class. Then share your observations about what went well during the lesson today.

Word Study
Whole-class Sort (Closed)

Day 3

In this lesson, the students:

- Read and sort words with the suffixes *-er*, *-or*, *-ist*, and *-est*

1 Gather and Get Ready to Sort

Gather the class with the students sitting, facing you. Review that yesterday the students learned about the suffixes *-er*, *-or*, and *-ist*. Explain that today the students will work together to sort words with the suffixes *-er*, *-or*, *-ist*, and *-est*.

2 Read the Sort Words

Display the "Week 16, Day 3 Sort" activity (WA1). Have the students read the words together as a class.

player	largest	sailor	slower
darker	illustrator	faster	artist
swimmer	lower	hunter	teacher
quicker	helper	clearest	brighter

🌐 ELL Vocabulary

English Language Learners may benefit from hearing the following vocabulary defined:

sailor: person who works on a sailboat

hunter: person who catches animals for food

clearest: most easily understood

Materials

- "Week 16, Day 3 Sort" (WA1)
- Copies of "Week 16, Day 3 Sort" (BLM1) in the word work area

Explain that the class will now sort the words by the meanings of the suffixes. Review the meanings of the suffixes *-er, -or, -ist,* and *-est* ("more," "a person who," and "most"). Create categories by writing the following as headings on the "Week 16, Day 3 Sort" activity (WA1): *more, most,* and *a person who.*

4 Sort by Meaning of Suffix

Point to the word *player* on the word list. Draw a dot between *play* and *er* and have the students read the word, first by syllables and then as a whole word. Use *player* in a sentence. (For example, "The soccer player scored a goal in the second half of the game.")

Ask and briefly discuss:

Q *In the word* player, *does the suffix* -er *mean "more" or "a person who"? Why do you think that?*

Repeat the procedure with the remaining words.

Click the reset icon on the CCC toolbar to clear the dots from the "Week 16, Day 3 Sort" activity (WA1). Point to *player* and ask:

Q *Which category does the word* player *belong in?*

Drag the word under the appropriate category. Repeat this procedure with the remaining words and then have the students read the sorted words by category.

WA1

more	most	a person who
slower	largest	player
faster	clearest	hunter
darker		helper
brighter		artist
quicker		swimmer
lower		teacher
		sailor
		illustrator

Teacher Note

If the students need additional support reading the words, consider framing the word parts as the students read them.

🌐 ELL Note

Check your English Language Learners' comprehension of the sort words and, if necessary, provide additional examples to clarify meaning.

💡 Facilitation Tip

Reflect on your experience over the past four weeks with **pacing class discussions**. Do the pacing techniques feel comfortable and natural for you? Do you find yourself using them throughout the school day? What effect has your focus on pacing had on your students' participation in discussions? We encourage you to continue to think about how to pace class discussions throughout the year.

Tell the students that you have put copies of the sort in the "Word Sorts" bin in the word work area. When they go to independent word work, they will sort the words again and record their sorts in their *Word Study Notebooks*.

5 Reflect on Sorting

Ask and briefly discuss:

Q *How did sorting go today? What was easy? What was hard?*

Teacher Note

If you prefer, you might suggest to the students that they can do the sort in pairs if they wish. Ask and briefly discuss:

Q *How will you find someone to do the sort with if you want to work with a partner?*

Q *What can you say if someone asks you to be his or her partner and you don't want to do the sort at that time?*

Word Study
Spelling Test
Day 4

In this lesson, the students:
- Spell words with the suffix *-ly*
- Handle materials responsibly

1 Get Ready to Spell

Have the students stay in their seats today. Ask and briefly discuss:

Q *How did you do with your independent spelling practice this week?*

2 Spelling Test

Distribute paper and pencils to the students. Have them write their names at the top and number the first eight lines 1 to 8. If necessary, review the procedure for writing and checking the spelling words.

Begin the test. Say "Number one: kindly." Use *kindly* in a sentence. (For example, "The vet always treats the animals kindly.") Say *kindly* again. Have the students write *kindly*. Allow enough time for all the students to finish before moving on to the next word.

Repeat this procedure for the remaining spelling words.

1. kindly   "The vet always treats the animals kindly."

2. sadly   "She looked at the broken toys sadly."

3. bravely   "He walked bravely into the dark forest."

4. friendly   "It is friendly to welcome new students to the school."

Materials
- Lined paper and a pencil for each student
- "Week 16, Day 4 Spelling Words" (WA2)
- "Class Assessment Record" sheet (CA1)

5.	slowly	"We trudged very slowly through the snow."
6.	neatly	"She wrote the note neatly, so it was easy to read."
7.	softly	"He spoke so softly that we could barely hear him."
8.	safely	"The pilot safely landed the airplane."

3 Check and Correct the Words

After the students are finished writing the last word, display the "Week 16, Day 4 Spelling Words" activity (WA2). Explain that the students will check their work by looking at each word they wrote and comparing it to the corresponding word in the word list.

Have the students check their work and correct mistakes. As they work, circulate and observe.

> **✓ CLASS ASSESSMENT NOTE**
>
> Ask yourself:
> - Are the students able to identify the base words and endings in the words?
> - Are they able to spell the words?
> - Do they notice when a word is spelled incorrectly?
>
> Record your observations on the "Class Assessment Record" sheet (CA1); see page 90 of the *Assessment Resource Book*. Support students who are struggling to check their work by reminding them to look at each word in the word list and ask themselves if they spelled the word the same way.

When the students are finished checking and correcting their work, collect the papers.

4 Reflect on Spelling

Have the students reflect on the spelling test. Ask and briefly discuss:

Q *What words were hard to spell this week? How did you figure out how to spell them?*

Q *If you have used any of the spelling words in your writing, which words did you use? What did you write about?*

Tell the students that they will learn more about base words and suffixes in the coming weeks.

Independent Work Connection

For next week's Independent Work, we suggest the following:

- Make additional copies of "Week 16, Day 3 Sort" (BLM1) to place in the word work area.

Independent Work

This week the students continue to rotate to and work in all three independent work areas around the room while you teach Small-group Reading. We suggest continuing any procedures that have worked effectively in previous weeks.

Independent Work Check-in

This week you will continue to teach an Independent Work Check-in lesson on the day of the week you do not teach Small-group Reading. The purpose of these check-in lessons is to ensure that the students are able to maintain successful independent work rotations. The lessons provide the time for you to assess your students, conduct conferences, and introduce new materials and activities. For more information about the check-in lessons, see Appendix B, "Independent Work Resources."

This week we suggest you teach the "Share a Book" check-in lesson in Appendix B, "Independent Work Resources." Depending on the needs of your students, you may decide to teach a different check-in lesson.

Week 17 OVERVIEW

Whole-class Instruction

Word Study

This week the students learn about the suffixes *-less* and *-ful* and discuss antonyms. They do an open pair sort using base words and the suffixes *-less* and *-ful*. The spelling words for the week are words with the suffixes *-er*, *-or*, and *-ist*. You may wish to assess your students' understanding of concepts taught in the previous nine weeks using the Word Study Progress Assessment. See the Word Study Progress Assessment Note at the end of the Day 4 lesson.

Independent Work Check-in

This week we suggest you teach the "Share Writing" check-in lesson in Appendix B, "Independent Work Resources." Depending on the needs of your students, you may decide to teach a different check-in lesson.

Small-group Reading Instruction and Independent Work Rotations

Small-group Reading

This week you will continue to teach Small-group Reading lessons at the small-group reading table while the students work independently in the reading, writing, and word work areas.

Independent Work

The students may have assigned work from Small-group Reading to do during Independent Work. The following are materials you might incorporate into independent work areas this week:

Word Work:

- "Week 16, Day 3 Sort" (see "Independent Work Connection" on page 353)

RESOURCES

Assessment Resource Book

- Week 17 assessments
- Word Study Progress Assessment 2

Word Study Notebook

- Word Sorts
- Spelling Practice

 Online Resources

Visit the CCC Learning Hub (ccclearninghub.org) to find your online resources for this week.

Whiteboard Activities

- WA1–WA3

Assessment Forms

- "Class Assessment Record" sheet (CA1)
- "Word Study Progress Assessment 2" recording form (WS2)
- "Word Study Progress Assessment 2 Student Card" (SC2)
- "Word Study Progress Assessment 2 Class Record" sheet (CR2)

Reproducible

- "Week 17, Day 3 Sort" (BLM1)

Professional Development Media

- "Asking Facilitative Questions" (AV8)

⏱ DO AHEAD

Word Study

✓ Prior to Day 1, familiarize yourself with the Day 1 Spelling Words.

✓ Prior to Day 2, familiarize yourself with the Day 2 Practice Words.

✓ Prior to Day 3, familiarize yourself with the Day 3 Sort Words.

✓ Prior to Day 3, visit the CCC Learning Hub (ccclearninghub.org) to access and print "Week 17, Day 3 Sort" (BLM1). Make enough copies for each pair of students to have one.

✓ Prior to Day 3, visit the CCC Learning Hub (ccclearninghub.org) to access and print the "Class Assessment Record" sheet (CA1); see page 91 of the *Assessment Resource Book.*

Independent Work Check-in

✓ Familiarize yourself with the "Share Writing" check-in lesson (or another check-in lesson of your choice) in Appendix B, "Independent Work Resources." Collect and prepare any necessary materials. For more information about the check-in lessons, see Appendix B, "Independent Work Resources."

📅 SUGGESTED WEEKLY SCHEDULE

Monday	Tuesday	Wednesday	Thursday	Friday
Word Study (20)	Word Study (20)		Word Study (20)	Word Study (20)
Independent Work Rotations/Small-group Reading (60)	Independent Work Rotations/Small-group Reading (60)	Independent Work Check-in (35)	Independent Work Rotations/Small-group Reading (60)	Independent Work Rotations/Small-group Reading (60)
80 minutes	80 minutes	35 minutes	80 minutes	80 minutes

Day 1 Spelling Words		Day 2 Practice Words		Day 3 Sort Words	
artist	*Challenge Words*	careful	hopeless	care	helpful
harder	driver	careless	joyful	careful	helping
helper	swimmer	cheerful	lifeless	careless	helpless
hunter		fearful	thoughtful	caring	hope
quicker		fearless	thoughtless	fear	hoped
sailor		helpful	truthful	fearful	hopeful
slower		helpless	useful	fearless	hopeless
teacher		hopeful	useless	help	hoping

Academic Focus

- Students spell words with the suffixes *-er*, *-ist*, and *-or*.
- Students learn the suffixes *-ful* and *-less*.
- Students read and sort words with the suffixes *-ful* and *-less*.
- Students discuss antonyms.

Social Development Focus

- Students work in a responsible way.
- Students handle materials responsibly.
- Students listen respectfully to the thinking of others and share their own.

Day 1 Word Study
Guided Spelling

Materials

- Wipe-off board, dry-erase marker, and tissue or cloth for each student

In this lesson, the students:

- Review the suffixes *-er*, *-or*, and *-ist*
- Spell words with the suffixes *-er*, *-or*, and *-ist*
- Handle materials responsibly

1 Get Ready to Spell

Have the students stay in their seats. Explain that today the students will spell words with the suffixes *-er*, *-or*, and *-ist*.

2 Review the Suffix -er

Review that the suffix -er can mean "more" or "a person who." Write the word *planner* where everyone can see it. Ask and briefly discuss:

Q *What is the base word in* planner? (plan)

Q *Does* planner *mean "more plans" or "a person who plans"? Why do you think that?*

3 Guide the Students' Spelling

Distribute the wipe-off boards, markers, and cloths or tissues.

hunter	"The hunter is a character in 'Little Red Riding Hood.'"

Say *hunter*. Use *hunter* in a sentence. Have the students say *hunter*. Then ask:

Q *What is the base word in* hunter? (hunt)

Have the students write *hunt*. Then ask:

Q *What is the suffix in* hunter? (-er)

Have the students write the rest of *hunter*.

Write *hunter* where everyone can see it, and have the students check their writing and erase and correct mistakes.

harder	"It is harder to climb a mountain than it is to climb a hill."

Say *harder*. Use *harder* in a sentence. Have the students say *harder*. Then ask:

Q *What is the base word in* harder? (hard)

Q *What vowel sound do you hear in* hard? (/är/)

Q *How do you spell* /är/? (a-r)

Have the students write *hard*.

Write *hard* where everyone can see it, and have the students check their writing and erase and correct mistakes. Then ask:

Q *What is the suffix in* harder? (-er)

Have the students write the rest of *harder*.

Write the rest of *harder* where everyone can see it, and have the students check their writing and erase and correct mistakes.

teacher	"I am your teacher."

Say *teacher*. Use *teacher* in a sentence. Have the students say *teacher*. Then ask:

Q *What is the base word in* teacher? (teach)

Q *What is the vowel sound in* teach? (long e)

Q *Is there more than one way to spell long e? (yes)*

Q *What ways can you spell long e?* (e-e, e-a, e_e)

Tell the students to think carefully about which spelling of long *e* to use.

Have the students write *teach*. Then ask:

Q *Does* teach *look right to you the way you spelled it? If not, do you want to change how you spelled long* e?

Write *teach* where everyone can see it, and have the students check their writing and erase and correct mistakes. Then ask:

Q *What is the suffix in* teacher? (-er)

Have the students write the rest of *teacher*.

Write the rest of *teacher* where everyone can see it, and have the students check their writing and erase and correct mistakes.

artist   "The artist painted a beautiful picture."

Say *artist*. Use *artist* in a sentence. Have the students say *artist*. Then ask:

Q *What is the base word in* artist? (art)

Q *How do you spell the vowel sound in* art? (a-r)

Have the students write *art*.

Write *art* where everyone can see it, and have the students check their writing and erase and correct mistakes. Then ask:

Q *What is the suffix in* artist? (-ist)

Have the students write the rest of *artist*.

Write the rest of *artist* where everyone can see it, and have the students check their writing and erase and correct mistakes.

Repeat the procedure with the words *helper*, *sailor*, *slower*, and *quicker*.

You may wish to challenge the students with the words *swimmer* and *driver*.

swimmer   "My brother is a very good swimmer."

Say *swimmer*. Use *swimmer* in a sentence. Then ask:

Q *What is the base word in* swimmer? (swim)

Q *What vowel sound do you hear in* swim? (short i)

Have the students write *swim*.

Write *swim* where everyone can see it, and have the students check their writing and erase and correct mistakes. Say *swimmer* again. Then ask:

Q *Is the vowel sound in* swim *short or long? (short)*

Q *What is the suffix in* swimmer? (-er)

Tell the students that before adding *e-r* to a base word with a short vowel sound, they must make sure there are two consonants before *e-r* just as they do for *i-n-g* and *e-d*. Explain that because *swim* has just one consonant at the end, they must add another *m* before adding *e-r*.

Have the students write the rest of *swimmer*. When most students are finished, call for their attention. Write the rest of *swimmer* where everyone can see it, and have the students check their writing and erase and correct mistakes.

driver   "She is always a very careful driver."

Say *driver*. Use *driver* in a sentence. Then ask:

Q *What is the base word in* driver? (drive)

If necessary, tell the students that in *drive* the long *i* sound is spelled with final *e*. Have the students write *drive*. Then ask:

Q *What is the suffix in* driver? (-er)

Tell the students that in words with the final *e* spelling, the *e* is dropped before adding *e-r*. To spell *driver*, they must drop the final *e* and then add *e-r*.

Have the students write the rest of *driver*.

When most students are finished, call for their attention. Write *driver* where everyone can see it, and have the students check their writing and erase and correct mistakes.

4 Wrap Up

Explain that the students will have a spelling test on Friday (or whichever day of the week you will teach the Day 4 lesson). Remind the students that it is important for them to practice these words in their *Word Study Notebooks* during the week so that they can remember how to spell the words.

Ask and briefly discuss:

Q *How will you make sure to do your spelling practice this week?*

Teacher Note

You may wish to post the *Word Study Notebook* page number for this week's spelling practice in the word work area for the students to refer to during Independent Work.

Materials

- "Week 17, Day 2 Words" (WA1)

Teacher Note

The suffixes *-less* and *-ful* are introduced in the vocabulary instruction in the *Making Meaning®* program from Center for the Collaborative Classroom. If you have taught the lesson in the *Vocabulary Teaching Guide*, you may want to briefly review *-less* and *-ful* and then continue to Step 4.

💡 Facilitation Tip

Practice **asking facilitative questions** during class discussions to help the students build on one another's thinking and respond directly to one another, not just to you. After a student comments, ask the class questions such as:

Q *Do you agree or disagree with [Deborah]? Why?*

Q *What questions can you ask [Deborah] about what she said?*

Q *What can you add to what [Deborah] said?*

To see this Facilitation Tip in action, view "Asking Facilitative Questions" (AV8).

In this lesson, the students:

- Learn the suffixes *-less* and *-ful*
- Read words with the suffixes *-less* and *-ful*
- Listen respectfully to the thinking of others and share their own

1 Gather and Review Base Words and Suffixes

Gather the class with partners sitting together, facing you. Explain that in this lesson you will ask partners to think and talk about some words. Ask and briefly discuss:

Q *What can you do to be respectful when you are working with your partner?*

Review that earlier the students read and spelled words with the suffixes *-er*, *-est*, and *-ly*. Then ask:

Q *What do you know about suffixes?*

Have a few volunteers share their ideas with the class.

> **Students might say:**
>
> "A suffix comes at the end of a word."
>
> "Suffixes make new words."
>
> "Sometimes you have to change *y* to *i* before you add a suffix."

2 Discuss the Words *Fearless* and *Fearful*

Write *fearless* where everyone can see it, and read it aloud. Use "Think, Pair, Share" to discuss:

 Q *What do you know about the word* fearless? [pause] *Turn to your partner.*

After a few moments, signal for the students' attention and have a few volunteers share their thinking with the class.

Explain that the word *fearless* means "without fear." Someone who is fearless is not afraid. Use *fearless* in a sentence. (For example, "My mother is fearless because she is not afraid of anything.")

Write *fearful* where everyone can see it and read it aloud. Then use "Think, Pair, Share" to discuss:

 Q *What do you know about the word* fearful? [pause] *Turn to your partner.*

After a few moments, signal for the students' attention and have a few volunteers share their thinking with the class.

Explain that the word *fearful* means "full of fear" or "afraid." Someone who is fearful is afraid. Use *fearful* in a sentence. (For example, "I am fearful of skydiving because it is dangerous.")

3 Introduce the Suffixes -*less* and -*ful*

Explain that readers who know how words work can understand more of what they read. Knowing the meaning of the suffixes -*less* and -*ful* can help the students if they come to a word they do not know that has one of these suffixes.

Direct the students' attention to the two words you have written, *fearless* and *fearful*. Ask:

Q *What is the same about these words?*

Have a few volunteers share their thinking with the class. If necessary, point out that *fear* is the base word in the words *fearless* and *fearful*. Then ask and briefly discuss:

Q *What is different about these words?*

Underline *less* and *ful* and explain that -*less* and -*ful* are both suffixes.

Tell the students that in the word *fearless*, the suffix -*less* means "without" so *fearless* means "without fear" or "not afraid." Draw a dot between the syllables *fear* and *less* and remind the students that the dot can help them see and read the syllables in a word. Have the students read *fearless*, first by syllables and then as a whole word.

Explain that in the word *fearful* the suffix -*ful* means "full of" so *fearful* means "full of fear" or "afraid." Draw a dot between the syllables *fear* and *ful*. Have the students read *fearful*, first by syllables and then as a whole word.

Write the words *hopeless* and *hopeful* where everyone can see them. Ask:

Q *What is the same about these words? What is different?*

Have a few volunteers share. Explain that when you hope for something, you wish for it to happen or to be true. Use *hope* in a sentence. (For example, "I hope we have nice weather this weekend.") Then ask:

 Q *Based on what you know about the suffixes* -less *and* -ful, *what do the words* hopeless *and* hopeful *mean? Turn to your partner.*

After a few moments, signal for the students' attention and have a few volunteers share.

4 Discuss Antonyms

Direct the students' attention to the word pairs *fearless/fearful* and *hopeless/hopeful* and point out that if two words have the same base word and end with the suffixes -*less* and -*ful*, they may be *antonyms*, or words with opposite meanings.

Write the word *painful* where everyone can see it. Ask:

 Q *What do you know about the word* painful? *Turn to your partner.*

After a few moments, signal for the students' attention and have a few volunteers share their thinking with the class.

> **Students might say:**
>
> "It has the suffix *-ful.*"
>
> "It has two syllables."
>
> "It means that something hurts."

Review that *painful* means "full of pain." Then write *painless* next to *painful*, and ask:

 Q *What do you think the word* painless *means? Why do you think that? Turn to your partner.*

After a few moments, signal for the students' attention and have a few volunteers share. If necessary, explain that if something is *painless*, it does not hurt at all. Point out that *painless* and *painful* are *antonyms*, or words with opposite meanings.

5 Read Words with the Suffixes *-less* and *-ful*

Tell the students that they will read more words with the suffixes *-less* and *-ful*; you will show them a word and they will say the suffix and then read the word. Display the "Week 17, Day 2 Words" activity (◖ WA1).

useful	useless	careful	joyful
careless	fearful	hopeless	cheerful
fearless	helpless	truthful	lifeless
thoughtful	hopeful	thoughtless	helpful

Suggested Vocabulary

useful: helpful

careless: doing things without thinking or planning

truthful: not lying

🌐 ELL Vocabulary

English Language Learners may benefit from hearing additional vocabulary defined, including:

helpless: not able to do things without help

thoughtless: not thinking about other people's feelings

joyful: very happy

cheerful: happy

lifeless: dead

Point to the first word and ask:

Q *What suffix do you see? (-ful)*

Draw a dot between *use* and *ful*. Have the students read the word, first by syllables and then as a whole word.

Repeat this procedure with several of the remaining words.

WA1

use·ful	use·less	care·ful	joy·ful
care·less	fear·ful	hope·less	cheer·ful
fear·less	help·less	truth·ful	life·less
thought·ful	hope·ful	thought·less	help·ful

Decoding Support

If the students need additional support reading the words, consider framing the word parts as the students read them.

6 Reflect on Working with Partners

Ask and briefly discuss:

Q *What did you and your partner do to be respectful when you were talking about the words?*

Tell the students that in the next lesson, they will work with partners to sort words.

Word Study
Pair Sort (Open)

Day 3

In this lesson, the students:
- Read and sort words with the suffixes *-less* and *-ful*
- Work responsibly with a partner
- Handle materials responsibly

1 Gather and Review the Suffixes *-less* and *-ful*

Have the students bring their pencils, pick up their independent work toolboxes, and gather with partners sitting together, facing you. Have

Materials

- "Week 17, Day 3 Sort" (WA2)
- Copy of "Week 17, Day 3 Sort" (BLM1) for each pair
- Scissors for each pair
- *Word Study Notebooks* (in student toolboxes)
- Pencils
- "Class Assessment Record" sheet (CA1)

them put their toolboxes on the floor next to them. Review that in the last lesson the students read words with the suffixes -*less* and -*ful*.

Use "Think, Pair, Share" to discuss:

 Q *What do you remember about the suffixes* -less *and* -ful? [pause] *Turn to your partner.*

After a few moments, signal for the students' attention and have a few pairs share their thinking with the class.

> **Students might say:**
>
> "The suffix -*ful* means 'full of.'"
>
> "The suffix -*less* means 'without.'"
>
> "They make words into opposites."

If necessary, review that the suffix -*less* means "without" and the suffix -*ful* means "full of."

2 Introduce the Sort

Explain that today partners will work together to do an open sort. Some of the words have the suffixes -*less* and -*ful* and some of the words are from earlier sorts.

Use "Think, Pair, Share" to discuss:

 Q *How does open sorting help you think carefully about words?* [pause] *Turn to your partner.*

After a few moments, signal for the students' attention and have a few pairs share their thinking with the class.

> **Students might say:**
>
> "It makes you look carefully at the word parts."
>
> "It makes you think about the meanings of the words."
>
> "It makes you figure out how the words are the same."

Display the "Week 17, Day 3 Sort" activity (WA2). Have pairs read the words together quietly.

hopeful	help	hoped	helpful
helping	hoping	fear	hope
careful	caring	careless	helpless
fearless	fearful	hopeless	care

Teacher Note

In this lesson, the students do not read all the word sort words as a class. The purpose of this is to encourage the students to read the words carefully with their partners. Base words are included in the sort to provide extra support for students who find it challenging to read the polysyllabic words.

When most pairs have finished reading, signal for the students' attention. Use "Think, Pair, Share" to discuss:

 Q *What are some words you could group together?* [pause] *Turn to your partner.*

After a few moments, signal for the students' attention and have a few pairs share their thinking with the class.

As volunteers share, ask follow-up questions, such as:

Q *What is alike about [careless and fearless]?*

Q *What other words could you group with [help and helpful]? Why does [helpless] go with [help and helpful]?*

Q *What did you notice about [care and hope] that made you think of grouping them together?*

Tell the students that the words can be sorted in many different ways. Remind the students that if they start to sort one way and find it does not make sense, they may try sorting another way.

3 Sort in Pairs

 Distribute a copy of "Week 17, Day 3 Sort" (BLM1) and scissors to each pair. Have each pair refer to the steps on the "Word Sort Steps" chart to cut apart and sort the words and then record their sort in their *Word Study Notebooks*.

Circulate and observe as the students work, offering support as necessary.

☑ CLASS ASSESSMENT NOTE

Ask yourself:

- Are the students able to generate ideas and start sorting?
- Do their categories make sense?
- Are they able to name their categories?

Record your observations on the "Class Assessment Record" sheet (CA1); see page 91 of the *Assessment Resource Book*. Support any pairs who struggle by asking questions such as:

Q *What is alike about these words? What other words might you group with them?*

Q *Why did you decide to group these words together?*

Q *How can you turn what you just told me into a name for the category?*

Teacher Note

If the students have difficulty generating ideas, prompt their thinking by reviewing the "Ways We Have Sorted" chart and sharing some of your own ideas.

Teacher Note

If your students need more support, you might use the "Week 17, Day 3 Sort" activity (WA2) to sort a few words as a class. Students may categorize by suffix or base word, or they may find other ways to sort.

Teacher Note

The pair sort allows you to observe and identify students who may need additional support. If you identify several students who are struggling, you might gather them at a different time during the day and repeat the sort as a group with your guidance.

4 Reflect on Sorting

Ask:

 Q *What is a word you sorted today that you would like to use in your writing? How would you use it? Turn to your partner.*

After a few moments, signal for the students' attention and have a few pairs share their thinking with the class. Share your observations about what went well during the open sort. Tell the students that in the next lesson they will take a spelling test with the words they have been practicing this week.

Day 4

Word Study
Spelling Test

Materials

- Lined paper and a pencil for each student
- "Week 17, Day 4 Spelling Words" (WA3)

In this lesson, the students:

- Spell words with -*er*, -*ist*, and -*or*
- Handle materials responsibly

1 Get Ready to Spell

Have the students stay in their seats today. Ask and briefly discuss:

Q *How did you do with your independent spelling practice this week?*

2 Spelling Test

Distribute paper and pencils to the students. Have them write their names at the top and number the first eight lines 1 to 8.

Begin the test. Say "Number one: hunter." Use *hunter* in a sentence. Say *hunter* again. Have the students write *hunter*. Allow enough time for all the students to finish before moving on to the next word.

Repeat this procedure for the remaining spelling words.

1. hunter   "The lion is a skillful hunter."
2. harder   "We can now spell harder words than earlier in the year."
3. teacher   "My teacher helped me learn math facts."
4. artist   "The artist drew a pretty vase with flowers."
5. helper   "I can be a helper by cleaning up after independent work."

6. sailor   "The sailor stayed on the ship for two weeks."

7. slower   "Drivers have to go at a slower speed when it is snowing."

8. quicker   "A rabbit is quicker than a turtle."

3 Check and Correct the Words

After the students are finished writing the last word, display the "Week 17, Day 4 Spelling Words" activity (WA3). Have the students check their work and correct mistakes. When the students are finished checking and correcting their work, collect the papers.

4 Reflect on Spelling

Have the students reflect on the spelling test. Ask and briefly discuss:

Q *Which words were hard to spell this week? What did you do to remember how to spell them?*

☑ WORD STUDY ASSESSMENT NOTE

Administer Word Study Progress Assessment 2 after this lesson, using "Word Study Progress Assessment 2" recording form (WS2) and "Word Study Progress Assessment 2 Student Card" (SC2); see pages 110–111 of the *Assessment Resource Book*.

Support any students who struggle to read the words by repeating instruction for concepts that are challenging for them, individually or in a small group. Keep in mind that the best assessment of students' reading is to notice how they use what they have learned when reading connected text.

Teacher Note

You may wish to use "Word Study Progress Assessment 2 Class Record" sheet (CR2) to record the assessment results for the whole class. See page 112 of the *Assessment Resource Book*.

Independent Work Connection

For next week's Independent Work, we suggest the following:

- Make several copies of "Week 17, Day 3 Sort" (BLM1) to place in the word work area.

Independent Work

This week the students continue to rotate to and work in all three independent work areas around the room while you teach Small-group Reading. We suggest continuing any procedures that have worked effectively in previous weeks.

Independent Work Check-in

This week you will continue to teach an Independent Work Check-in lesson on the day of the week you do not teach Small-group Reading. The purpose of these check-in lessons is to ensure that the students are able to maintain successful independent work rotations. The lessons provide the time for you to assess your students, conduct conferences, and introduce new materials and activities. For more information about the check-in lessons, see Appendix B, "Independent Work Resources."

This week we suggest you teach the "Share Writing" check-in lesson in Appendix B, "Independent Work Resources." Depending on the needs of your students, you may decide to teach a different check-in lesson.

Week 18 OVERVIEW

Whole-class Instruction

Word Study

This week the students review suffixes, including *-less* and *-ful*, and apply what they know to reading longer words. On Day 3, they read words as you transform them by adding and removing suffixes. "Build That Word" is included as an optional activity. The week's spelling words are words with the suffixes *-less* and *-ful*.

Independent Work Check-in

This week we suggest you teach the "Independent Work Observation" check-in lesson in Appendix B, "Independent Work Resources." Depending on the needs of your students, you may decide to teach a different check-in lesson.

Small-group Reading Instruction and Independent Work Rotations

Small-group Reading

This week you will continue to teach Small-group Reading lessons at the small-group reading table while the students work independently in the reading, writing, and word work areas.

Independent Work

The students may have assigned work from Small-group Reading to do during Independent Work. The following are materials you might incorporate into independent work areas this week:

Word Work:

- "Week 17, Day 3 Sort" (see "Independent Work Connection" on page 369)

Week 18

RESOURCES

Extension
- "Play 'Build That Word'"

Assessment Resource Book
- Week 18 assessment

Word Study Notebook
- Spelling Practice

 Online Resources

Visit the CCC Learning Hub (ccclearninghub.org) to find your online resources for this week.

Whiteboard Activities
- WA1–WA2

Assessment Form
- "Class Assessment Record" sheet (CA1)

Reproducible
- (Optional) "Week 18, 'Build That Word'" (BLM1)

⏱ DO AHEAD

Word Study

✓ Prior to Day 1, familiarize yourself with the Day 1 Spelling Words.

✓ Prior to Day 2, familiarize yourself with the Day 2 Practice Words.

✓ Prior to Day 3, familiarize yourself with the Day 3 Practice Words and think of examples of their use.

✓ Prior to Day 3, visit the CCC Learning Hub (ccclearninghub.org) to access and print the "Class Assessment Record" sheet (CA1); see page 92 of the *Assessment Resource Book*.

✓ (Optional) Prior to Day 3, write down the morphemic transformation sequences on an index card to expedite your delivery of the lesson (see Step 3).

✓ (Optional) If you plan to integrate "Build That Word" in the word work area, visit the CCC Learning Hub (ccclearninghub.org) to access and print "Week 18, 'Build That Word'" (BLM1). See "Independent Work Connection" on page 383.

Independent Work Check-in

✓ Familiarize yourself with the "Independent Work Observation" check-in lesson (or another check-in lesson of your choice) in Appendix B, "Independent Work Resources." Collect and prepare any necessary materials. For more information about the check-in lessons, see Appendix B, "Independent Work Resources."

📅 SUGGESTED WEEKLY SCHEDULE

Monday	Tuesday	Wednesday	Thursday	Friday
Word Study (20)	Word Study (20)		Word Study (20)	Word Study (20)
Independent Work Rotations/Small-group Reading (60)	Independent Work Rotations/Small-group Reading (60)	Independent Work Check-in (35)	Independent Work Rotations/Small-group Reading (60)	Independent Work Rotations/Small-group Reading (60)
80 minutes	**80 minutes**	**35 minutes**	**80 minutes**	**80 minutes**

Day 1 Spelling Words		Day 2 Practice Words		Day 3 Practice Words	
careful	*Challenge Words*	careful	helper	care	hoped
careless	beautiful	carefully	helplessly	cared	hopeful
fearful	penniless	fearless	hopelessly	careful	hopefully
fearless		gladly	joyfully	carefully	hopeless
helpful				careless	slow
helpless				fear	slowed
hopeful				feared	slower
hopeless				fearful	slowest
				fearfully	slowly
				fearless	use
				fearlessly	used
				help	useful
				helped	useless
				helpful	uselessly
				helpfully	user
				hope	

Academic Focus

- Students spell words with *-less* and *-ful*.
- Students review suffixes.
- Students use suffixes to read two- and three-syllable words.
- Students read morphemic transformations.

Social Development Focus

- Students work in a responsible way.
- Students handle materials responsibly.
- Students listen respectfully to the thinking of others and share their own.

In this lesson, the students:

- Review the suffixes -*less* and -*ful*
- Spell words with the suffixes -*less* and -*ful*
- Handle materials responsibly

1 Get Ready to Spell

Have the students stay in their seats. Explain that today the students will spell words with the suffixes -*less* and -*ful*.

2 Review the Suffixes -*less* and -*ful*

Write the words *joyful* and *joyless* where everyone can see them. Ask and briefly discuss:

Q *What is the base word in these words?* (joy)

Q *From what you know about* -ful *and* -less, *what do* joyful *and* joyless *mean?*

If necessary, review that the suffix -*less* means "without" and that *joyless* means "without happiness, or sad." Also review that the suffix -*ful* means "full of" and that *joyful* means "full of joy, or happy."

3 Guide the Students' Spelling

Distribute the wipe-off boards, markers, and tissues or cloths.

> helpful   "My sister is always very helpful around the house."

Say *helpful*. Use *helpful* in a sentence. Have the students say *helpful*. Then ask:

Q *What is the base word in* helpful? (help)

Have the students write *help*. Ask:

Q *What is the suffix in* helpful? (-ful)

Have the students write the rest of *helpful*.

Write *helpful* where everyone can see it, and have the students check their writing and erase and correct mistakes.

Materials

- Wipe-off board, dry-erase marker, and tissue or cloth for each student

Teacher Note

If necessary, explain that *joy* means "happiness."

Spelling Support

If necessary, continue to support the students in writing words with vowel sounds that can be spelled in more than one way. You might point to the correct spelling on the "Spelling-Sound Chart."

Spelling Support

You may have to tell the students the base word because of the change in pronunciation. *Beauty* is an irregular high-frequency word. You may wish to support your students by writing *beauty* where everyone can see it before you discuss the suffix.

Teacher Note

You may wish to support the students by asking:

Q *From what you know about the base word* penny *and the suffix* -less, *what do you think* penniless *means?*

If necessary, explain that *penniless* means "without money." If you are penniless, you do not have any money, not even a penny.

Teacher Note

You may wish to post the *Word Study Notebook* page number for this week's spelling practice in the word work area for the students to refer to during Independent Work.

Repeat the procedure with the words *fearless, hopeless, hopeful, careful, fearful, helpless,* and *careless.* Support the students in spelling the base words as needed.

fearless	"My cat is fearless; she isn't scared of anything."
hopeless	"The girl felt hopeless when she lost her homework."
hopeful	"I am hopeful that the weather will be nice this weekend."
careful	"We must always be careful when crossing the street."
fearful	"My dog is fearful—he's even afraid of the cat!"
helpless	"Helpless babies need grown-ups to take care of them."
careless	"I was careless and accidentally broke a glass."

You may wish to challenge the students with the words *beautiful* and *penniless.*

beautiful	"The sky was beautiful this morning at sunrise."

Say *beautiful.* Use *beautiful* in a sentence. Then ask:

Q *What is the base word in* beautiful? *(beauty)*

Have the students write *beauty.* Then ask:

Q *What is the suffix in* beautiful? *(-ful)*

Remind the students that when the base word ends with *y,* they must change the *y* to *i* before adding a suffix. Have the students erase *y* to write the rest of *beautiful.* When most students are finished, call for their attention and write *beautiful* where everyone can see it. Have the students check their writing and erase and correct mistakes.

penniless	"The girl spent all her allowance on a toy and was penniless for the rest of the week."

Use the same procedure with the word *penniless.*

4 Wrap Up

Explain that the students will have a spelling test on Friday (or whichever day of the week you will teach the Day 4 lesson). Remind the students that it is important for them to practice these words in their *Word Study Notebooks* during the week so that they can remember how to spell the words.

In this lesson, the students:

- Read words with multiple suffixes
- Learn a strategy for finding the meanings of unfamiliar words
- Listen respectfully to the thinking of others and share their own

1 Gather and Review Suffixes

Gather the class with partners sitting together, facing you. Ask and briefly discuss:

Q *When we are talking as a class, why is it important to listen carefully to what your classmates say?*

> **Students might say:**
>
> "It helps you think more about the question."
>
> "Sometimes you agree or disagree."

Remind the students that noticing the parts of words can help readers read the words more easily. Explain that in the next few lessons, the students will use what they know about base words and suffixes to read long words and talk about the words in pairs and as a class.

2 Read Words with One Suffix

Tell the students that they will read words with suffixes; you will show them a word and they will say the suffix and then read the word. Display the "Week 18, Day 2 Words" activity (WA1).

Point to the word *careful* and ask:

Q *Which suffix do you see? (-ful)*

Draw a dot between *care* and *ful*. Have the students read *careful*, first by syllables and then as a whole word.

Repeat this procedure with *gladly*, *fearless*, and *helper*.

Materials

- "Week 18, Day 2 Words" (WA1)

 ELL Note

If necessary, explain that *gladly* means "happily."

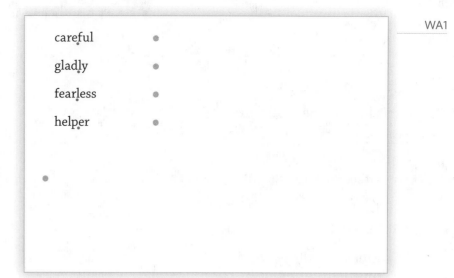

careful   •

gladly   •

fearless   •

helper   •

    •

3 Discuss and Read Words with Multiple Suffixes

Explain that you will show another word and the students will talk with partners about which suffix they see. Click to reveal *hopelessly.*

Point to the word *hopelessly* and use "Think, Pair, Share" to discuss:

 Q *Which suffix do you see?* [pause] *Turn to your partner.*

After a few moments, signal for the students' attention and have a few pairs share their thinking with the class.

Draw a dot between *hope* and *less* and one between *less* and *ly.* Point out that *hopelessly* has two suffixes, *-less* and *-ly.* Have the students read *hopelessly,* first by syllables and then as a whole word. Remind the students that *-ly* means "in a certain way." Ask and briefly discuss:

Q *What do you think* hopelessly *might mean?*

Click to reveal *carefully,* and ask:

Q *Which suffixes do you see?* (-ful, -ly)

As the students share, draw a dot between *care* and *ful* and one between *ful* and *ly.* Have the students read *carefully,* first by syllables and then as a whole word. Ask and briefly discuss:

Q *What do you think* carefully *might mean?*

Then use the same procedure to have the students analyze *helplessly* and *joyfully.*

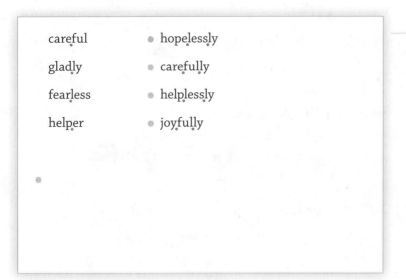

careful	• hopelessly
gladly	• carefully
fearless	• helplessly
helper	• joyfully

4 Discuss Checking to See Whether a Word Makes Sense

Tell the students that if they read a long word like *carelessly* and are not sure what it means, they may be able to use what they know about suffixes to help them figure out the meaning.

Click to reveal the sentence "She read carelessly, skipping over words and not thinking about whether the story made sense." Read it aloud with the students. Then ask and briefly discuss:

Q *From what you know about suffixes, what do you think* carelessly *means?*

> **Students might say:**
>
> "She cared less."
>
> "I disagree with [Haruki]. I think it means she didn't care."
>
> "In addition to what [Savannah] said, *-ly* means 'act in a certain way.'"

Reread the sentence and ask:

Q *Does [act in a way like she did not care] make sense in this sentence?*

Have a few volunteers share their thinking with the class. Review that thinking about suffixes is a strategy the students can use to help them understand words they read. Then, thinking about whether the word they read makes sense in the sentence will help them check the meaning.

5 Reflect on Listening Carefully

Ask and briefly discuss:

Q *How did you do with listening carefully to one another today?*

Tell the students that in the next lesson, they will have more opportunities to read long words.

 Facilitation Tip

Continue to **ask facilitative questions** to build accountability and participation during class discussions. Redirect students' comments to the class by asking:

Q *Do you agree or disagree with what [Ramon] just said? Why?*

Q *What can you add to what [Ramon] said?*

Materials

- "Class Assessment Record" sheet (CA1)

In this lesson, the students:

- Learn about morphemic transformations
- Listen respectfully to the thinking of others and share their own

ABOUT MORPHEMIC TRANSFORMATIONS

In morphemic transformations, the students read a series of words as you change the affixes (prefixes and suffixes) one at a time. The activity reinforces the students' understanding that many words are composed of base words and affixes, and that the addition of affixes can transform a word's meaning. The activity also demonstrates how pronunciation and spelling sometimes change with the addition of affixes. We suggest that you write the words for this activity where all the students can clearly see how you are changing a word each time they read it. Providing an example sentence for each word adds a layer of meaning and is particularly helpful for English Language Learners.

1 Gather and Review

Gather the class with partners sitting together, facing you. Remind the students that noticing the parts of long words can help readers read the words more easily. Explain that the students will use what they know about base words and suffixes to read long words today.

2 Introduce Morphemic Transformations

Explain that the students will read a base word first and then read a series of words that use the base word. For each word, the students will first read the syllables and then the whole word. Ask:

 Q *Why is it fair to wait for the signal to read before we start reading the first word in a list or sentence? Turn to your partner.*

After a few moments, signal for the students' attention and have a few volunteers share their thinking with the class.

> **Students might say:**
>
> "Everyone can read the word together."
>
> "We can all read the word to ourselves first before the class reads it."

Tell the students that when they wait for your signal and read together, all the students have a chance to think carefully about what they are reading.

3 Read Morphemic Transformations

Write the word *help* where everyone can see it. Have the students read the word.

Add *ful*. Have the students read *helpful*, first by syllables and then as a whole word.

Use *helpful* in a sentence. (For example, "My sister is very helpful to me when I am doing my homework.") Then add *ly*. Have the students read *helpfully*, first by syllables and then as a whole word. Then use *helpfully* in a sentence. (For example, "He helpfully asked if he could clean up the book corner.")

Follow the same procedure for the following words, erasing parts as needed to make changes:

- *hope, hopeful, hopefully, hopeless, hoped*
- *use, useless, uselessly, useful, user, used*
- *care, careful, carefully, careless, cared*
- *fear, fearless, fearlessly, fearful, fearfully, feared*
- *slow, slower, slowly, slowest, slowed*
- *help, helpful, helpfully, helped*

☑ CLASS ASSESSMENT NOTE

After this lesson, ask yourself:

- Are the students able to identify word parts?
- Are they able to read syllables and then read the word?
- Do the students understand how suffixes change the meanings of the words?

Record your observations on the "Class Assessment Record" sheet (CA1); see page 92 of the *Assessment Resource Book*.

4 Reflect on Reading

Ask and briefly discuss:

Q *How did you do with reading the words together today?*

Tell the students that in the next few weeks, they will have more opportunities to read long words.

Teacher Note

If the students struggle to read the words, consider framing the syllables as they read them.

Teacher Note

Using the word in a sentence after the students read it clarifies the meaning and the way the word is used.

Day 4

Word Study
Spelling Test

Materials

- Lined paper and a pencil for each student
- "Week 18, Day 4 Spelling Words" (WA2)

In this lesson, the students:

- Spell words with -*less* and -*ful*
- Handle materials responsibly

1 Get Ready to Spell

Have the students stay in their seats today. Explain that the students will take a spelling test.

2 Spelling Test

Distribute paper and pencils to the students. Have them write their names at the top and number the first eight lines 1 to 8.

Begin the test. Say "Number one: helpful." Use *helpful* in a sentence. Say *helpful* again. Have the students write *helpful*. Allow enough time for all the students to finish before moving on to the next word.

Repeat this procedure for the remaining spelling words.

1. helpful — "I try to be helpful by picking up my toys when I am done with them."

2. fearless — "She is fearless when she sees a snake; she stays calm and walks right by."

3. hopeless — "The team felt hopeless after losing another game."

4. hopeful — "I am hopeful that it will stop raining before recess."

5. careful — "You have to be careful when using scissors."

6. fearful — "I am fearful of spiders."

7. helpless — "I felt helpless when my foot got stuck in the mud."

8. careless — "She was careless with her toys, and many of them got broken."

3 Check and Correct the Words

After the students are finished writing the last word, display the "Week 18, Day 4 Spelling Words" activity (WA2). Have the students check their work and correct mistakes. When the students are finished checking and correcting their work, collect the papers.

4 Reflect on Spelling

Have the students reflect on the spelling test. Ask and briefly discuss:

Q *How did you do with spelling this week? What might you do differently next week?*

Tell the students they will have more opportunities to practice spelling in the coming weeks.

EXTENSION

Play "Build That Word"

You may wish to have partners play "Build That Word" using base words and suffixes. Distribute "Week 18 'Build That Word'" (BLM1) and scissors to each pair and have partners cut the tiles apart.

Remind the students that to start a game of "Build That Word," you will say a word and they will build that word with the tiles. Explain that in today's game, the students will build words with suffixes.

Have each pair clear a space and make sure all of the tiles are visible. Say *hopefully* and use it in a sentence. Have the students say and build *hopefully*. After a few moments, ask:

Q *What word did you build? (hopefully)*

Write *hopefully* where everyone can see it. Have the students check and correct their work.

Repeat this procedure with the words *wishful, dancer, painlessly, kindly,* and *baked.*

Explain that "Build That Word" will be available for the students to play during independent word work. Refer to "Week 18 'Build That Word'" (BLM1) and explain that pairs of students will be able to do this activity. Ask and briefly discuss:

Q *If you and your partner decide to play "Build That Word," how will you decide who will read and who will make the words?*

Independent Work Connection

For next week's Independent Work, we suggest the following:

- Make additional copies of "Week 18 'Build That Word'" (BLM1) to place in the word work area.

Teacher Note

Prior to teaching this activity, you will need to visit the CCC Learning Hub (ccclearninghub.org) to access and print "Week 18 'Build That Word'" (BLM1). Make enough copies for each pair of students to have one, plus extras to place in the word work area.

Teacher Note

If time allows, have the students think of other words they can build with the letter tiles.

OVERVIEW   Independent Work

This week the students continue to rotate to and work in all three independent work areas around the room while you teach Small-group Reading. We suggest continuing any procedures that have worked effectively in previous weeks.

Independent Work Check-in

This week you will continue to teach an Independent Work Check-in lesson on the day of the week you do not teach Small-group Reading. The purpose of these check-in lessons is to ensure that the students are able to maintain successful independent work rotations. The lessons provide the time for you to assess your students, conduct conferences, and introduce new materials and activities. For more information about the check-in lessons, see Appendix B, "Independent Work Resources."

This week we suggest you teach the "Independent Work Observation" check-in lesson in Appendix B, "Independent Work Resources." Depending on the needs of your students, you may decide to teach a different check-in lesson.

Week 19 OVERVIEW

Whole-class Instruction

Word Study

This week, the students learn about the prefix -un and discuss synonyms.
On Day 3, they do an open sort in pairs using words with prefixes and suffixes.
An optional morphemic transformation activity is included as an extension.
The week's spelling words are a review of affixes the students have learned.

Independent Work Check-in

This week we suggest you introduce new materials to an independent work
area using the "Introduce New Materials" check-in lesson in Appendix B,
"Independent Work Resources." Depending on the needs of your students,
you may decide to teach a different check-in lesson.

Small-group Reading Instruction and Independent Work Rotations

Small-group Reading

This week you will continue to teach Small-group Reading lessons at the
small-group reading table while the students work independently in the
reading, writing, and word work areas.

Independent Work

The students may have assigned work from Small-group Reading to do
during Independent Work. The following are materials you might incorporate
into independent work areas this week:

Word Work:

- "Week 18 'Build That Word'" (see "Independent Work Connection" on page 383)

Week 19

RESOURCES

Extension
- "Read Morphemic Transformations"

Assessment Resource Book
- Week 19 assessment
- Social skills assessment

Word Study Notebook
- Word Sorts
- Spelling Practice

 Online Resources

Visit the CCC Learning Hub (ccclearninghub.org) to find your online resources for this week.

Whiteboard Activities
- WA1–WA3

Assessment Forms
- "Class Assessment Record" sheet (CA1)
- "Social Skills Assessment Record" sheet (SS1)

Reproducible
- "Week 19, Day 3 Sort" (BLM1)

⏱ DO AHEAD

Word Study

✓ Prior to Day 1, familiarize yourself with the Day 1 Spelling Words.

✓ Prior to Day 2, familiarize yourself with the Day 2 Practice Words.

✓ Prior to Day 3, familiarize yourself with the Day 3 Sort Words.

✓ Prior to Day 3, visit the CCC Learning Hub (ccclearninghub.org) to access and print "Week 19, Day 3 Sort" (BLM1). Make enough copies for each pair of students to have one.

✓ Prior to Day 3, visit the CCC Learning Hub (ccclearninghub.org) to access and print the "Class Assessment Record" sheet (CA1); see page 93 of the *Assessment Resource Book*.

Independent Work Check-in

✓ Familiarize yourself with the "Introduce New Materials" check-in lesson (or another check-in lesson of your choice) in Appendix B, "Independent Work Resources." Collect and prepare any necessary materials. For more information about the check-in lessons, see Appendix B, "Independent Work Resources."

📅 SUGGESTED WEEKLY SCHEDULE

Monday	Tuesday	Wednesday	Thursday	Friday
Word Study (20)	Word Study (20)		Word Study (20)	Word Study (20)
Independent Work Rotations/Small-group Reading (60)	Independent Work Rotations/Small-group Reading (60)	Independent Work Check-in (35)	Independent Work Rotations/Small-group Reading (60)	Independent Work Rotations/Small-group Reading (60)
80 minutes	80 minutes	35 minutes	80 minutes	80 minutes

Word Study

Day 1 Spelling Words		Day 2 Practice Words		Day 3 Sort Words	
cheerful	needle	under	unpacked	careful	hopeless
fairly	playful	undo	unsnap	careless	lock
friendless	purple	unfair	unsnapped	fair	pack
gladly	worker	unfriendly	until	fearful	unfair
		unhelpful	unwrap	fearless	unlock
		unlock	unwrapped	helpful	unpack
		unlocked	unzip	helpless	unzipped
		unpack	unzipped	hopeful	zipped

Academic Focus

- Students spell review words.
- Students learn the prefix *un-*.
- Students read and sort words with the prefix *un-*.
- Students discuss synonyms.

Social Development Focus

- Students work in a responsible way.
- Students handle materials responsibly.
- Students listen respectfully to the thinking of others and share their own.

Day 1

Word Study
Guided Spelling

Materials

- Wipe-off board, dry-erase marker, and tissue or cloth for each student

In this lesson, the students:

- Review suffixes
- Spell words with more than one suffix
- Handle materials responsibly

1 Get Ready to Spell

Have the students stay in their seats. Explain that today the students will spell words with more than one suffix.

2 Review Suffixes

Review that a word can have more than one suffix. Remind the students that noticing the suffixes at the end of a word can help readers read and understand the word more easily.

Write the word *fearlessly* where everyone can see it. Ask:

Q *What is the base word in* fearlessly? *(fear)*

Q *What are the suffixes? (-less, -ly)*

Then ask:

 Q *What do you think* fearlessly *means? Why do you think that? Turn to the person sitting next to you.*

After a few moments, signal for the students' attention and have a few volunteers share their thinking with the class. If necessary, explain that if you act fearlessly, you act in a way that is without fear. Use *fearlessly* in a sentence. (For example, "She fearlessly jumped off the diving board into the pool.")

3 Guide the Students' Spelling

Distribute the wipe-off boards, markers, and cloths or tissues. Explain that the spelling words this week use everything the students have learned over the past several weeks.

fairly　　　　"The students played the game fairly."

Say *fairly*. Use *fairly* in a sentence. Have the students say *fairly*. Then ask:

Q *What is the base word in* fairly? *(fair)*

Have the students write *fair*.

Then ask:

Q *What is the suffix in* fairly? *(-ly)*

Have the students add *ly* to *fair*.

Write *fairly* where everyone can see it, and have the students check their writing and erase and correct mistakes.

Use the same procedure with the words *friendless, playful, cheerful, gladly, worker, purple,* and *needle*.

friendless　"The dragon was lonely because he was friendless."

playful　　　"The playful kitten chased the string."

cheerful　　"*Cheerful* is a synonym for *happy*."

gladly　　　 "The mother gladly read the book to the baby again."

Spelling Support

If necessary, continue to support the students in writing words with vowel sounds that can be spelled in more than one way and with unusual spellings. You might point to the correct spelling on the "Spelling-Sound Chart" or tell the students the spelling if a word is not on the word wall.

worker	"The school gardener is a hard worker."
purple	"Janelle's sweater today is purple."
needle	"I used a needle to sew the button back on my shirt."

4 Wrap Up

Explain that the students will have a spelling test on Friday (or whichever day of the week you will teach the Day 4 lesson). Remind the students that when they go to independent word work, they will practice spelling these words in their *Word Study Notebooks* before choosing another activity.

Teacher Note

You may wish to post the *Word Study Notebook* page number for the spelling practice in the word work area for the students to refer to during Independent Work.

Day 2

Word Study
Introduce the Prefix *un-*

Materials

- "Week 19, Day 2 Words" (WA1)

In this lesson, the students:

- Review suffixes
- Learn the prefix *un-*
- Read words with the prefix *un-*
- Discuss synonyms
- Listen respectfully to the thinking of others and share their own

1 Gather and Review Suffixes

Gather the class with partners sitting together, facing you. Review that the students have been reading and spelling words with suffixes. Ask:

Q *What do you know about suffixes?*

Have a few volunteers share their ideas with the class.

2 Discuss the Words *Unzip* and *Unhappy*

Write the word *unzip* where everyone can see it and read it aloud. Ask:

 Q *What do you know about the word* unzip? *Turn to your partner.*

After a few moments, signal for the students' attention and have a few volunteers share their thinking with the class. If necessary, explain that the word *unzip* means "open something using a zipper." Use *unzip* in a sentence. (For example, "I will unzip my jacket if I get too warm.")

Then write the word *unhappy* where everyone can see it and read it aloud. Ask:

 Q *What do you know about the word* unhappy? *Turn to your partner.*

After a few moments, signal for the students' attention and have a few volunteers share their thinking with the class. If necessary, explain that the word *unhappy* means "sad." Use *unhappy* in a sentence. (For example, "I was very unhappy when I couldn't go to the zoo.")

3 Introduce the Prefix *un-*

Direct the students' attention to the two words you have written, *unzip* and *unhappy*. Ask and briefly discuss:

Q *What is the same about these words?*

Q *What do you think* un- *might mean?*

Underline *un* and explain that *un-* is a prefix. Tell the students that a *prefix* is a letter or group of letters that is added to the beginning of a base word to make a new word.

Tell the students that adding the prefix *un-* to the base word *zip* makes the word *unzip*. In the word *unzip*, the prefix *un-* means "the opposite of." Draw a dot between the syllables *un* and *zip* and remind the students that the dot can help them see and read the syllables in a word. Have the students read *unzip*, first by syllables and then as a whole word.

Tell the students that adding the prefix *un-* to the base word *happy* makes the word *unhappy*. Explain that in the word *unhappy*, the prefix *un-* means "not." Draw a dot between the syllables *un* and *happy* and have the students read the word, first by syllables and then as a whole word.

Point out that when the prefix *un-* is added to a word, it often makes an *antonym*—a word with the opposite meaning. *Happy* and *unhappy* are antonyms.

Teacher Note

The prefix *un-* is introduced in the vocabulary instruction in the *Making Meaning*® program from Center for the Collaborative Classroom. If you have taught the lesson in the *Vocabulary Teaching Guide*, you may want to briefly review *un-* and then continue to Step 4.

Remind the students that *unhappy* means "sad." Explain that *unhappy* and *sad* are synonyms, and that *synonyms* are words that mean the same thing or almost the same thing. Remind the students that in a previous week they learned the word *joyful*, and that *joyful* means "happy." *Joyful* and *happy* are synonyms. Ask and briefly discuss:

Q *What other synonyms, or words that mean the same thing or almost the same thing, do you know?*

Add any word pairs the students suggest to your "Synonyms" chart, if you have started one, or begin a chart with the words the class discusses today.

5 Read the Words

Tell the students that they will read more words with the prefix *un-*. Display the "Week 19, Day 2 Words" activity (◖ WA1).

unzip	unzipped	unsnap	unfriendly
unpacked	unwrapped	unlocked	unhelpful
unlock	unfair	unwrap	under
undo	unpack	unsnapped	until

🌐 ELL Vocabulary

English Language Learners may benefit from hearing the following vocabulary defined:

undo: open or loosen something, like a button or knot

unsnap: open something that is fastened with a snap

Point to the first word and ask:

Q *What prefix do you see?* (un-)

Draw a dot between *un* and *zip*. Have the students read the word, first by syllables and then as a whole word.

Repeat this procedure with the next thirteen words. For *under* and *until*, have the students read both words with you. Then ask:

Q *What do you notice about these words?*

> **Students might say:**
>
> "*Under* starts with *u-n*, but *der* is not a base word."
>
> "*Until* starts with *u-n*, but *un* is part of the word."
>
> "Both words start with *u-n* but *un* doesn't mean 'not.' "

Teacher Note

If the students struggle to answer the question, provide a few words that you have already worked with in Word Study, such as *fearful*, *fearless*, and *faster*, and ask the students for their synonyms. Ask:

Q *What is another word for [fearful]?*

Explain that the letters *u-n* at the beginning of a word are not always the prefix that means "not." Point out that noticing *u-n* at the beginning of a word can help the students read the word even when the letters are not a prefix.

WA1

unzip	unzipped	unsnap	unfriendly
unpacked	unwrapped	unlocked	unhelpful
unlock	unfair	unwrap	under
undo	unpack	unsnapped	until

6 Reflect on Reading

Ask and briefly discuss:

Q *How did you do with reading the words together today?*

Tell the students that in the next lesson, they will work with partners to sort words.

Word Study
Pair Sort (Open)

Day 3

In this lesson, the students:

- Read and sort words with prefixes and suffixes
- Work responsibly with a partner
- Handle materials responsibly

1 Gather and Review

Have the students bring their pencils, pick up their independent work toolboxes, and gather with partners sitting together, facing you. Have them put their toolboxes on the floor next to them. Review that in the last lesson the students read words with the prefix *un-*. Remind them

Materials

- "Week 19, Day 3 Sort" (WA2)
- Copy of "Week 19, Day 3 Sort" (BLM1) for each pair
- Scissors for each pair
- "Word Sort Steps" chart
- *Word Study Notebooks* (in student toolboxes)
- Pencils
- "Class Assessment Record" sheet (CA1)

that a *prefix* is a letter or group of letters that is added to the beginning of a base word to make a new word. Review that noticing a prefix at the beginning of a word can help readers see the parts of the word and read the whole word.

Use "Think, Pair, Share" to discuss:

Q *What do you remember about the prefix* un-? [pause] *Turn to your partner.*

After a few moments, signal for the students' attention and have a few pairs share their thinking with the class.

> **Students might say:**
>
> "It comes at the beginning of words."
>
> "It changes the meaning of words."
>
> "It can make words into opposites."

Review that in many words the prefix *un-* means "the opposite of" or "not."

2 Introduce the Sort

Explain that today partners will work together to do an open sort. Some of the words have the prefix *un-* and some are words from earlier sorts.

Use "Think, Pair, Share" to discuss:

Q *When you do an open sort, what do you do or notice?* [pause] *Turn to your partner.*

After a few moments, signal for the students' attention and have a few pairs share their thinking with the class.

> **Students might say:**
>
> "I look carefully at the word parts."
>
> "I think about the meanings of the words."
>
> "I notice how the words are the same."

Display the "Week 19, Day 3 Sort" activity (◖ WA2). Have pairs read the words together quietly.

zipped	fearless	fearful	hopeless
helpless	unzipped	fair	helpful
hopeful	unlock	pack	lock
careful	unpack	careless	unfair

When most pairs have finished reading, signal for the students' attention. Use "Think, Pair, Share" to discuss:

 Q *What are some words you could group together?* [pause] *Turn to your partner.*

After a few moments, signal for the students' attention and have a few pairs share their thinking with the class.

As volunteers share, ask follow-up questions such as:

Q *What is alike about [*unzipped *and* unpack*]?*

Q *What other words could you group with [*fair *and* pack*]? Why does [*lock*] go with [*fair *and* pack*]?*

Q *What did you notice about [*fearless *and* hopeless*] that made you think of grouping them together?*

Tell the students that the words can be sorted in many different ways. Remind the students that if they start to sort one way and find it does not make sense, they may try sorting another way.

3 Sort in Pairs

 Distribute a copy of "Week 19, Day 3 Sort" (BLM1) and scissors to each pair of students. Have each pair refer to the steps on the "Word Sort Steps" chart to cut apart and sort the words and then record their sort in their *Word Study Notebooks*.

Circulate and observe as the students work, offering support as necessary.

☑ CLASS ASSESSMENT NOTE

Ask yourself:

- Are the students able to generate ideas and start sorting?
- Do their categories make sense?
- Are they able to name their categories?

Record your observations on the "Class Assessment Record" sheet (CA1); see page 93 of the *Assessment Resource Book*. Support any pairs who struggle by asking questions such as:

Q *What is alike about these words? What other words might you group with them?*

Q *Why did you decide to group these words together?*

Q *How can you turn what you just told me into a name for the category?*

Teacher Note

If the students have difficulty generating ideas, prompt their thinking by reviewing the "Ways We Have Sorted" chart and sharing some of your own ideas.

Teacher Note

If your students need more support, you might use the "Week 19, Day 3 Sort" activity (WA2) to sort a few words as a class. Students may categorize by prefix, suffix, or base word, or they may find other ways to sort.

Teacher Note

The pair sort allows you to observe and identify students who may need additional support. If you identify several students who are struggling, you might gather them at a different time during the day and repeat the sort as a group with your guidance.

4 Reflect on Sorting

Ask:

 Q *What is a word you sorted today that you would like to use in your writing? How would you use it? Turn to your partner.*

After a few moments, signal for the students' attention and have a few pairs share their thinking with the class. Share your observations about what went well during the open sort. Tell the students that in the next lesson, they will take a spelling test with the words they have been practicing this week.

Day 4

Word Study
Spelling Test

Materials

- Lined paper and a pencil for each student
- "Week 19, Day 4 Spelling Words" (WA3)

In this lesson, the students:
- Spell review words
- Handle materials responsibly

1 Get Ready to Spell

Have the students stay in their seats today. Tell the students that they will have a spelling test.

2 Spelling Test

Distribute paper and pencils to the students. Have them write their names at the top and number the first eight lines 1 to 8.

Begin the test. Say "Number one: fairly." Use *fairly* in a sentence. Say *fairly* again. Have the students write *fairly*. Allow enough time for all the students to finish before moving on to the next word.

Repeat this procedure for the remaining spelling words.

1. fairly   "We play games fairly."
2. friendless   "When he started at a new school, the friendless boy wished he had someone to play with."
3. playful   "The playful puppies like to run in circles."
4. cheerful   "Mia had a cheerful smile on her face."
5. gladly   "Kenji will gladly help you with your homework."
6. worker   "Samara is a hard worker."
7. purple   "We ate purple grapes for a snack."
8. needle   "Dad fixed his shirt with a needle and thread."

3 Check and Correct the Words

After the students are finished writing the last word, display the "Week 19, Day 4 Spelling Words" activity (🌙 WA3). Have the students check their work and correct mistakes.

4 Reflect on Spelling

Have the students reflect on the spelling test. Ask and briefly discuss:

Q *What is challenging about spelling words with suffixes? What is easy?*

Tell the students they will have more opportunities to practice spelling in the coming weeks.

EXTENSION

Read Morphemic Transformations

Write the word *kind* where everyone can see it. Have the students read it.

Add *un-* to the beginning of *kind*. Draw a dot between the syllables *un* and *kind*. Have the students read *unkind*, first by syllables and then as a whole word.

Use *unkind* in a sentence. (For example, "It was unkind of him not to help his sister.") Then add *ly*. Draw a dot between the syllables *kind* and *ly*. Have the students read *unkindly*.

Use *unkindly* in a sentence. (For example, "The older boys treated him unkindly.")

Follow the same procedure for the following words, erasing word parts as needed to make changes:

- *clear, clearly, clearer, unclear, cleared, clearest*
- *bright, brightly, brightest, brighter*
- *thought, thoughtful, thoughtfully, thoughtless*
- *pack, packed, unpacked, unpacking, packing*
- *help, helper, helpful, unhelpful, unhelpfully*

Independent Work Connection

For next week's Independent Work, we suggest the following:

- Make additional copies of "Week 19, Day 3 Sort" (BLM1) to place in the word work area.

Teacher Note

If the students struggle to read the words, consider framing the syllables.

Teacher Note

If necessary, have the students read by syllables before reading the whole word.

OVERVIEW | Independent Work

This week the students continue to rotate to and work in all three independent work areas around the room while you teach Small-group Reading. We suggest continuing any procedures that have worked effectively in previous weeks.

Independent Work Check-in

This week you will continue to teach an Independent Work Check-in lesson on the day of the week you do not teach Small-group Reading. The purpose of these check-in lessons is to ensure that the students are able to maintain successful independent work rotations. The lessons provide the time for you to assess your students, conduct conferences, and introduce new materials and activities. For more information about the check-in lessons, see Appendix B, "Independent Work Resources."

This week we suggest you teach the "Introduce New Materials" check-in lesson in Appendix B, "Independent Work Resources." Depending on the needs of your students, you may decide to teach a different check-in lesson.

Week 20 OVERVIEW

Whole-class Instruction

Word Study

This week the students learn about the prefix *re-* and read words with the prefix. On Day 3, they do an open sort in pairs using base words and the prefixes *re-* and *un-*. The week's spelling words are words with the prefix *un-*.

Independent Work Check-in

This week we suggest you teach the "Self-selecting Work Areas" check-in lesson in Appendix B, "Independent Work Resources." Depending on the needs of your students, you may decide to teach a different check-in lesson.

Small-group Reading Instruction and Independent Work Rotations

Small-group Reading

This week you will continue to teach Small-group Reading lessons at the small-group reading table while the students work independently in the reading, writing, and word work areas.

Independent Work

The students may have assigned work from Small-group Reading to do during Independent Work. The following are materials you might incorporate into independent work areas this week:

Word Work:

- "Week 19, Day 3 Sort" (see "Independent Work Connection" on page 397)

RESOURCES

Extension
- "Connect Spelling to Writing"

Assessment Resource Book
- Week 20 assessment

Word Study Notebook
- Word Sorts
- Spelling Practice

 Online Resources

Visit the CCC Learning Hub (ccclearninghub.org) to find your online resources for this week.

Whiteboard Activities
- WA1-WA3

Assessment Form
- "Class Assessment Record" sheet (CA1)

Reproducibles
- "Week 20, Day 3 Sort" (BLM1)
- (Optional) "Week 20 High-frequency Words" (BLM2)

⏱ DO AHEAD

Word Study

✓ Prior to Day 1, familiarize yourself with the Day 1 Spelling Words.

✓ Prior to Day 2, decide how you will randomly assign partners to work together during the next several weeks.

✓ Prior to Day 2, familiarize yourself with the Day 2 Practice Words.

✓ Prior to Day 3, familiarize yourself with the Day 3 Sort Words.

✓ Prior to Day 3, visit the CCC Learning Hub (ccclearninghub.org) to access and print "Week 20, Day 3 Sort" (BLM1). Make enough copies for each pair of students to have one.

✓ Prior to Day 4, visit the CCC Learning Hub (ccclearninghub.org) to access and print the "Class Assessment Record" sheet (CA1); see page 94 of the *Assessment Resource Book*.

✓ (Optional) If you plan to integrate the new high-frequency words in the word work area, visit the CCC Learning Hub (ccclearninghub.org) to access and print "Week 20 High-frequency Words" (BLM2). See "Independent Work Connections" on page 411.

Independent Work Check-in

✓ Familiarize yourself with the "Self-selecting Work Areas" check-in lesson (or another check-in lesson of your choice) in Appendix B, "Independent Work Resources." Collect and prepare any necessary materials. For more information about the check-in lessons, see Appendix B, "Independent Work Resources."

📅 SUGGESTED WEEKLY SCHEDULE

Monday	Tuesday	Wednesday	Thursday	Friday
Word Study (20)	Word Study (20)		Word Study (20)	Word Study (20)
Independent Work Rotations/Small-group Reading (60)	Independent Work Rotations/Small-group Reading (60)	Independent Work Check-in (35)	Independent Work Rotations/Small-group Reading (60)	Independent Work Rotations/Small-group Reading (60)
80 minutes	**80 minutes**	**35 minutes**	**80 minutes**	**80 minutes**

Day 1 Spelling Words		Day 2 Practice Words		Day 3 Sort Words	
undo	unpack	redo	repaint	lock	retell
unfair	unpacking	refill	reptile	packing	review
unlock	unsnap	reflect	reread	read	reviewer
unlocked	unzip	reheat	retell	reader	tell
		reload	retie	reheat	unfair
		remove	reuse	reheating	unlock
		rename	review	repack	unpack
		repack	rewrite	reread	unzip

Academic Focus

- Students spell words with the prefix *un-*.
- Students learn the prefix *re-*.
- Students read and sort words with the prefix *re-*.

Social Development Focus

- Students work in a responsible way.
- Students handle materials responsibly.
- Students listen respectfully to the thinking of others and share their own.

Day 1 Word Study
Guided Spelling

Materials

- Wipe-off board, dry-erase marker, and tissue or cloth for each student

In this lesson, the students:

- Review the prefix *un-*
- Spell words with the prefix *un-*
- Handle materials responsibly

1 Get Ready to Spell

Have the students stay in their seats. Review that last week, the students practiced spelling words with more than one suffix. Explain that today the students will spell words with the prefix *un-*.

2 Review the Prefix *un-*

Write the word *unpleasant* on the board. Ask and briefly discuss:

Q *What is the prefix in* unpleasant? *What is the base word?*
(un-, pleasant)

Then ask:

 Q *What do you think* unpleasant *means? Turn to the person sitting next to you.*

After a few moments, signal for the students' attention and have a few volunteers share their thinking with the class.

Underline *un* and remind the students that *un-* is a prefix. Review that the prefix *un-* means "not" or "the opposite of" and that when *un-* is added to the base word *pleasant*, it makes the word *unpleasant*, which means "not nice or enjoyable." Use *unpleasant* in a sentence. (For example, "We left the kitchen because the smell of the burnt toast was unpleasant.")

Teacher Note
You may wish to explain that *pleasant* is a synonym of "enjoyable."

3 Guide the Students' Spelling

Distribute the wipe-off boards, markers, and tissues or cloths.

unzip	"You can unzip your coat if you get too warm."

Say *unzip*. Use *unzip* in a sentence. Have the students say *unzip*. Then ask:

Q *What is the first syllable in* unzip? *(un-)*

Have the students write *un-*. Then ask:

Q *What is the second syllable in* unzip? *(zip)*

Have the students write the rest of *unzip*.

Write *unzip* where everyone can see it, and have the students check their writing and erase and correct mistakes.

Use the same procedure with the words *unlock, unlocked, unpack, unpacking, unfair, undo*, and *unsnap*.

unlock	"One time I lost my keys and I couldn't unlock the door to my house."
unlocked	"I unlocked my car door and drove away."
unpack	"The first thing I do when I get home from a trip is unpack my suitcase."
unpacking	"My friend thinks that unpacking suitcases is boring."
unfair	"It is unfair to cheat at sports."

Spelling Support

Support your students by providing guidance for sounds with multiple spellings, such as the sound of hard *c* (as in *cat*), and by identifying the high-frequency words *do* and *fair*.

| undo | "The knot was tied so tightly it was hard to undo." |
| unsnap | "We can snap our math cubes together and then we can unsnap them." |

4 Discuss and Reflect on Spelling

Remind the students that they will have a spelling test on Friday (or whichever day of the week you will teach the Day 4 lesson). Tell them that when they go to independent word work, they will practice spelling the words before choosing another activity.

Teacher Note

You may wish to post the *Word Study Notebook* page number for the spelling practice in the word work area for the students to refer to during Independent Work.

Day 2

Word Study
Introduce the Prefix *re-*

Materials

- "Week 20, Day 2 Words" (WA1)

Teacher Note

The students may work in partnerships already established, or you may assign new partners for the Word Study lessons. The partners you assign today will work together for the next five weeks of Word Study.

In this lesson, the students:
- Begin working with new partners
- Learn the prefix *re-*
- Read words with the prefix *re-*
- Listen respectfully to the thinking of others and share their own

1 Gather and Review Prefixes

Randomly assign partners and gather the class with partners sitting together, facing you. Review that the students have been reading and spelling words with the prefix *un-*. Ask:

Q *What do you know about the prefix* un-?

Have a few volunteers share their ideas with the class.

> **Students might say:**
>
> "It comes at the beginning of a word."
>
> "It makes a new word."
>
> "It makes words into opposites."

2 Discuss the Words *Reread* and *Reuse*

Write the word *reread* where everyone can see it and read it aloud. Ask:

 Q *What do you know about the word* reread? *Turn to your partner.*

After a few moments, signal for the students' attention and have a few volunteers share their thinking with the class.

> **Students might say:**
>
> "I see the word *read*."
>
> "Maybe the first part is a prefix."

If necessary, explain that the word *reread* means "read again." Use *reread* in a sentence. (For example, "I will reread the paragraph if I don't understand it.")

Then write the word *reuse* where everyone can see it and read the word. Ask:

 Q *What do you know about the word* reuse? *Turn to your partner.*

After a few moments, signal for the students' attention and have a few volunteers share their thinking with the class.

If necessary, explain that the word *reuse* means "use again." Use *reuse* in a sentence. (For example, "I can reuse that bag to take my shopping home.")

3 Introduce the Prefix *re-*

Direct the students' attention to the two words you have written. Ask and briefly discuss:

Q *What is the same about these words?*

Q *What do you think* re- *might mean?*

Underline *re* and explain that *re-* is a prefix. Review that a *prefix* is a letter or group of letters that is added to the beginning of a base word to make a new word.

If necessary, explain that in the word *reread*, the prefix *re-* means "again." Draw a dot between the syllables *re* and *read* and remind the students that the dot can help them see and read the syllables in a word. Have the students read *reread*, first by syllables and then as a whole word.

Repeat the procedure with the word *reuse*.

4 Read the Words

Tell the students that they will read more words that begin with *re-*. Display the "Week 20, Day 2 Words" activity (WA1).

retell	refill	remove	reheat
reread	review	repack	rename
reuse	rewrite	repaint	reflect
retie	redo	reload	reptile

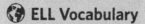

🌐 ELL Vocabulary

English Language Learners may benefit from hearing the following vocabulary defined:

review: look at something again

remove: take away

Point to the first word and ask:

Q *Which prefix do you see? (re-)*

Draw a dot between *re* and *tell*. Have the students read the word, first by syllables and then as a whole word.

Repeat this procedure with the next thirteen words. When you come to *reflect* and *reptile*, have the students read both words with you. Then ask:

Q *What do you notice about these words?*

> **Students might say:**
>
> *"Reflect* starts with *r-e,* but *flect* is not a base word."
>
> *"Reptile* starts with *r-e,* but *r-e* is part of the word."
>
> "Both words start with *r-e,* but *re* doesn't mean 'again.'"

Explain that the letters *r-e* at the beginning of a word are not always the prefix that means "again." Draw a dot at the syllable juncture in each word. Point out that noticing *r-e* at the beginning of a word can sometimes help the students read the word even when the letters are not a prefix.

WA1

re·tell	re·fill	re·move	re·heat
re·read	review	re·pack	re·name
re·use	rewrite	re·paint	re·flect
re·tie	re·do	re·load	rep·tile

Teacher Note

If the students need additional support reading the words, consider framing the word parts as the students read them.

5 Reflect on Reading

Ask:

 Q *What did you like about reading words today? Turn to your partner.*

After a few moments, signal for the students' attention and have a few pairs share their thinking with the class.

Tell the students that in the next few weeks, they will sort words with prefixes, like the ones they read today.

Word Study
Pair Sort (Open)
Day 3

In this lesson, the students:
- Read and sort words with prefixes and suffixes
- Work responsibly with a partner
- Handle materials responsibly

1 Gather and Review Prefixes

Have the students bring their pencils, pick up their independent work toolboxes, and gather with partners sitting together, facing you. Have them put their toolboxes on the floor next to them.

Review that in the last lesson the students read words with the prefix *re-* and that noticing a prefix at the beginning of a word can help readers see the first part of the word and read the whole word.

Use "Think, Pair, Share" to discuss:

 Q *What do you remember about the prefix* re-? *[pause] Turn to your partner.*

After a few moments, signal for the students' attention and have a few pairs share their thinking with the class.

> **Students might say:**
>
> "It comes at the beginning of a word."
>
> "It changes the meaning of a word."
>
> "It means 'again.'"

Materials
- "Week 20, Day 3 Sort" (WA2)
- Copy of "Week 20, Day 3 Sort" (BLM1) for each pair
- Scissors for each pair
- *Word Study Notebooks* (in student toolboxes)
- Pencils

 Facilitation Tip

Reflect on your experiences over the past few weeks with **asking facilitative questions**. Does this technique feel comfortable and natural to you? Do you find yourself using it throughout the school day? What effect has using this technique had on your students' listening and participation in discussions? We encourage you to continue to use and reflect on this technique throughout the year.

2 Introduce the Sort

Explain that today partners will work together to do an open sort. Some of the words have the prefix *re-* and some of them are words from earlier sorts. Ask:

Q *What can you and your partner do to share the work while you are sorting?*

Then use "Think, Pair, Share" to discuss:

 Q *How does open sorting help you think carefully about words?* [pause] *Turn to your partner.*

After a few moments, signal for the students' attention and have a few pairs share their thinking with the class.

 Display the "Week 20, Day 3 Sort" activity (WA2). Have pairs read the words together quietly.

reread	lock	reader	unlock
unpack	packing	repack	tell
reheating	reheat	review	unzip
retell	reviewer	read	unfair

When most pairs have finished reading, signal for the students' attention. Use "Think, Pair, Share" to discuss:

Q *What are some words you could group together?* [pause] *Turn to your partner.*

After a few moments, signal for the students' attention and have a few pairs share their thinking with the class.

As volunteers share, ask follow-up questions, such as:

Q *What is alike about* [reheat *and* reread]?

Q *What other words could you group with* [unzip *and* unlock]? *Why does* [unpack] *go with* [unzip *and* unlock]?

Q *What did you notice about* [reviewer *and* reader] *that made you think of grouping them together?*

Tell the students that the words can be sorted in many different ways. Remind the students that if they start to sort one way and find it does not make sense, they may try sorting another way.

3 Sort in Pairs

 Distribute a copy of "Week 19, Day 3 Sort" (BLM1) and scissors to each pair of students. Have each pair refer to the steps on the "Word Sort Steps" chart to cut apart and sort the words and then record their sort in their *Word Study Notebooks*.

4 Reflect on Sorting

Ask:

 Q *How did open sorting go today? Turn to your partner.*

After a few moments, signal for the students' attention and have a few volunteers share their thinking with the class. Share your observations about what went well during the open sort. Tell the students that in the next lesson, they will take a spelling test with the words they have been practicing this week.

Word Study
Spelling Test
Day 4

In this lesson, the students:

- Spell words with *un-*
- Handle materials responsibly

Materials

- Lined paper and a pencil for each student
- "Week 20, Day 4 Spelling Words" (WA3)
- "Class Assessment Record" sheet (CA1)

1 Get Ready to Spell

Have the students stay in their seats today. Tell the students that they will have a spelling test.

2 Spelling Test

Distribute paper and pencils to the students. Have them write their names at the top and number the first eight lines 1 to 8.

Begin the test. Say "Number one: unzip." Use *unzip* in a sentence. Say *unzip* again. Have the students write *unzip*. Allow enough time for all the students to finish before moving on to the next word.

Repeat this procedure for the remaining spelling words.

1. unzip   "Unzip your jacket and take it off."

2. unlock   "I unlock the door when I get to the classroom in the morning."

3. unlocked   "Victor unlocked the gate and went in."

4. unpack   "When you get to school, you unpack your backpack."

5. unpacking   "When I was unpacking my backpack, I found my missing pencil."

6. unfair   "He said it was unfair that Sayuri got twice as many cookies."

7. undo   "Undo your shoelaces before trying to take off your shoes."

8. unsnap   "I unsnap the dog's leash from its collar when I get home from a walk."

3 Check and Correct the Words

After the students are finished writing the last word, display the "Week 20, Day 4 Spelling Words" activity (WA3). Have the students check their work and correct mistakes.

Circulate and observe as the students work, offering support as necessary.

☑ CLASS ASSESSMENT NOTE

Ask yourself:

- Do the students stay focused during the spelling test?
- Do they spell most words correctly?
- Is there a pattern to the types of errors they make?

Record your observations on the "Class Assessment Record" sheet (CA1); see page 94 of the *Assessment Resource Book*.

---

4 Reflect on Spelling

Without mentioning any students' names, share some observations about how the students are doing with spelling.

EXTENSION

Connect Spelling to Writing

Review that one reason writers spell words correctly is to make sure readers can understand and enjoy their writing. Remind the students that sometimes you will ask them to think about how they might use the spelling words in their writing. Think aloud about how one of the words reminds you of something that happened to you.

> **You might say:**
>
> "When I read the word *unpack*, it reminds me of lunchtime today. I unpacked my backpack when I got to school, and I discovered that I had left my lunch at home."

Ask:

Q *Which of these words reminds you of something that happened to you?*
What is a story you could write about that? Turn to your partner.

After a few moments, signal for the students' attention and have a few
volunteers share their thinking with the class. Encourage the students
to use the spelling words and other words from the week's sort in their
writing.

Independent Work Connections

For next week's Independent Work, we suggest the following:

- Make additional copies of "Week 20, Day 3 Sort" (BLM1) to place in
  the word work area.

- Make several copies of "Week 20 High-frequency Words" (BLM2)
  and place them in the independent word work area. The students can
  use these words to play any word games you have introduced, such
  as "Word Memory" and "Word Go Fish."

Independent Work

This week the students continue to rotate to and work in all three independent work areas around the room while you teach Small-group Reading. We suggest continuing any procedures that have worked effectively in previous weeks.

Independent Work Check-in

This week you will continue to teach an Independent Work Check-in lesson on the day of the week you do not teach Small-group Reading. The purpose of these check-in lessons is to ensure that the students are able to maintain successful independent work rotations. The lessons provide the time for you to assess your students, conduct conferences, and introduce new materials and activities. For more information about the check-in lessons, see Appendix B, "Independent Work Resources."

This week we suggest you teach the "Self-selecting Work Areas" check-in lesson in Appendix B, "Independent Work Resources." Depending on the needs of your students, you may decide to teach a different check-in lesson.

Week 21 OVERVIEW

Whole-class Instruction

Word Study

This week the students begin to learn about open and closed syllables, the basis for polysyllabic decoding. The students have many opportunities to read open and closed syllables on Days 2 and 3. The week's spelling words are words with the prefix re-.

Independent Work Check-in

This week we suggest you teach the "Work Habits" check-in lesson in Appendix B, "Independent Work Resources." Depending on the needs of your students, you may decide to teach a different check-in lesson.

Small-group Reading Instruction and Independent Work Rotations

Small-group Reading

This week you will continue to teach Small-group Reading lessons at the small-group reading table while the students work independently in the reading, writing, and word work areas.

Independent Work

The students may have assigned work from Small-group Reading to do during Independent Work. The following are materials you might incorporate into independent work areas this week:

Word Work:

- "Week 20, Day 3 Sort" (see "Independent Work Connections" on page 411)
- "Week 20 High-frequency Words" (see "Independent Work Connections" on page 411)

Week 21

RESOURCES

Assessment Resource Book
- Week 21 assessment

Word Study Notebook
- Spelling Practice

Online Resources

Visit the CCC Learning Hub (ccclearninghub.org) to find your online resources for this week.

Whiteboard Activities
- WA1–WA5

Assessment Form
- "Class Assessment Record" sheet (CA1)

Reproducible
- (Optional) "Week 21, Day 4 'Build That Word'" (BLM1)

⏱ DO AHEAD

Word Study

✓ Prior to Day 1, familiarize yourself with the Day 1 Spelling Words.

✓ Prior to Day 2, familiarize yourself with the Day 2 Syllables and Words.

✓ Prior to Day 2, visit the CCC Learning Hub (ccclearninghub.org) to access and print the "Class Assessment Record" sheet (CA1); see page 95 of the *Assessment Resource Book*.

✓ Prior to Day 3, familiarize yourself with the Day 3 Syllables.

✓ (Optional) If you plan to integrate "Build That Word" in the word work area, visit the CCC Learning Hub (ccclearninghub.org) to access and print "Week 21, Day 4 'Build That Word'" (BLM1). See "Independent Work Connection" on page 426.

Independent Work Check-in

✓ Familiarize yourself with the "Work Habits" check-in lesson (or another check-in lesson of your choice) in Appendix B, "Independent Work Resources." Collect and prepare any necessary materials. For more information about the check-in lessons, see Appendix B, "Independent Work Resources."

📅 SUGGESTED WEEKLY SCHEDULE

Monday	Tuesday	Wednesday	Thursday	Friday
Word Study (20)	Word Study (20)		Word Study (20)	Word Study (20)
Independent Work Rotations/Small-group Reading (60)	Independent Work Rotations/Small-group Reading (60)	Independent Work Check-in (35)	Independent Work Rotations/Small-group Reading (60)	Independent Work Rotations/Small-group Reading (60)
80 minutes	80 minutes	35 minutes	80 minutes	80 minutes

Day 1 Spelling Words		Day 2 Syllables and Words		Day 3 Syllables	
reheat	*Challenge Words*	ba	pen	ba	po
reload	review	bacon	pilot	bat	pre
remake	rewrite	cat	pom-pom	co	prep
rename		con	pre	cot	pro
repack		dis	pro	me	prob
repaint		discuss	prob	met	ra
reread		final	problem	mo	rat
rethink		fit	re	mop	
		go	si		
		he	so		
		lem	subject		
		less	tub		
		li	un		
		mis	va		
		moment	we		
		mu			

Academic Focus

- Students spell words with the prefix *re-*.
- Students learn about open and closed syllables.
- Students read two-syllable words.

Social Development Focus

- Students work in a responsible way.
- Students handle materials responsibly.
- Students listen respectfully to the thinking of others and share their own.

In this lesson, the students:

- Review the prefix *re-*
- Spell words with the prefix *re-*
- Handle materials responsibly

1 Get Ready to Spell

Have the students stay at their seats. Explain that today the students will spell words with the prefix *re-*.

2 Review the Prefix *re-*

Write the word *redo* where everyone can see it. Ask and briefly discuss:

Q *What is the base word in this word? What do you think* redo *might mean?*

If necessary, review that the prefix *re-* means "again" and that *redo* means "do again." Use *redo* in a sentence. (For example, "I had to redo my homework because I lost it.")

3 Guide the Students' Spelling

Distribute the wipe-off boards, dry-erase markers, and cloths or tissues.

> reread "I loved the book so much that I am going to reread it."

Say *reread*. Use *reread* in a sentence. Have the students say *reread*. Then ask:

Q *How many syllables are in* reread? *(two)*

Q *What is the first syllable in* reread? *(re-)*

Have the students write *re-*. Then ask:

Q *What is the second syllable in* reread? *(read)*

Have the students finish writing *reread*. Then ask:

Q *Does* reread *look right to you the way you spelled it? If not, do you want to change how you spelled it?*

Write *reread* where everyone can see it and have the students check their writing and erase and correct mistakes.

Repeat the procedure with the words *repack, repaint, reload, remake, rethink, reheat,* and *rename*.

> repack "My book bag wouldn't zip up, so I had to repack it."

Materials

- Wipe-off board, dry-erase marker, and tissue or cloth for each student

Teacher Note

Use this question only for words you are confident the students will recognize.

Spelling Support

Support the students by providing guidance for sounds with more than one spelling, such as long vowel sounds and the sound /k/.

repaint	"We need to repaint the fence because the old paint is peeling."
reload	"When you get a new phone, you have to reload your music and contacts."
remake	"My dog tore all the covers off the bed, so I had to remake it."
rethink	"I had to rethink my plan about going to the beach when it rained on Saturday."
reheat	"When I eat leftovers for dinner, I reheat them in the microwave."
rename	"If I think of a better title for my story, I will rename it."

Teacher Note

You may wish to explain that *rethink* means "think about again."

You may wish to challenge the students with the words *review* and *rewrite*.

review	"I will review my writing before I publish it."

Say *review*. Use *review* in a sentence. Have the students say *review*. Then ask:

Q *How many syllables are in* review? *(two)*

Q *What is the first syllable in* review? *(re-)*

Have the students write *re*.

Write *re* where everyone can see it and have the students check their writing and erase and correct mistakes. Then ask:

Q *What is the second syllable in* review? *(view)*

Q *What vowel sound do you hear in* review? *(long* u*)*

Explain that in *review* the long *u* sound in *view* is spelled *i-e-w*. Tell the students that the spelling *i-e-w* is used only in a few words, such as *view*.

Have the students finish writing *review*.

Write *review* where everyone can see it and have the students check their writing and erase and correct mistakes.

rewrite	"My teacher asked me to rewrite the sentence."

Say *rewrite*. Use *rewrite* in a sentence. Have the students say *rewrite*. Ask:

Q *What is the base word in* rewrite? *What is the prefix? (write, re-)*

Have the students write *rewrite*. When most students are finished, signal for their attention and ask:

Q *Does* rewrite *look right to you the way you spelled it? If not, do you want to change how you spelled it?*

Write *rewrite* where everyone can see it and have the students check their writing and erase and correct mistakes.

4 Wrap Up

Remind the students that they will have a spelling test on Friday (or whichever day of the week you will teach the Day 4 lesson). Tell them that when they go to independent word work, they will practice spelling these words before they choose another activity.

Teacher Note

You may wish to post the *Word Study Notebook* page number for the spelling practice in the word work area for the students to refer to during Independent Work.

Word Study
Introduce Open and Closed Syllables
Day 2

In this lesson, the students:

- Learn about open and closed syllables
- Read open and closed syllables
- Listen respectfully to the thinking of others and share their own

ABOUT OPEN AND CLOSED SYLLABLES

Syllables are the building blocks of the words students see every day. Understanding open and closed syllables (those that end in a vowel or a consonant) allows students to make a judgment about the probable vowel sound in a syllable. In a closed syllable, the vowel sound is usually short, and in an open syllable, the vowel sound is usually long. Providing guidelines for ways to break words into syllables gives students tools to analyze longer words. Open and closed syllables are introduced this week, practiced next week, and then applied throughout the remainder of the year.

Materials

- "Week 21, Day 2 Closed Syllables" (WA1)
- "Week 21, Day 2 Open Syllables" (WA2)
- "Class Assessment Record" sheet (CA1)

1 Gather and Review Prefixes

Gather the class with partners sitting together, facing you.

Write *replay* where everyone can see it and read the word with the students. Ask and briefly discuss:

Q *From what you know about the prefix* re-, *what do you think* replay *means?*

Use the same procedure to review the prefix *un-*, using the word *unplug*.

2 Introduce Closed Syllables

Display the "Week 21, Day 2 Closed Syllables" activity (◖ WA1). Read the words with the students.

tub

cat

fit

Ask:

Q *Do you hear a long vowel sound or a short vowel sound in these words? (short vowel sound)*

Click to reveal the group of syllables and explain that these are syllables that often appear in longer words.

un	lem
less	pen
mis	con
dis	prob

Point to *un*. Have the students read *un*. Say that a guideline that the students can use to read syllables like *un* is that when there is a consonant at the end of the syllable, the vowel in the syllable usually has a short vowel sound. Have the students read the remaining syllables in this group.

Click to reveal the two-syllable words. Do not read them to the class.

problem

discuss

pom-pom

subject

Review that when there is a consonant at the end of a syllable, the vowel usually has a short vowel sound. Knowing about the vowel sound in a syllable will help the students read longer words when they come to them.

> **You might say:**
> "If you know that when there is a consonant at the end of a syllable the vowel usually has a short vowel sound, that can help you read longer words."

Explain that the students will read these longer words one syllable at a time. Draw a dot between *prob* and *lem*. Frame *prob* with your hands and have the students read it. Then frame *lem* and have the students

Teacher Note

The schwa sound in unstressed syllables is not formally introduced in this lesson. The vowel pronunciations in open and closed syllables are introduced as guidelines rather than rules, because of the variation in sound in unstressed and stressed syllables. Your students may notice that the vowel does not have exactly the same sound in the word as a whole as it does in an isolated syllable. If they do, we suggest that you acknowledge the fact and move on without prolonged discussion.

Teacher Note

Keeping the guideline as concise as possible will help the students remember it.

read that syllable. Point to *problem* and have the students read the whole word. Use the same procedure for *discuss*, *pom-pom*, and *subject*.

> **You might say:**
>
> "Here is a longer word you might not recognize. We will use what we know to read the syllables and then put the syllables together to read the word. We will read the first syllable. [Frame *prob* and have the students read it.] Now we will read the second syllable. [Frame *lem* and have the students read it.] Now let's read the whole word."

WA1

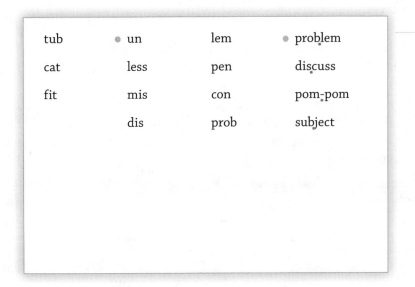

tub	• un	lem	• problem
cat	less	pen	discuss
fit	mis	con	pom-pom
	dis	prob	subject

3 Introduce Open Syllables

Display the "Week 21, Day 2 Open Syllables" activity (WA2). Read the four words with the students.

we

go

so

he

Ask:

Q *Do you hear a long or short vowel sound in these words? (long vowel sound)*

Click to reveal the group of syllables and explain that these are syllables that often appear in longer words.

re	mu
pre	li
pro	ba
va	si

Teacher Note

If the students struggle to read open syllables, you may wish to create another open syllable list and have the students practice.

 ELL Note

You may wish to explain that *final* means "last" and that *moment* means a "very short time."

Point to *re*. Have the students read *re*. Explain that a guideline that the students can use to read syllables like *re* is that the vowel sound is usually long in a syllable that ends with a vowel. Have the students read the remaining syllables in this group.

Click to reveal the two-syllable words. Do not read them to the class.

final

bacon

pilot

moment

Review that when there is a vowel at the end of a syllable, the vowel usually has a long vowel sound. Knowing about the vowel sound will help the students read longer words when they come to them. Draw a dot between *fi* and *nal*. Frame the syllable *fi* and have the students read it. Frame *nal* and have the students read the syllable. Point to *final* and have the students read the word. Use the same procedure to have the students read the remaining words.

WA2

we	• re	mu	• final
go	pre	li	bacon
so	pro	ba	pilot
he	va	si	moment

CLASS ASSESSMENT NOTE

After the lesson, take time to ask yourself:

- Do the students understand the difference between open and closed syllables?
- Are the students able to read open and closed syllables in isolation?

Record your observations on the "Class Assessment Record" sheet (CA1); see page 95 of the *Assessment Resource Book*. If many students are struggling with open and closed syllables, have the students read minimal word pairs such as *we/wet, so/sock, me/men, go/got, he/hem,* and *she/shed*. For each word, have the students identify whether there is a consonant at the end and whether the vowel has the long or short vowel sound.

4 Wrap Up

Tell the students that reading longer words takes practice and that the students will work more on reading longer words in the next lesson and in the coming weeks. Explain that when the students go to independent word work, they will do any sort they wish from a previous week before choosing another activity.

Word Study
Review Open and Closed Syllables

Day 3

In this lesson, the students:

- Review open and closed syllables
- Read open and closed syllables
- Listen respectfully to the thinking of others and share their own

1 Gather and Review Open and Closed Syllables

Gather the class with partners sitting together, facing you. Tell the students that today they will read a list of syllables. Ask and briefly discuss:

Q *Why is it important to wait for my signal before reading syllables and words?*

2 Read the Syllables

Display the "Week 21, Day 3 Syllables" activity (◖ WA3). Point to *met* and have the students read the word. Ask and briefly discuss:

Q *What do you remember about the vowel sound in a syllable with a consonant at the end?*

> **Students might say:**
>
> "In *met* there is a *t* at the end. The *e* has the short vowel sound."
>
> "The vowel in the syllable usually has a short sound."

Have the students read the remaining syllables. If necessary, support the students by having them identify whether there is a consonant at

Materials

- "Week 21, Day 3 Syllables" (WA3)
- "Week 21, Day 3 Syllable Practice" (WA4)

💡 **Facilitation Tip**

Continue to practice **asking facilitative questions** during class discussions to help the students respond directly to one another.

the end of the syllable and whether the vowel will have a short or long vowel sound.

met

rat

bat

cot

mop

prob

prep

Click to reveal the second column of syllables.

me

po

ba

mo

ra

co

pre

pro

Ask and briefly discuss:

Q *What do you remember about the vowel sound in a syllable with no consonant at the end?*

Have the students read each syllable. If necessary, have the students identify whether there is a consonant at the end of the syllable and whether the vowel will have a short or long vowel sound.

3 Syllable Practice

Display the "Week 21, Day 3 Syllable Practice" activity (◖ WA4). Explain that these are the same syllables the students just read, but they are not in the same order. This time, as the students read each syllable, they will have to watch closely to see whether there is a consonant at the end to know whether the vowel has a short or long vowel sound.

Have the students read each syllable. If necessary, have the students identify whether there is a consonant at the end of the syllable and whether the vowel will have a short or long vowel sound.

4 Reflect on Reading

Ask:

Q *How did you do with reading the syllables and words today?*

Q *What is easy about reading syllables? What is challenging?*

Tell the students that in the next few weeks they will have more opportunities to use what they know about syllables to read words.

Word Study
Spelling Test
Day 4

In this lesson, the students:

- Spell words with the prefix *re-*
- Handle materials responsibly

1 Get Ready to Spell

Have the students stay in their seats. Ask and briefly discuss:

Q *How did you do with your independent spelling practice this week?*

2 Spelling Test

Distribute paper and pencils to the students. Have them write their names at the top and number the first eight lines 1 to 8.

Begin the test. Say "Number one: reread." Use *reread* in a sentence. Say *reread* again. Have the students write *reread*. Allow enough time for all the students to finish before moving on to the next word.

Repeat this procedure for the remaining spelling words.

1.	reread	"I love to reread my favorite books."
2.	repack	"The student had to repack his lunchbox after his snack fell out."
3.	repaint	"I would like to repaint the walls in the classroom."
4.	reload	"I had to reload my games and music when I got a new cell phone."

Materials

- "Week 21, Day 4 Spelling Words" (WA5)
- Lined paper and a pencil for each student

5. remake   "The girl had to remake her bed after the baby pulled the blankets off."

6. rethink   "We had to rethink our plan to go to the park after it started to rain."

7. reheat   "She is going to reheat leftovers for dinner."

8. rename   "The town is going to rename the park in honor of the mayor."

3 Check and Correct the Words

After the students are finished writing the last word, display the "Week 21, Day 4 Spelling Words" activity (◖ WA5). Have the students check their work and correct mistakes. When the students are finished checking and correcting their work, collect the papers.

4 Reflect on Spelling

Have the students reflect on the spelling test. Ask and briefly discuss:

Q *How did you do with spelling the words today?*

Q *How does learning spelling words help you in your writing?*

Independent Work Connection

For next week's Independent Work, we suggest the following:

▪ Make several copies of "Week 21, Day 4 'Build That Word'" (BLM1) to place in the word work area.

Independent Work  OVERVIEW

This week the students continue to rotate to and work in all three independent work areas around the room while you teach Small-group Reading. We suggest continuing any procedures that have worked effectively in previous weeks.

Independent Work Check-in

This week you will continue to teach an Independent Work Check-in lesson on the day of the week you do not teach Small-group Reading. The purpose of these check-in lessons is to ensure that the students are able to maintain successful independent work rotations. The lessons provide the time for you to assess your students, conduct conferences, and introduce new materials and activities. For more information about the check-in lessons, see Appendix B, "Independent Work Resources."

This week we suggest you teach the "Work Habits" check-in lesson in Appendix B, "Independent Work Resources." Depending on the needs of your students, you may decide to teach a different check-in lesson.

Week 22 OVERVIEW

Whole-class Instruction

Word Study

This week the students continue to learn about open and closed syllables. They read and sort syllables, and they read polysyllabic words with teacher guidance. In spelling, the students review and write compound words.

Independent Work Check-in

This week we suggest you teach the "Independent Work Observation" check-in lesson in Appendix B, "Independent Work Resources." Depending on the needs of your students, you may decide to teach a different check-in lesson.

Small-group Reading Instruction and Independent Work Rotations

Small-group Reading

This week you will continue to teach Small-group Reading lessons at the small-group reading table while the students work independently in the reading, writing, and word work areas.

Independent Work

The students may have assigned work from Small-group Reading to do during Independent Work. The following are materials you might incorporate into independent work areas this week:

Word Work:

- "Week 21, Day 4 'Build That Word'" (see "Independent Work Connection" on page 426)

Week 22

RESOURCES

Assessment Resource Book
- Week 22 assessment

Word Study Notebook
- Spelling Practice

 ## Online Resources

Visit the CCC Learning Hub (ccclearninghub.org) to find your online resources for this week.

Whiteboard Activities
- WA1–WA4

Assessment Form
- "Class Assessment Record" sheet (CA1)

Reproducibles
- "Week 22, Day 2 Sort" (BLM1)
- (Optional) "Week 22, Day 4 'Build That Word'" (BLM2)

⏱ DO AHEAD

Word Study

✓ Prior to Day 1, familiarize yourself with the Day 1 Spelling Words.

✓ Prior to Day 2, familiarize yourself with the Day 2 Practice Words and Day 2 Sort Syllables.

✓ Prior to Day 2, visit the CCC Learning Hub (ccclearninghub.org) to access and print "Week 22, Day 2 Sort" (BLM1). Make several copies to place in the word work area before the lesson.

✓ Prior to Day 3, familiarize yourself with the Day 3 Words.

✓ Prior to Day 4, visit the CCC Learning Hub (ccclearninghub.org) to access and print the "Class Assessment Record" sheet (CA1); see page 96 of the *Assessment Resource Book*.

✓ (Optional) If you plan to integrate "Build That Word" in the word work area, visit the CCC Learning Hub (ccclearninghub.org) to access and print "Week 22, Day 4 'Build That Word'" (BLM2).

Independent Work Check-in

✓ Familiarize yourself with the "Independent Work Observation" check-in lesson (or another check-in lesson of your choice) in Appendix B, "Independent Work Resources." Collect and prepare any necessary materials. For more information about the check-in lessons, see Appendix B, "Independent Work Resources."

📅 SUGGESTED WEEKLY SCHEDULE

Monday	Tuesday	Wednesday	Thursday	Friday
Word Study (20)	Word Study (20)		Word Study (20)	Word Study (20)
Independent Work Rotations/Small-group Reading (60)	Independent Work Rotations/Small-group Reading (60)	Independent Work Check-in (35)	Independent Work Rotations/Small-group Reading (60)	Independent Work Rotations/Small-group Reading (60)
80 minutes	80 minutes	35 minutes	80 minutes	80 minutes

Day 1 Spelling Words		Day 2 Practice Words		Day 2 Sort Syllables		Day 3 Words	
backpack	hillside	absent	pencil	al	fum	carpenter	passenger
bedtime	rainfall	discuss	problem	bo	me	excellent	splendid
farmland	snowball	escape	reptile	bu	mem	insect	wonderful
goldfish	sunshine	except	rescue	de	se	mistake	yesterday
		excite	survive	dem	semp		
		garden	thirteen	em	ul		
		insect	walrus	fli	va		
		mistake	yellow	flim	val		

Academic Focus

- Students spell compound words.
- Students divide words into syllables.
- Students read two- and three-syllable words.

Social Development Focus

- Students work in a responsible way.
- Students handle materials responsibly.
- Students listen respectfully to the thinking of others and share their own.

Day 1

Word Study
Guided Spelling

Materials

- Wipe-off board, dry-erase marker, and tissue or cloth for each student

In this lesson, the students:

- Spell compound words
- Handle materials responsibly

1 Get Ready to Spell

Have the students stay at their seats. Explain that this week the students will spell compound words.

2 Review Compound Words

Ask and briefly discuss:

Q *What do you remember about compound words?*

If necessary, review that *compound words* are made up of two smaller words. Explain that knowing the two small words in a compound word can help in spelling the compound word.

3 Guide the Students' Spelling

Distribute the wipe-off boards, markers, and cloths or tissues.

> bedtime   "I brush my teeth every night at bedtime."

Say *bedtime*. Use *bedtime* in a sentence. Have the students say *bedtime*. Then ask:

Q *What is the first small word in* bedtime? *(bed)*

Have the students write *bed*. Then ask:

Q *What is the second small word in* bedtime? *(time)*

Have the students finish writing *bedtime*.

Write *bedtime* where everyone can see it and have the students check their writing and erase and correct mistakes. Repeat the procedure with the words *backpack, farmland, goldfish, hillside, rainfall, snowball,* and *sunshine.*

> backpack   "Tyreese carries his books in a backpack."
>
> farmland   "Fruits and vegetables are grown on farmland."
>
> goldfish   "My brother once had a pet goldfish."
>
> hillside   "I know a walking path that goes up a hillside."
>
> rainfall   "I got soaked in the heavy rainfall."
>
> snowball   "Lily made a perfect snowball after the storm."
>
> sunshine   "Plants need water and sunshine to grow."

4 Wrap Up

Remind the students that they will have a spelling test on Friday (or whichever day of the week you will teach the Day 4 lesson). Tell them that when they go to independent word work, they will practice spelling these words before they choose another activity.

Spelling Support

If necessary, remind the students not to leave a space between the smaller words when writing a compound word.

Spelling Support

Support your students by providing guidance for sounds with multiple spellings, such as long vowel sounds and the sounds /k/ and /l/.

Teacher Note

You may wish to post the *Word Study Notebook* page number for the spelling practice in the word work area for the students to refer to during Independent Work.

Word Study
Introduce Dividing Between Syllables

Materials

- "Week 22, Day 2 Words" (WA1)
- "Week 22, Day 2 Sort" (WA2)
- Copies of "Week 22, Day 2 Sort" (BLM1) in the word work area

In this lesson, the students:

- Learn about dividing words into syllables
- Read and sort two-syllable words
- Listen respectfully to the thinking of others and share their own

ABOUT READING TWO-SYLLABLE WORDS

To read polysyllabic words, students cannot use the familiar strategy of sounding out the word from left to right. The students have already read many two-syllable words with inflectional endings and affixes. Now they apply what they have learned to see other kinds of polysyllabic words in syllable, or word part, units. This challenging skill develops over time with a great deal of reading practice. As the students read more words, they develop automaticity with reading syllables. Dividing words into syllables is a preliminary step to building easy recognition of word parts. Throughout this lesson, you support the students in identifying syllables to accustom them to the procedure.

1 Gather and Review

Gather the class with partners sitting together, facing you.

Write *unhelpful* where everyone can see it, inserting a dot between the syllables *un*, *help*, and *ful*. Do not read the word for the students.

Have the students read *unhelpful*, first as you frame each syllable and then as a whole word. Point out that *unhelpful* has a prefix, *un-*, and a suffix, *-ful*. Review that each word part is a *syllable*, which has one vowel sound, and that many prefixes and suffixes are syllables. Review that recognizing syllables and putting the syllables together helps in reading longer words.

Explain that longer words can be divided into syllables even when they do not have prefixes or suffixes. Reading each syllable separately and then putting the syllables together helps in reading longer words.

Teacher Note

This is a key concept to communicate to your students. Repeating it several times is helpful.

2 Introduce Dividing Words Between Two Consonants

Display the "Week 22, Day 2 Words" activity (◖ WA1). Point to the word *rescue* and read it for the students. Have the students clap on and say the syllables. Draw a dot between *res* and *cue*. Have the students read *rescue*.

Click to reveal the word *walrus* and read it for the students. Have the students clap on and say the syllables. Draw a dot between *wal* and *rus*. Have the students read *walrus*.

Ask:

 Q *What do you notice about the letters before and after the dot? Turn to your partner.*

After a few moments, signal for the students' attention and have a few volunteers share their thinking with the class.

Explain that there are several ways to divide words into syllables to make them easier to read. One way is to divide between two consonants that come between two vowels in a word.

Click to reveal the remaining words, one at a time, drawing a dot between the syllables of each word. Do not read the words for the students. Instead, have the students read each word first by syllables and then as a whole word. When you come to the word *except*, explain that for words that begin with *ex*, they will always keep the *x* with the *e* to make the first syllable. Repeat this guideline when you get to the word *excite*. If time allows, provide more examples of words that begin with *ex* for the students, such as *explode*, *explore*, *explain*, and *extra*.

WA1

rescue	reptile	survive	pencil
walrus	insect	mistake	garden
absent	thirteen	discuss	except
yellow	escape	problem	excite

Teacher Note

You may wish to explain that a *walrus* is an animal that looks a bit like a seal or a sea lion and that lives in the Arctic, a very cold place.

Teacher Note

If your students need more support, frame each syllable for them instead of relying only on the dot to show the syllable break.

3 Sort the Syllables

Display the "Week 22, Day 2 Sort" activity (WA2). Ask and briefly discuss:

Q *What do you remember about a syllable that has a vowel at the end?*

If necessary, remind the students that in a syllable that has a vowel at the end, the vowel usually has the long vowel sound. Do not yet read the syllables aloud.

al	de	fli	fum
mem	se	flim	ul
bo	dem	va	me
val	em	bu	semp

Explain that this week, the students will sort syllables by vowel sound. One category will be syllables with a long vowel sound and the other will be syllables with the short vowel sound. Ask and briefly discuss:

Q *How will you tell whether the syllable has a long vowel sound or a short vowel sound?*

Create categories by writing *long vowel* and *short vowel* as headings on the chart. Point to *al* on the "Week 22, Day 2 Sort" activity (WA2) and ask:

Q *What vowel sound will be in this syllable? How do you know?*

As the students respond, drag and drop *al* under the appropriate category. Use the same procedure to sort the remaining syllables.

After all the syllables have been sorted, have the students read the syllables in each group together.

long vowel	short vowel
bo	al
de	mem
se	val
fli	dem
va	em
bu	flim
me	fum
	ul
	semp

Facilitation Tip

Continue to practice **asking facilitative questions** during class discussions to help the students respond directly to one another.

Tell the students that you have put copies of the sort in the word work area for them to sort during Independent Work. Explain that when they go to independent word work, the students will repeat this week's sort before starting another activity.

4 Wrap Up

Tell the students that dividing words into syllables is challenging and that the students will practice more in the coming weeks.

Word Study
Read Longer Words
Day 3

In this lesson, the students:

- Apply knowledge of syllables to reading longer words
- Listen respectfully to the thinking of others and share their own

1 Gather and Review Dividing Between Consonants

Gather the class with partners sitting together, facing you. Ask and briefly discuss:

Q *How did it go doing this week's sort in Independent Work?*

Display the "Week 22, Day 3 Words" activity (WA3). Point to and read aloud *mistake* and *insect*. Ask:

Q *Where did you divide these words into syllables yesterday?*

As the students respond, draw a dot between the syllables.

Review that when there are two consonants between vowels, the word is often divided between the consonants.

2 Read Longer Words

Explain that this guideline can be used for even longer words. Click to reveal the word *carpenter* on the "Week 22, Day 3 Words" activity (WA3). Remind the students that when two consonants come between two vowels in a word, the word is usually divided into syllables between the consonants.

Materials

- "Week 22, Day 3 Words" (WA3)

Ask:

 Q *Where will you divide this word into syllables? Why do you think that? Turn to your partner.*

After a few moments, signal for the students' attention and have a few volunteers share. Point out that there are two places in the word where two consonants come between two vowels. Write a small *v* above each vowel. Underline each consonant. Draw a dot between the syllables *car*, *pen*, and *ter*, just below the word. Frame each syllable and have the students read *carpenter*, first by syllables and then as a whole word.

Click to reveal the next word and use the same procedure to have the students read the words *splendid*, *yesterday*, *excellent*, *passenger*, and *wonderful*.

> ### 🌐 ELL Vocabulary
>
> English Language Learners may benefit from hearing the following vocabulary defined:
>
> **carpenter:** person who builds things using wood
> **splendid:** very beautiful

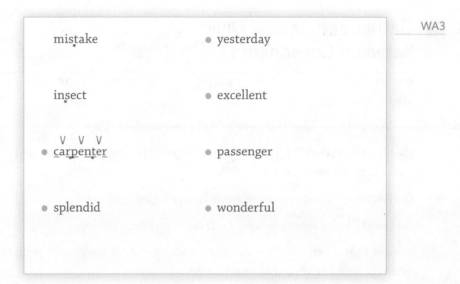

mistake	• yesterday
insect	• excellent
v v v • <u>carpenter</u>	• passenger
• splendid	• wonderful

3 Reflect on Reading

Ask:

 Q *How can dividing words into syllables help you in your reading? Turn to your partner.*

After a few moments, signal for the students' attention and have a few students share their thinking with the class. Tell the students that in the next few weeks, they will have more opportunities to read long words.

Teacher Note

You may wish to point out to the students that when there is a double consonant in a word (as in *excellent* and *passenger*), they only say the consonant sound once when they read the whole word. This concept was introduced with consonant-*l-e* syllables in Week 13.

In this lesson, the students:

- Spell compound words
- Handle materials responsibly

Materials

- "Week 22, Day 4 Spelling Words" (WA4)
- Lined paper and a pencil for each student
- "Class Assessment Record" sheet (CA1)

1 Get Ready to Spell

Have the students stay in their seats. Ask and briefly discuss:

Q *How did you do with your independent spelling practice this week?*

2 Spelling Test

Distribute paper and pencils to the students. Have them write their names at the top and number the first eight lines 1 to 8.

Begin the test. Say "Number one: bedtime." Use *bedtime* in a sentence. Say *bedtime* again. Have the students write *bedtime*. Allow enough time for all the students to finish before moving on to the next word.

Repeat this procedure for the remaining spelling words.

1. bedtime   "Some parents read their children stories at bedtime."

2. backpack   "You carry your books in a backpack."

3. farmland   "Fruits and vegetables are grown on farmland."

4. goldfish   "A goldfish is a popular pet."

5. hillside   "Our puppy rolled down the hillside."

6. rainfall   "Lots of water ran down the street in the heavy rainfall."

7. snowball   "We used a big snowball for the snowman's body."

8. sunshine   "Cats like to sleep in the sunshine."

3 Check and Correct the Words

After the students are finished writing the last word, display the "Week 22, Day 4 Spelling Words" activity (◖ WA4). Have the students check their work and correct mistakes.

4 Reflect on Spelling

Have the students reflect on the spelling test. Ask and briefly discuss:

Q *How did the spelling test go?*

Q *How does learning spelling words help you in your writing?*

Independent Work Connections

For next week's Independent Work, we suggest the following:

- Make additional copies of "Week 22, Day 2 Sort" (BLM1) to place in the word work area before the lesson.

- Make several copies of "Week 22, Day 4 'Build That Word'" (BLM2). Place these in the word work area.

Independent Work  OVERVIEW

This week the students continue to rotate to and work in all three independent work areas around the room while you teach Small-group Reading. We suggest continuing any procedures that have worked effectively in previous weeks.

Independent Work Check-in

This week you will continue to teach an Independent Work Check-in lesson on the day of the week you do not teach Small-group Reading. The purpose of these check-in lessons is to ensure that the students are able to maintain successful independent work rotations. The lessons provide the time for you to assess your students, conduct conferences, and introduce new materials and activities. For more information about the check-in lessons, see Appendix B, "Independent Work Resources."

This week we suggest you teach the "Independent Work Observation" check-in lesson in Appendix B, "Independent Work Resources." Depending on the needs of your students, you may decide to teach a different check-in lesson.

Week 23 OVERVIEW

Whole-class Instruction

Word Study ....

This week the students continue to learn about open and closed syllables. They learn about breaking words that have one consonant between two vowels into syllables, and they read polysyllabic words with teacher guidance. In spelling, the students practice breaking two-syllable words into syllables and then writing them.

Independent Work Check-in ....

This week we suggest you teach the "Introduce New Materials" check-in lesson in Appendix B, "Independent Work Resources." Depending on the needs of your students, you may decide to teach a different check-in lesson.

Small-group Reading Instruction and Independent Work Rotations

Small-group Reading

This week you will continue to teach Small-group Reading lessons at the small-group reading table while the students work independently in the reading, writing, and word work areas.

Independent Work

The students may have assigned work from Small-group Reading to do during Independent Work. The following are materials you might incorporate into independent work areas this week:

Word Work:

- "Week 22, Day 2 Sort" (see "Independent Work Connections" on page 440)
- "Week 22, Day 4 'Build That Word'" (see "Independent Work Connections" on page 440)

Week 23

RESOURCES

Assessment Resource Book
- Week 23 assessment

Word Study Notebook
- Spelling Practice

 Online Resources

Visit the CCC Learning Hub (ccclearninghub.org) to find your online resources for this week.

Whiteboard Activities
- WA1–WA4

Assessment Form
- "Class Assessment Record" sheet (CA1)

Reproducible
- "Week 23, Day 3 Sort" (BLM1)

Professional Development Media
- "Responding Neutrally with Interest" (AV9)

⏱ DO AHEAD

Word Study

✓ Prior to Day 1, familiarize yourself with the Day 1 Spelling Words.

✓ Prior to Day 2, familiarize yourself with the Day 2 Practice Syllables and Words.

✓ Prior to Day 3, familiarize yourself with the Day 3 Sort Words.

✓ Prior to Day 3, visit the CCC Learning Hub (ccclearninghub.org) to access and print "Week 23, Day 3 Sort" (BLM1). Make several copies to place in the independent word work area before the lesson.

✓ Prior to Day 3, visit the CCC Learning Hub (ccclearninghub.org) to access and print the "Class Assessment Record" sheet (CA1); see page 97 of the *Assessment Resource Book*.

Independent Work Check-in

✓ Familiarize yourself with the "Introduce New Materials" check-in lesson (or another check-in lesson of your choice) in Appendix B, "Independent Work Resources." Collect and prepare any necessary materials. For more information about the check-in lessons, see Appendix B, "Independent Work Resources."

📅 SUGGESTED WEEKLY SCHEDULE

Monday	Tuesday	Wednesday	Thursday	Friday
Word Study (20)	Word Study (20)		Word Study (20)	Word Study (20)
Independent Work Rotations/Small-group Reading (60)	Independent Work Rotations/Small-group Reading (60)	Independent Work Check-in (35)	Independent Work Rotations/Small-group Reading (60)	Independent Work Rotations/Small-group Reading (60)
80 minutes	**80 minutes**	**35 minutes**	**80 minutes**	**80 minutes**

Day 1 Spelling Words		Day 2 Practice Syllables and Words		Day 3 Sort Words	
absent	*Challenge Words*	con	pro	confuse	refill
escape	except	de	re	decide	reread
insect	explode	decide	refill	lizard	ribbon
mistake		detail	reread	model	seldom
problem		hi	retell	moment	spider
reptile		moment	so	predict	travel
rescue		paper	student	prevent	until
thirteen		predict	we		
		prevent			

Academic Focus

- Students spell two-syllable words.
- Students divide words into syllables.
- Students read two- and three-syllable words.

Social Development Focus

- Students work in a responsible way.
- Students handle materials responsibly.
- Students listen respectfully to the thinking of others and share their own.

Day 1

Word Study
Guided Spelling

Materials

- Wipe-off board, dry-erase marker, and tissue or cloth for each student

In this lesson, the students:

- Spell two-syllable words
- Handle materials responsibly

1 Review Dividing a Word into Syllables

Have the students stay at their seats. Review that last week, the students spelled compound words. Explain that today the students will spell words with two syllables. Review that when reading a longer word, it is helpful to divide the word into syllables and read each syllable. When spelling, it is also helpful to divide a word into syllables and spell each syllable.

Say *reptile*; then ask:

Q *What are the syllables in* reptile? *(rep, tile)*

Explain that when writing *reptile*, thinking about how to spell each syllable helps you as you write the word.

> **You might say:**
> "The first syllable in *reptile* is *rep*. I will sound it out slowly, and then write *r-e-p*. The second syllable is *tile*. I know that *tile* is spelled with the final *e* spelling for *i*, so I will write *t-i-l-e*. Now I'll read the word to check the spelling: *reptile*."

Erase *reptile*.

2 Guide the Students' Spelling

Distribute the wipe-off boards, markers, and cloths or tissues.

reptile   "The iguana is a reptile."

Say *reptile*. Use *reptile* in a sentence. Have the students say *reptile*. Then ask:

Q *How many syllables are in* reptile? *(two)*

Q *What is the first syllable in* reptile? *(rep)*

Have the students write *rep*. Then ask:

Q *What is the second syllable in* reptile? *(tile)*

Q *What is the vowel sound in* tile? *(long i)*

Tell the students to think carefully about which spelling of the long *i* sound to use.

Have the students finish writing *reptile*.

Write *reptile* where everyone can see it and have the students check their writing and erase and correct mistakes.

insect   "The ladybug is a colorful insect."

Say *insect*. Use *insect* in a sentence. Have the students say *insect*. Then ask:

Q *How many syllables are in* insect? *(two)*

Q *What is the first syllable in* insect? *(in)*

Have the students write *in*. Then ask:

Q *What is the second syllable in* insect? *(sect)*

Explain that in *sect*, the sound /k/ is spelled *c*. Have the students finish writing *insect*.

Write *insect* where everyone can see it and have the students check their writing and erase and correct mistakes.

Spelling Support

If necessary, continue to support the students in spelling vowels by pointing to the correct spelling on the "Spelling-Sound Chart."

Spelling Support

Support the students by providing guidance for sounds with multiple spellings, such as long *a* (/ā/), long *u* (/ū/), long *e* (/ē/), *r*-controlled vowel (/ər/), and /k/.

Then use the same procedure to guide the students in spelling the following words.

mistake	"Someone might call you the wrong name by mistake."
problem	"I lost my keys one time, and it was a problem."
escape	"We keep the class pet in its cage so it doesn't escape."
absent	"Tahlia was absent from school because she was sick and had to stay in bed."
rescue	"Firefighters rescue people every day."
thirteen	"Many eighth graders are thirteen years old."

You may wish to challenge your students with the words *explode* and *except*.

explode	"Fireworks explode with bright colors."
except	"All of my pets have been dogs, except one."

3 Reflect on Working Responsibly

Have the students reflect on how they worked today. Ask and briefly discuss:

Q *What did you do to handle your materials in a responsible way?*

Remind the students that they will have a spelling test on Friday (or whichever day of the week you will teach the Day 4 lesson). Tell them that when they go to independent word work, they will practice spelling these words before they choose another activity.

Teacher Note

You may wish to post the *Word Study Notebook* page number for the spelling practice in the word work area for the students to refer to during Independent Work.

In this lesson, the students:

- Review open syllables
- Learn about dividing words before or after a single consonant
- Read two-syllable words
- Listen respectfully to the thinking of others and share their own

Materials

- "Week 23, Day 2 Syllables" (WA1)
- "Week 23, Day 2 Words" (WA2)

1 Gather and Review Dividing a Word into Syllables

Gather the class with partners sitting together, facing you. Remind the students that there are several ways to divide words into syllables to make them easier to read. The students have learned that one way is to divide between two consonants that come between two vowels in a word. Today they will learn another way to divide words.

2 Review Open Syllables

Display the "Week 23, Day 2 Syllables" activity (WA1) and have the students read the syllables *we*, *so*, and *hi*.

Ask:

Q *What do you remember about syllables with a vowel at the end?*

Have a few volunteers share. If necessary, review that when a syllable ends with a vowel, the vowel usually has a long vowel sound.

Click to reveal the remaining syllables, and have the students read them.

WA1

we	• pro
so	re
hi	con
	de

3 Introduce Dividing Before a Single Consonant

Display the "Week 23, Day 2 Words" activity (WA2). Point to the word *detail* and read it aloud.

Have the students say the syllables. Draw a dot between *de* and *tail*. Frame each syllable and have the students read *detail*, first by syllables and then as a whole word.

Click to reveal the word *retell*, and read it for the students. Have the students clap on and say the syllables. Draw a dot between *re* and *tell*. Frame each syllable and have the students read *retell*, first by syllables and then as a whole word.

Explain that a way to divide a word that has one consonant between two vowels is to try dividing the word before the consonant and try a long vowel sound in the first syllable.

Click to reveal the remaining words, one at a time, drawing a dot between the syllables. Do not read the words for the students; instead, frame each syllable and have the students read each word first by syllables and then as a whole word.

> 🌐 **ELL Vocabulary**
>
> English Language Learners may benefit from hearing additional vocabulary defined, including:
>
> **detail:** small part; something that might not be noticed
> **predict:** say what will happen next
> **prevent:** stop something from happening

WA2

detail	• moment	• paper
• retell	• reread	• student
• predict	• prevent	
• decide	• refill	

4 Introduce Making a Match with a Real Word

Write the word *salad* where everyone can see it. Divide the word according to the above procedure by drawing a dot between *sa* and *lad*: *sa.lad*. Have the students read *salad*, first by syllables and then as a whole word. Ask:

Q *Is /sāləd/ a word? (no)*

Explain that when reading longer words, the students will sometimes try syllables that do not make a real word. When this happens, they can try dividing the word after the consonant and try a short vowel sound in the first syllable. Erase the dot after *sa* and place a dot between *sal* and *ad*: *sal.ad*. Have the students read the word again, first by syllables and then as a whole word. Then ask:

Q *Is /săləd/ a word? (yes)*

Write *cabin* where everyone can see it, and draw a dot between *ca* and *bin*. Have the students read *cabin*, first by syllables and then as a whole word. Ask:

Q *Is /cābən/ a word? (no)*

Erase the dot and write it between *cab* and *in*: *cab.in*. Have the students read the word, first by syllables and then as a whole word. Ask:

Q *Is /căbən/ a word? (yes)*

Use the same procedure to have the students read the words *siren*, *robin*, *music*, *motor*, and *dragon*.

Review that for words with one consonant between two vowels, the students can divide before the vowel and try saying a long vowel sound in the first syllable. If that does not make a word they recognize, they can try dividing after the vowel and try saying a short vowel sound in the first syllable.

Remind the students that they have learned several ways to divide words into syllables—using prefixes and suffixes, dividing between consonants, and dividing before or after a single consonant.

5 Reflect

Ask:

 Q *What did you like about reading words today? Turn to your partner.*

After a few moments, signal for attention and have a few students share their thinking with the class. Tell the students that in the next few weeks, they will have more opportunities to read long words.

Teacher Note

Note that by dividing the syllables in this way, the word should be read with a long *a* sound (/sāləd/). If the students read the word with a short *a* sound (/săləd/), ask:

Q *What do you know about syllables with a vowel at the end? (They have a long vowel sound.)*

 ELL Note

Asking themselves if something is a word does not always help English Language Learners who have limited vocabulary. Provide definitions and context sentences as needed for additional support.

Teacher Note

You may wish to tell the students that a *cabin* is a small house and that a *siren* is a loud warning sound, such as on a fire truck.

Materials

- "Week 23, Day 3 Sort" (WA3)
- "Class Assessment Record" sheet (CA1)
- Copies of "Week 23, Day 3 Sort" (BLM1) in the word work area

Teacher Note

All the words with an open first syllable in this list are recognizable with a long vowel sound in the first syllable, although some people may use a schwa sound there. The schwa is introduced in Week 24.

In this lesson, the students:
- Review dividing words into syllables
- Read and sort two-syllable words
- Listen respectfully to the thinking of others and share their own

1 Gather and Review Dividing Before or After a Consonant

Gather the class with partners sitting together, facing you. Review that dividing longer words into syllables can help readers read the words more easily.

Review that when dividing a longer word into syllables, the students can first divide the word before the consonant and try saying a long vowel sound in the first syllable. If the word does not sound right, they can divide it after the consonant and try saying a short vowel sound in the first syllable.

2 Read the Sort Words

Display the "Week 23, Day 3 Sort" activity (WA3). Point to *predict* and ask:

Q *Where will you try dividing first? What sound will the vowel in the first syllable have? Turn to your partner.*

After a few moments, signal for the students' attention and have a few volunteers share. As they share, draw a dot between *pre* and *dict*. Have the students read *predict*. Ask:

Q *Is /predict/ a word? (yes)*

Point to *decide* and ask:

Q *Where will you try dividing first? What sound will the vowel in the first syllable have?*

As a volunteer shares, draw a dot between *de* and *cide*; then have the students read *decide*.

Ask:

Q *Is /decide/ a word? (yes)*

Use the same procedure for the remaining words on the list. For *model*, *travel*, and *lizard*, guide the students to break before the consonant and try saying a long vowel sound; then break after the consonant and try saying a short vowel sound.

Suggested Vocabulary

predict: say what will happen in the future

seldom: not very often

prevent: stop from happening

confuse: make a person unsure about something

🌐 ELL Vocabulary

English Language Learners may benefit from hearing additional vocabulary defined, including:

moment: very short time

ribbon: long strip of cloth used to tie hair or tie a package

WA3

predict	seldom	refill	confuse
decide	reread	spider	travel
moment	prevent	ribbon	lizard
model	until		

3 Introduce the Word Sort

Click the reset button on the CCC toolbar to clear the dots from the "Week 23, Day 3 Sort" activity (WA3). Explain that this week, the students will sort the words into two groups. One group will have two consonants between the vowels and the other will have just one consonant between the vowels. Write *one consonant* and *two consonants* as category headings on the chart, and have the students sort the first five words, using the procedure for whole-class sorting.

one consonant	two consonants	
predict	seldom	
decide		
moment		
model		
	refill	confuse
reread	spider	travel
prevent	ribbon	lizard
until		

Tell the students that you have placed copies of the sort in the word work area for them to sort during Independent Work. Explain that when they go to independent word work, they will repeat this week's sort before choosing another activity.

 CLASS ASSESSMENT NOTE

After this lesson, ask yourself:

- Do the students recognize the two types of words: one consonant between two vowels and two consonants between two vowels?

- Are the students able to consistently try saying a long vowel sound in an open syllable first?

Record your observations on the "Class Assessment Record" sheet (CA1); see page 97 of the *Assessment Resource Book*. If your students struggle to recognize open and closed syllables, support them by creating practice lists for them to read.

4 Reflect on Syllabication

Have the students reflect on syllabication. Ask and briefly discuss:

Q *What is easy about dividing words into syllables? What is hard?*

Facilitation Tip

We invite you to practice **responding neutrally with interest** during class discussions. To respond neutrally means to refrain from overtly praising (for example, "Great idea" or "Good job") or criticizing (for example, "That's wrong") the students' responses. While it may feel more natural to avoid criticism rather than praise, research shows that both kinds of responses encourage students to look to you, rather than to themselves, for validation. To see this Facilitation Tip in action, view "Responding Neutrally with Interest" (AV9).

In this lesson, the students:

- Spell two-syllable words
- Handle materials responsibly

Materials

- "Week 23, Day 4 Spelling Words" (WA4)
- Lined paper and a pencil for each student

1 Get Ready to Spell

Have the students stay in their seats. Ask and briefly discuss:

Q *How did you do with your independent spelling practice this week?*

2 Spelling Test

Distribute paper and pencils to the students. Have them write their names at the top and number the first eight lines 1 to 8.

Begin the test. Say "Number one: reptile." Use *reptile* in a sentence. Say *reptile* again. Have the students write *reptile*. Allow enough time for all the students to finish before moving on to the next word.

Repeat this procedure for the remaining spelling words.

1.	reptile	"Snakes are one kind of reptile."
2.	insect	"The honeybee is a helpful insect."
3.	mistake	"If I make a mistake, I erase the word and try again."
4.	problem	"We solved the math problem by working together."
5.	escape	"My sister's dog sometimes tries to escape from the yard."
6.	absent	"Joseph was absent because he had the flu."
7.	rescue	"Lifeguards watch carefully in case they have to rescue a swimmer."
8.	thirteen	"Nine plus four equals thirteen."

Spelling Support

We suggest that you pronounce the vowel sound in unstressed, or unaccented, syllables clearly rather than saying the schwa sound (/ə/).

3 Check and Correct the Words

After the students are finished writing the last word, display the "Week 23, Day 4 Spelling Words" activity (WA4). Have the students check their work and correct mistakes. When the students are finished checking and correcting their work, collect the papers.

Explain that using everything they know about words to spell the words correctly helps writers know what to do when they spell words they have not written before.

4 Reflect on Spelling

Have the students reflect on the spelling test. Ask and briefly discuss:

Q *Which words were hard to spell this week? What did you do to remember how to spell them?*

Tell the students they will have more opportunities to practice spelling in the coming weeks.

Independent Work Connection

For next week's Independent Work, we suggest the following:

- Make additional copies of "Week 23, Day 3 Sort" (BLM1) to place in the word work area.

Independent Work

This week the students continue to rotate to and work in all three independent work areas around the room while you teach Small-group Reading. We suggest continuing any procedures that have worked effectively in previous weeks.

Independent Work Check-in

This week you will continue to teach an Independent Work Check-in lesson on the day of the week you do not teach Small-group Reading. The purpose of these check-in lessons is to ensure that the students are able to maintain successful independent work rotations. The lessons provide the time for you to assess your students, conduct conferences, and introduce new materials and activities. For more information about the check-in lessons, see Appendix B, "Independent Work Resources."

This week we suggest you teach the "Introduce New Materials" check-in lesson in Appendix B, "Independent Work Resources." Depending on the needs of your students, you may decide to teach a different check-in lesson.

Week 24 OVERVIEW

Whole-class Instruction

Word Study 462

This week the students learn about the schwa sound and the different spellings for the sound. They learn about the suffixes *-ion*, *-sion*, and *-tion*, and they read and sort words with these suffixes. There is no spelling test this week; the spelling focus is on the different spellings for the schwa sound.

Independent Work Check-in 473

This week we suggest you teach the "Conferring" check-in lesson in Appendix B, "Independent Work Resources." Depending on the needs of your students, you may decide to teach a different check-in lesson.

Small-group Reading Instruction and Independent Work Rotations

Small-group Reading

This week you will continue to teach Small-group Reading lessons at the small-group reading table while the students work independently in the reading, writing, and word work areas.

Independent Work

The students may have assigned work from Small-group Reading to do during Independent Work. The following are materials you might incorporate into independent work areas this week:

Word Work:

- "Week 23, Day 3 Sort" (see "Independent Work Connection" on page 456)

Week 24

RESOURCES

Assessment Resource Book
- Week 24 assessment

Word Study Notebook
- Word Sorts
- Spelling Practice

 Online Resources

Visit the CCC Learning Hub (ccclearninghub.org) to find your online resources for this week.

Whiteboard Activities
- WA1-WA4

Assessment Form
- "Class Assessment Record" sheet (CA1)

Reproducible
- "Week 24, Day 3 Sort" (BLM1)

⏱ DO AHEAD

Word Study

✓ Prior to Day 1, familiarize yourself with the Day 1 Spelling Words.

✓ Prior to Day 2, familiarize yourself with the Day 2 Practice Words.

✓ Prior to Day 3, visit the CCC Learning Hub (ccclearninghub.org) to access and print "Week 24, Day 3 Sort" (BLM1). Make enough copies for each pair of students to have one.

✓ Prior to Day 3, visit the CCC Learning Hub (ccclearninghub.org) to access and print the "Class Assessment Record" sheet (CA1); see page 98 of the *Assessment Resource Book*.

✓ Prior to Day 4, familiarize yourself with the Day 4 Practice Words.

Independent Work Check-in

✓ Familiarize yourself with the "Conferring" check-in lesson (or another check-in lesson of your choice) in Appendix B, "Independent Work Resources." Collect and prepare any necessary materials. For more information about the check-in lessons, see Appendix B, "Independent Work Resources."

📅 SUGGESTED WEEKLY SCHEDULE

Monday	Tuesday	Wednesday	Thursday	Friday
Word Study (20)	Word Study (20)		Word Study (20)	Word Study (20)
Independent Work Rotations/Small-group Reading (60)	Independent Work Rotations/Small-group Reading (60)	Independent Work Check-in (35)	Independent Work Rotations/Small-group Reading (60)	Independent Work Rotations/Small-group Reading (60)
80 minutes	**80 minutes**	**35 minutes**	**80 minutes**	**80 minutes**

OVERVIEW Word Study

Day 1 Spelling Words		Day 2 Practice/ Day 3 Sort Words		Day 4 Practice Words	
about	below	action	invention	alive	divide
ago	mistake	confusion	motion	confuse	predict
around	prepare	connection	prediction	connect	protect
before	ribbon	discussion	prevention		
		division	question		
		fiction	revision		
		instruction	station		
		invasion	vacation		

Academic Focus

- Students learn about the schwa sound.
- Students learn about the suffixes -*tion*, -*sion*, and -*ion*.
- Students read and sort words with the suffixes -*tion*, -*sion*, and -*ion*.

Social Development Focus

- Students work in a responsible way.
- Students handle materials responsibly.
- Students listen respectfully to the thinking of others and share their own.

Day 1

Word Study
Introducing the Schwa Sound

Materials

- "Week 24, Day 1 Words" (WA1)

In this lesson, the students:

- Learn about the schwa sound
- Handle materials responsibly

1 Review Syllables

Have the students stay in their seats. Review that last week, the students spelled two-syllable words. Ask and briefly discuss:

Q *What do you remember about spelling two-syllable words?*

Remind the students that noticing syllables can help readers read, spell, and understand words.

2 Introduce the Schwa Sound

Display the "Week 24, Day 1 Words" activity (◗ WA1) and read the displayed words with the students.

about

ago

around

Ask and briefly discuss:

Q *What vowel sound do you hear in the first syllable of these words? What do you notice?*

Point out that the letter *a* stands for the sound /ə/ in these words. Explain that there is a name for this sound. The /ə/ sound is called the *schwa sound*. Point to the schwa square on the "Spelling-Sound Chart" and explain that any of these letters (vowels) can stand for the schwa sound.

Click to reveal the next three words.

below

before

prepare

Have the students read *below*, first by syllables and then as a whole word. Point out that some people pronounce this word with a long *e* and long *o* (/bēlō/), and some people pronounce it /bəlō/. In this case, the *e* is read using the schwa sound /ə/, not the long *e* sound. Use the same procedure to explain the schwa sound in the first syllables of *before* and *prepare*. Point out that when a letter stands for the schwa sound, it is difficult to know which spelling to use. For words with the schwa sound, writers just have to remember the spelling.

Click to reveal the last two words and have the students read the words *mistake* and *ribbon*.

Teacher Note

There are no spelling practice words or a spelling test this week. Instead, instruction is focused on issues surrounding the schwa sound (/ə/, the unaccented vowel sound similar to short *u*) and its spellings.

Teacher Note

You may wish to explain that *prepare* means "get ready."

about	● below	● mistake
ago	before	ribbon
around	prepare	

3 Reflect

Ask:

 Q *What did you find out about the schwa sound today? Turn to the person sitting next to you.*

After a few moments, signal for the students' attention and have a few volunteers share their thinking with the class.

Day 2

Word Study
Introduce the Suffixes *-tion*, *-sion*, and *-ion*

Materials

- "Week 24, Day 2 Words" (WA2)

In this lesson, the students:

- Learn about the suffixes *-tion*, *-sion*, and *-ion*
- Read words with the suffixes *-tion*, *-sion*, and *-ion*
- Listen respectfully to the thinking of others and share their own

1 Gather and Review Dividing a Word into Syllables

Gather the class with partners sitting together, facing you. Review that the students have been learning about dividing words into syllables. Review that when dividing a longer word that has two vowels with one consonant between them, the students can first divide the word before the middle consonant and try saying the long vowel sound. If the word does not sound right, they can divide it after the consonant and try saying the short vowel sound.

Write *spider* where everyone can see it. Draw a dot between *spi* and *der*. Point out that in this word, the first syllable ends with a vowel. Review that when a syllable ends with a vowel, it is called an *open syllable*, and that the vowel sound is usually long. Have the students read *spider*, first by syllables and then as a whole word.

Write *gentle* where everyone can see it. Draw a dot between *gen* and *tle*. Point out that in this word, the first syllable ends with a consonant. Review that when a syllable ends with a consonant, it is called a *closed syllable*, and that the vowel sound in a closed syllable is usually short. Also review that the second syllable is a consonant-*l-e* syllable. Have the students read *gentle*, first by syllables and then as a whole word.

2 Review Prefixes and Suffixes

Review that the students have been reading and sorting words with more than one syllable. Review that a syllable may be a prefix or suffix—a letter or group of letters added to the beginning (a *prefix*) or end (a *suffix*) of a base word to make a new word.

Write *colorful* where everyone can see it. Draw a dot between *color* and *ful*, just below the word. Ask and briefly discuss:

Q *Based on what you know about the word* color *and the suffix* -ful, *what do you think* colorful *means?*

Repeat the procedure to review other prefixes and suffixes, using the words *unequal*, *lazier*, and *artist*.

3 Introduce *-tion*, *-sion*, and *-ion*

Explain that some suffixes are not easy to define, but they do give the reader information about words.

Display the "Week 24, Day 2 Words" activity (◖ WA2) and read the displayed words for the students.

invention

discussion

confusion

station

Suggested Vocabulary

confusion: feeling of not knowing what to do or not understanding something

Teacher Note

You may wish to write *lazy* where everyone can see it, and point out that when the base word ends with *y*, you need to change the *y* to *i* before adding the suffix.

Teacher Note

The suffixes *-tion* and *-ion* are introduced in an earlier week in the vocabulary instruction in the *Making Meaning*® program from Center for the Collaborative Classroom. If you have taught the lesson in the *Vocabulary Teaching Guide*, you may want to review *-tion* and *-ion* and simply introduce *-sion*.

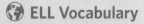 **ELL Vocabulary**

English Language Learners may benefit from hearing additional vocabulary defined, including:

station: place where buses and trains stop for people to get on or off

Ask:

Q *What do you notice about these words?*

Have a few volunteers share their thinking with the class.

> **Students might say:**
>
> "They have *i-o-n* at the end."
>
> "Some end with /shən/."

Point to the word *invention*. Draw a dot between *invent* and *ion*, just below the word, and underline *ion*. Tell the students this is the suffix /ən/. Cover the suffix -*ion*, and have the students read the base word. Explain that *invent* means "make something new for the first time." Use *invent* in a sentence. (For example, "Many people have tried to invent a way to see in the dark.")

Point to *invention* again and read the word with the students. Explain that the word *invention* means "something new that is made for the first time." Use *invention* in a sentence. (For example, "The light bulb was an important invention.") Explain that *invent* is the verb, or action word, that we use to tell what we do. *Invention* is the noun, or thing, that happens because of the action. Inventing something to see in the dark resulted in the invention of the light bulb. Explain that we make the noun *invention* by adding the suffix -*ion* to the verb *invent*.

Point to the *t* in *invention* and explain that when -*ion* is added after *t*, the syllable -*tion* is usually pronounced /shən/. Tell the students that the vowel sound in -*tion* is the schwa sound.

Repeat the procedure for the words *discussion* and *discuss*. Explain that the suffixes -*ion* and -*tion* can often be added to verbs to create nouns. Tell the students that the pronunciation of the base word often changes when the suffix -*ion* or -*tion* is added. Point out that -*tion* is usually pronounced /shən/.

Repeat the procedure for the words *confusion* and *confuse*. Point out that the final *e* in *confuse* was dropped when the suffix -*ion* was added. Also remind the students that the pronunciation of the base word often changes when the suffix -*ion* or -*tion* is added. Point out that -*sion* is often pronounced /zhən/.

Facilitation Tip

Continue to focus on **responding neutrally with interest** during class discussions by refraining from overtly praising or criticizing the students' responses.

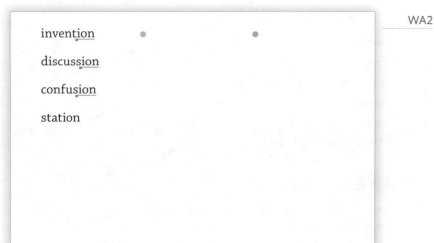

invention   •   •

discussion

confusion

station

Point to the word *station*. Explain that some words that end with *-tion*, such as *station*, do not have base words, but *-ion* and *-tion* still show that the words are nouns, or words that name things.

Click the reset icon on the CCC toolbar to clear the dots and underlining from the "Week 24, Day 2 Words" activity (WA2).

4 Read the Words

Explain that now the students will read more words with the suffixes *-tion* and *-ion*.

Click to reveal the remaining words on the "Week 24, Day 2 Words" activity (WA2).

fiction	connection
motion	instruction
vacation	question
prediction	division
action	revision
prevention	invasion

Point to *fiction*. Draw a dot between *fic* and *tion*. Have the students read *fiction*, first by syllables and then as a whole word.

Repeat this procedure for the remaining words, drawing a dot between syllables. When you get to the word *division*, read it for the students and point out that when the suffix *-ion* comes after one *s*, the *s* usually stands for the sound /zh/. Also point out that in the first syllable, *i* has the schwa sound and not a long vowel sound. Have the students read *division* and then the remaining words.

Teacher Note

If the students need additional support reading the words, consider framing the word parts as the students read them.

Reading by syllables is challenging, because there are many exceptions to the pronunciation guidelines students learn. Support the students as necessary by suggesting they try a different pronunciation if the first one does not produce a word they know.

Suggested Vocabulary

motion: movement

prediction: statement about what will happen in the future

prevention: stopping something from happening

connection: joining two or more things

revision: change

invasion: taking over a place, usually by soldiers

🌐 ELL Vocabulary

English Language Learners may benefit from hearing additional vocabulary defined, including:

instruction: something written or said that tells you how to do something

invention	• fiction	• connection
discussion	motion	instruction
confusion	vacation	question
station	prediction	division
	action	revision
	prevention	invasion

5 Reflect

Have the students reflect on their learning. Ask and briefly discuss:

Q *How can recognizing a suffix at the end of a word help you in your reading?*

> **Students might say:**
>
> "It can help you pronounce a word you don't know."
>
> "Sometimes it can help you know what a word means, if you can take off the suffix and see the base word."

Tell the students that they will talk more about the suffixes *-tion*, *-sion*, and *-ion* tomorrow.

In this lesson, the students:

- Read and sort words with the suffixes *-tion, -sion,* and *-ion*
- Work responsibly with a partner
- Handle materials responsibly

1 Gather and Review *-tion, -sion,* and *-ion*

Have the students bring their pencils, pick up their independent work toolboxes, and gather with partners sitting together, facing you. Have them put their toolboxes on the floor next to them. Review that in the last lesson the students read words with the suffixes *-tion, -sion,* and *-ion,* and that adding these suffixes to a verb or action word usually makes a noun, or thing that happens because of the action.

Write *direct* and *direction* where everyone can see them and have the students read the pair of words. Explain that *direct* means "tell which way to go." Use *direct* in a sentence. (For example, "The police officer will direct you to the post office; she will tell you which way to go.") Ask:

Q *What do you think the word* direction *means?*

Review that *-tion* is usually pronounced /shən/ and that *-sion* is often pronounced /zhən/.

2 Introduce the Sort

Explain that today partners will work together to do an open sort with words that have the suffixes *-tion, -sion,* and *-ion.* Ask and briefly discuss:

Q *What do you remember about sorting with a partner?*

Q *What will you do to work respectfully with your partner today?*

Then use "Think, Pair, Share" to discuss:

 Q *How does open sorting help you think carefully about words?* [pause] *Turn to your partner.*

After a few moments, signal for the students' attention and have a few pairs share their thinking with the class.

> **Students might say:**
>
> "It makes you look carefully at the word parts."
>
> "It makes you think about the meanings of the words."
>
> "It makes you figure out how the words are the same."

Materials

- "Week 24, Day 3 Sort" (WA3)
- Copy of "Week 24, Day 3 Sort" (BLM1) for each pair
- Scissors for each pair
- "Word Sort Steps" chart
- *Word Study Notebooks* (in student toolboxes)
- Pencils
- "Class Assessment Record" sheet (CA1)

3 Sort in Pairs

Display the "Week 24, Day 3 Sort" activity (WA3) and read the words with the students.

invention	motion	question	prevention
discussion	revision	prediction	connection
station	vacation	division	confusion
fiction	invasion	action	instruction

🌐 ELL Vocabulary

English Language Learners may benefit from hearing the following vocabulary defined:

motion: movement

revision: change made to something to fix it or make it better

invasion: going into a place and taking over

prevention: stopping something from happening

connection: joining two or more things together

confusion: the feeling of not understanding what is happening

instruction: something written or said that tells you how to do something

Ask:

Q *What is one way to sort these words? Turn to your partner.*

After a few moments, signal for the students' attention and have a few volunteers share. Then distribute a copy of "Week 24, Day 3 Sort" (BLM1) and scissors to each pair. Have each pair refer to the steps on the "Word Sort Steps" chart to cut apart and sort the words and then record their sort in their *Word Study Notebooks*.

📋 CLASS ASSESSMENT NOTE

Ask yourself:

- Are the students able to create categories for sorting?
- Are they able to correctly sort the words into their categories?
- Are partners able to work together to sort the words?

Record your observations on the "Class Assessment Record" sheet (CA1); see page 98 of the *Assessment Resource Book*.

Teacher Note

If necessary, provide a few examples, such as by suffix or by number of syllables.

Teacher Note

Pair sorting allows you to observe and identify students who may need additional support. If your students need more support, you might use the "Week 24, Day 3 Sort" activity (WA3) to sort a few words as a class.

4 Reflect on Partner Work

Ask and briefly discuss:

Q *What did your partner do to be respectful when you were talking about the words?*

Tell the students that next week, they will work with partners again to sort words.

Word Study
More About the Schwa

Day 4

In this lesson, the students:

- Review the schwa sound
- Handle materials responsibly

Materials

- "Week 24, Day 4 Words" (WA4)

1 Gather and Review the Schwa Sound

Gather the class with partners sitting together, facing you. Ask and briefly discuss:

Q *What do you remember about the schwa sound?*

Review that the schwa is the sound /ə/ and that the students hear this sound in many words with more than one syllable.

2 Read the Words

Write the words *about*, *around*, and *ago* where everyone can see them, and read the words aloud. Remind the students that they hear the schwa in the first syllable of each of these words. Display the "Week 24, Day 4 Words" activity (WA4) and read the first word, *alive*, with the students. Ask:

Q *Where do you hear the schwa sound in this word? Which letter stands for the schwa sound? Turn to your partner.*

After a few moments, signal for the students' attention and have a few volunteers share. Use the same procedure to read and discuss the remaining words on the list. For *predict* and *protect*, your students may pronounce the first syllable with a long vowel sound. This is an opportunity to discuss again that words can be pronounced in different ways.

alive	predict
divide	confuse
connect	protect

3 Reflect

Ask and briefly discuss:

Q *What might you tell someone at home about the schwa sound?*

Tell the students that next week they will talk more about the schwa sound.

Independent Work Connection

For next week's Independent Work, we suggest the following:

• Make several copies of "Week 24, Day 3 Sort" (BLM1) to place in the word work area.

Independent Work  OVERVIEW

This week the students continue to rotate to and work in all three independent work areas around the room while you teach Small-group Reading. We suggest continuing any procedures that have worked effectively in previous weeks.

Independent Work Check-in

This week you will continue to teach an Independent Work Check-in lesson on the day of the week you do not teach Small-group Reading. The purpose of these check-in lessons is to ensure that the students are able to maintain successful independent work rotations. The lessons provide the time for you to assess your students, conduct conferences, and introduce new materials and activities. For more information about the check-in lessons, see Appendix B, "Independent Work Resources."

This week we suggest you teach the "Conferring" check-in lesson in Appendix B, "Independent Work Resources." Depending on the needs of your students, you may decide to teach a different check-in lesson.

Week 25 OVERVIEW

Whole-class Instruction

Word Study

This week the students apply all they have learned about reading syllables to reading longer words. They learn a three-step procedure for analyzing an unknown word: first, look for prefixes and suffixes; second, divide the rest of the word into syllables; and third, say the whole word to see if they recognize it. On Day 3, an open pair sort focuses their attention on syllables in words.

The students will be able to read the words in the lesson with teacher support and using established procedures. However, these words are too challenging for grade 2 students to be expected to spell. Beginning this week, spelling focuses on irregular high-frequency words. Have the students use the Word Bank in their *Word Study Notebooks* or the word wall to spell the words on Day 1.

Independent Work Check-in

This week we suggest you teach the "Conferring" check-in lesson in Appendix B, "Independent Work Resources." Depending on the needs of your students, you may decide to teach a different check-in lesson.

Small-group Reading Instruction and Independent Work Rotations

Small-group Reading

This week you will continue to teach Small-group Reading lessons at the small-group reading table while the students work independently in the reading, writing, and word work areas.

Independent Work

The students may have assigned work from Small-group Reading to do during Independent Work. The following are materials you might incorporate into independent work areas this week:

Word Work:

- "Week 24, Day 3 Sort" (see "Independent Work Connection" on page 472)

Week 25

RESOURCES

Extension
- "Connect Spelling to Writing"

Assessment Resource Book
- Week 25 assessment

Word Study Notebook
- Word Sorts
- Spelling Practice
- (Optional) Word Bank

 ## Online Resources

Visit the CCC Learning Hub (ccclearninghub.org) to find your online resources for this week.

Whiteboard Activities
- WA1–WA2

Assessment Form
- "Class Assessment Record" sheet (CA1)

Reproducibles
- "Week 25, Day 3 Sort" (BLM1)
- (Optional) "Week 25, Day 4 'Build That Word'" (BLM2)

⏲ DO AHEAD

Word Study

✓ Prior to Day 1, familiarize yourself with the Day 1 Spelling Words.

✓ Prior to Day 2, decide how you will randomly assign partners to work together over the next several weeks.

✓ Prior to Day 3, familiarize yourself with the Day 3 Sort Words.

✓ Prior to Day 3, visit the CCC Learning Hub (ccclearninghub.org) to access and print "Week 25, Day 3 Sort" (BLM1). Make enough copies for each pair of students to have one.

✓ Prior to Day 3, visit the CCC Learning Hub (ccclearninghub.org) to access and print the "Class Assessment Record" sheet (CA1); see page 99 of the *Assessment Resource Book*.

✓ (Optional) If you plan to integrate "Build That Word" in the word work area, visit the CCC Learning Hub (ccclearninghub.org) to access and print "Week 25, Day 4 'Build That Word'" (BLM2). Make several copies to place in the word work area before the lesson. See "Independent Work Connections" on page 486.

Independent Work Check-in

✓ Familiarize yourself with the "Conferring" check-in lesson (or another check-in lesson of your choice) in Appendix B, "Independent Work Resources." Collect and prepare any necessary materials. For more information about the check-in lessons, see Appendix B, "Independent Work Resources."

📅 SUGGESTED WEEKLY SCHEDULE

Monday	Tuesday	Wednesday	Thursday	Friday
Word Study (20)	Word Study (20)		Word Study (20)	Word Study (20)
Independent Work Rotations/Small-group Reading (60)	Independent Work Rotations/Small-group Reading (60)	Independent Work Check-in (35)	Independent Work Rotations/Small-group Reading (60)	Independent Work Rotations/Small-group Reading (60)
80 minutes	80 minutes	35 minutes	80 minutes	80 minutes

Word Study

Day 1 Spelling Words		Day 3 Sort Words	
almost	idea	cleverly	paper
away	never	complicate	proper
ever	over	computer	reread
father	under	later	river
		level	shiver
		limited	spider
		moment	vacation
		never	vanishes
		over	

Academic Focus

- Students spell words with irregular spellings.
- Students read and sort two- and three-syllable words.

Social Development Focus

- Students work in a responsible way.
- Students handle materials responsibly.
- Students listen respectfully to the thinking of others and share their own.

Day 1

Word Study
Guided Spelling

Materials

- Wipe-off board, dry-erase marker, and tissue or cloth for each student
- (Optional) *Word Study Notebooks*

Spelling Support

Spelling instruction in Weeks 25–30 focuses on high-frequency words. To support the students in spelling these words, you might have them refer to the Word Bank at the end of their *Word Study Notebooks* or to the word wall.

In this lesson, the students:

- Spell words with irregular spellings
- Handle materials responsibly

1 Get Ready to Spell

Have the students stay in their seats. Review that last week, the students talked about the schwa sound. Ask and briefly discuss:

Q *What do you know about the schwa sound?*

If necessary, review that the schwa sound can be spelled in different ways. Explain that this week the students will spell high-frequency words. Explain that *high-frequency words* are words that are helpful to remember because the students will use them often in their writing and see them often in their reading. Explain that some of these words use different spellings for the schwa sound.

2 Guide the Students' Spelling

Explain that for the next few weeks, the students will spell words with unusual spellings. Distribute the wipe-off boards, markers, and cloths or tissues.

Teacher Note

If you plan to have the students use their Word Banks, have them turn to that section in their *Word Study Notebooks*.

> father   "Anouk's father visited our class to tell us what it is like to be a doctor."

Say *father*. Use *father* in a sentence. Have the students say *father* and write *father*.

Write *father* where everyone can see it and have the students check their writing and erase and correct mistakes.

Then use the same procedure to have the students write *almost*, *idea*, *over*, *under*, and *away*.

> almost   "We were almost ready for recess when it started to rain."
>
> idea   "I have a great idea!"
>
> over   "The clock is on the wall over the door."
>
> under   "The little boy hid under the bed."
>
> away   "When the dog barked, the cat ran away."

Tell the students that they will write two words that rhyme and have similar spellings.

> ever   "Have you ever seen an anteater?"
>
> never   "I have never seen an anteater."

Say *ever*. Use *ever* in a sentence. Have the students say *ever*. Explain that in *ever*, the sound /ər/ is spelled *e-r*. Have the students write *ever*.

Write *ever* where everyone can see it and have the students check their writing and erase and correct mistakes.

Say *never*. Tell the students that *never* rhymes with *ever* and most of the word is spelled the same way. Have the students say *never*. Ask:

Q   *What sound do you hear at the beginning of* never? (/n/)

Have the students write *never*.

Write *never* where everyone can see it and have the students check their writing and erase and correct mistakes.

3 Reflect

Have the students reflect on their spelling. Ask and briefly discuss:

Q *Which word was hardest to spell? What will you do to remember how to spell it the next time you write it?*

Remind the students that they will have a spelling test on Friday (or whichever day of the week you will teach the Day 4 lesson). Tell them that when they go to independent word work, they will practice spelling these words before choosing another activity.

Day 2 | Word Study
Syllabication

In this lesson, the students:

- Begin working with new partners
- Review and practice strategies for reading longer words
- Listen respectfully to the thinking of others and share their own

1 Gather and Review Reading Strategies

Randomly assign partners and gather the class with partners sitting together, facing you. Review that students have learned two strategies for reading longer words and that one strategy is to look for prefixes or suffixes in the word. Ask:

Q *What do you know about prefixes and suffixes?*

Have a few volunteers share their thinking with the class.

> **Students might say:**
>
> "A suffix comes at the end of a word."
>
> "A prefix comes at the beginning of a word."
>
> "They make new words."

Write *unbutton* where everyone can see it. Have the students read *unbutton*, first as you frame each syllable and then as a whole word. Ask:

 Q *What does* unbutton *mean? How do you know? Turn to your partner.*

After a few moments, signal for the students' attention and have a few volunteers share their thinking with the class.

Students might say:

"It means to take the button out of the buttonhole. That's how you open a shirt."

"The prefix *un-* means 'the opposite of' so it means the opposite of *button*."

Repeat the procedure with the following words that have prefixes or suffixes the students have learned: *revisit*, *smoothly*, and *brightest*.

Review that noticing the prefixes and suffixes in words can help the students read and understand the meanings of longer words.

Review that another strategy for reading longer words is to divide the words into syllables. Review that when dividing a longer word into syllables, the students can divide a word between two consonants. If there is just one consonant between two vowels, they can try dividing the word before the consonant and try a long vowel sound in the first syllable. If that does not sound like a word, they can try dividing after the consonant and try a short vowel sound in the first syllable.

Write *wagon* where everyone can see it. Draw a dot between *wa* and *gon*, just below the word. Have the students read *wagon*, first by syllables and then as a whole word. Ask:

Q *Is /wāgən/ a word? (no)*

Erase the dot and draw another dot between *wag* and *on*. Have the students read *wagon*, first by syllables and then as a whole word. Ask and briefly discuss:

Q *Is /wăgən/ a word? (yes)*

Q *What sound do you hear in the second syllable? What do you know about that sound?*

If necessary, remind the students that sometimes a vowel stands for the schwa sound.

2 Introduce a Word-analysis Strategy

Explain that when the students come to a longer word they do not recognize, it is helpful to always follow the same process: first, look for prefixes and suffixes; second, divide the rest of the word into syllables; and third, say the whole word to see if they recognize it.

Write the word *unfriendly* where everyone can see it. Model the process of looking for affixes.

You might say:

"If I'm not sure what this word is, I will first look for a prefix or a suffix in the word. I see the prefix *un-*, so I'll draw a dot between *un* and *f*. I also see the suffix *-ly*, so I'll draw a dot between *d* and *ly*. Now I see that the base word in this longer word is *friend*. I will try to read the word: *un-friend-ly; unfriendly*. I recognize that. It means 'not very nice' as in 'The dog was unfriendly. It growled at me.'"

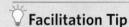 **Facilitation Tip**

Reflect on your experience over the past three weeks with **responding neutrally with interest** during class discussions. Does this practice feel natural to you? Are you integrating it into class discussions throughout the school day? What effect is it having on the students? We encourage you to continue to use this practice and reflect on students' responses as you facilitate class discussions in the future.

Teacher Note

Note that by dividing syllables in this way, the word should be read with a long *a* sound (/wāgən/). If the students read the word with a short *a* sound (/wăgən/), ask:

Q *What do you know about syllables with a vowel at the end? (They have a long vowel sound.)*

Use the same procedure to model analyzing and reading the word *unwashed*. Tell the students they can use this strategy when they come to words they are not sure of in their reading.

3 Reflect on Reading

Ask:

 Q *What might you tell someone at home about how to read longer words? Turn to your partner.*

After a few moments, signal for attention and have a few students share their thinking with the class. Tell the students that in the next few weeks, they will have more opportunities to read longer words.

Day 3 | Word Study
Pair Sort (Open)

Materials

- "Week 25, Day 3 Sort" (WA1)
- Copy of "Week 25, Day 3 Sort" (BLM1) for each pair
- Scissors for each pair
- *Word Study Notebooks* (in student toolboxes)
- Pencils
- "Word Sort Steps" chart
- "Class Assessment Record" sheet (CA1)

In this lesson, the students:

- Read and sort two- and three-syllable words
- Work responsibly in pairs
- Handle materials responsibly

1 Gather and Review a Word-analysis Strategy

Have the students bring their pencils, pick up their independent work toolboxes, and gather with partners sitting together, facing you. Have them put their toolboxes on the floor next to them. Review that looking for prefixes and suffixes in words and dividing words into syllables, if needed, can help readers read and understand longer words.

Review that a helpful process for reading longer words is to: first, look for prefixes and suffixes in the word; second, divide the rest of the word into syllables, if needed; and third, say the whole word to see if you recognize it.

2 Sort in Pairs

Explain that today partners will work together to do an open sort with longer words. Ask and briefly discuss:

Q *What can you do if you come to a longer word you don't know?*

Q *What can you do if you and your partner have different ideas about how to divide a word into syllables?*

Students might say:

"We can count the consonants between the vowels and then divide between two consonants."

"If there is just one consonant, we can try dividing one way and then try the other way if we don't recognize the word."

"We can try both our ideas and see if we recognize the word."

"If you forget to look for the prefixes, your partner can remind you."

Then ask:

 Q *How does open sorting help you think carefully about words?* [pause] *Turn to your partner.*

After a few moments, signal for the students' attention and have a few pairs share their thinking with the class.

Students might say:

"It makes you look carefully at the word parts."

"It makes you think about the meanings of the words."

"It makes you figure out how the words are the same."

Display the "Week 25, Day 3 Sort" activity (◖ WA1) and read the words with the students.

proper	never	over	reread
vanishes	river	later	spider
limited	cleverly	vacation	paper
level	complicate	moment	computer
shiver			

Teacher Note

If necessary, support the students by framing syllables or drawing dots between them.

 ELL Vocabulary

English Language Learners may benefit from hearing the following vocabulary defined:

proper: right way to do something

vanishes: disappears

limited: not a lot

cleverly: in a smart way

complicate: make something difficult

Ask:

Q *What is a way to group these words? Which words can you put together?*

Distribute a copy of "Week 25, Day 3 Sort" (BLM1) and scissors to each pair of students. Have each pair refer to the steps on the "Word Sort Steps" chart to cut apart and sort the words and then record their sorts in their *Word Study Notebooks*.

Teacher Note

Pair sorting allows you to observe and identify students who may need additional support. If the students need more support, you might use the "Week 25, Day 3 Sort" activity (WA1) to sort a few of the words as a class.

 CLASS ASSESSMENT NOTE

Ask yourself:

- Are the students able to recognize affixes?
- Are they able to divide words between consonants?
- Do they try dividing before a single consonant and then after?

Record your observations on the "Class Assessment Record" sheet (CA1); see page 99 of the *Assessment Resource Book*. Notice whether the students can read the words and sort them into categories. Support any students who struggle by guiding them to identify affixes and syllable breaks.

Reading words by syllables is challenging. If your students continue to struggle, identify their points of confusion and reteach needed content. You may wish to select polysyllabic words from the students' content-area reading and guide the students through reading them by framing the syllables.

3 Reflect on Partner Work

Ask:

Q *What did you do to work well with your partner today?*

Have a few volunteers share their thinking with the class.

In this lesson, the students:

- Spell words with irregular spellings
- Handle materials responsibly

Materials

- "Week 25, Day 4 Spelling Words" (WA2)
- Lined paper and a pencil for each student

1 Get Ready to Spell

Have the students stay in their seats. Ask and briefly discuss:

Q *How did you do with your spelling practice this week?*

2 Spelling Test

Distribute paper and pencils to the students. Have them write their names at the top and number the first eight lines 1 to 8.

Begin the test. Say "Number one: father." Use *father* in a sentence. Say *father* again. Have the students write *father*. Allow enough time for all the students to finish before moving on to the next word.

1.	father	"My father watches the TV news every night."
2.	almost	"I am almost ready to say the next spelling word."
3.	idea	"Jaime had an idea for a project about spiders."
4.	over	"An airplane flew over the playground."
5.	under	"The pencil rolled under the bookcase."
6.	away	"When you are sick, you stay away from your friends."
7.	ever	"Have you ever gone to the beach?"
8.	never	"No, I have never gone to the beach."

3 Check and Correct the Words

After the students are finished writing the last word, display the "Week 25, Day 4 Spelling Words" activity (WA2). Have the students check their work and correct mistakes. As they work, circulate and observe. When the students are finished checking and correcting their work, collect the papers.

4 Wrap Up

Tell the students they will have more opportunities to practice spelling in the coming weeks.

EXTENSION

Connect Spelling to Writing

Review that one reason writers spell words correctly is to make sure readers can understand and enjoy their writing. Think aloud about how one of the words reminds you of something that happened to you.

> **You might say:**
>
> "When I read the word *away*, it reminds me of the time my dog got out of the yard and ran away. We put up posters with our phone number, and someone found him and called us. I could write about that."

Ask:

Q *Which of these words reminds you of something that happened to you? What is a story you could write about that? Turn to your partner.*

After a few moments, signal for the students' attention and have a few volunteers share their thinking with the class. Encourage the students to use the spelling words and other words from the week's sort in their writing.

Independent Work Connections

For next week's Independent Work, we suggest the following:

- Make additional copies of "Week 25, Day 3 Sort" (BLM1) to place in the word work area.

- Make several copies of "Week 25, Day 4 'Build That Word'" (BLM2) and place them in the word work area.

Independent Work

This week the students continue to rotate to and work in all three independent work areas around the room while you teach Small-group Reading. We suggest continuing any procedures that have worked effectively in previous weeks.

Independent Work Check-in

This week you will continue to teach an Independent Work Check-in lesson on the day of the week you do not teach Small-group Reading. The purpose of these check-in lessons is to ensure that the students are able to maintain successful independent work rotations. The lessons provide the time for you to assess your students, conduct conferences, and introduce new materials and activities. For more information about the check-in lessons, see Appendix B, "Independent Work Resources."

This week we suggest you teach the "Conferring" check-in lesson in Appendix B, "Independent Work Resources." Depending on the needs of your students, you may decide to teach a different check-in lesson.

Week 26 OVERVIEW

Whole-class Instruction

Word Study

This week the students learn about the suffixes *-ment* and *-ness* and do an open sort in pairs. The spelling words this week are again high-frequency words.

Independent Work Check-in

This week we suggest you teach the "Share a Book" check-in lesson in Appendix B, "Independent Work Resources." Depending on the needs of your students, you may decide to teach a different check-in lesson.

Small-group Reading Instruction and Independent Work Rotations

Small-group Reading

This week, you will continue to teach Small-group Reading lessons at the small-group reading table while the students work independently in the reading, writing, and word work areas.

Independent Work

The students may have assigned work from Small-group Reading to do during Independent Work. The following are materials you might incorporate into independent work areas this week:

Word Work:

- "Week 25, Day 3 Sort" (see "Independent Work Connections" on page 486)
- "Week 25, 'Build That Word' Tiles" and "Week 25, 'Build That Word' Word List" (see "Independent Work Connections" on page 486)

Week 26

RESOURCES

Extension
- "Connect Spelling to Writing"

Assessment Resource Book
- Week 26 assessment

Word Study Notebook
- Word Sorts
- Spelling Practice
- (Optional) Word Bank

 Online Resources

Visit the CCC Learning Hub (ccclearninghub.org) to find your online resources for this week.

Whiteboard Activities
- WA1–WA3

Assessment Form
- "Class Assessment Record" sheet (CA1)

Reproducible
- "Week 26, Day 3 Sort" (BLM1)

Professional Development Media
- "Asking Questions Once and Using Wait-time" (AV11)

⏲ DO AHEAD

Word Study

✓ Prior to Day 1, familiarize yourself with the Day 1 Spelling Words.

✓ Prior to Day 2, familiarize yourself with the Day 2 Practice/Day 3 Sort Words.

✓ Prior to Day 3, visit the CCC Learning Hub (ccclearninghub.org) to access and print "Week 26, Day 3 Sort" (BLM1). Make enough copies for each pair of students to have one.

✓ Prior to Day 3, visit the CCC Learning Hub (ccclearninghub.org) to access and print the "Class Assessment Record" sheet (CA1); see page 100 of the *Assessment Resource Book*.

Independent Work Check-in

✓ Familiarize yourself with the "Share a Book" check-in lesson (or another check-in lesson of your choice) in Appendix B, "Independent Work Resources." Collect and prepare any necessary materials. For more information about the check-in lessons, see Appendix B, "Independent Work Resources."

📅 SUGGESTED WEEKLY SCHEDULE

Monday	Tuesday	Wednesday	Thursday	Friday
Word Study (20)	Word Study (20)		Word Study (20)	Word Study (20)
Independent Work Rotations/Small-group Reading (60)	Independent Work Rotations/Small-group Reading (60)	Independent Work Check-in (35)	Independent Work Rotations/Small-group Reading (60)	Independent Work Rotations/Small-group Reading (60)
80 minutes	80 minutes	35 minutes	80 minutes	80 minutes

Word Study

Day 1 Spelling Words		Day 2 Practice/ Day 3 Sort Words	
answer	color	agreement	happiness
because	letter	amazement	improvement
better	mother	announcement	punishment
brother	other	appointment	sadness
		brightness	softness
		darkness	soreness
		excitement	tidiness
		gladness	treatment

Academic Focus

- Students spell high-frequency words.
- Students learn about the suffixes -*ment* and -*ness*.
- Students read and sort words with the suffixes -*ment* and -*ness*.

Social Development Focus

- Students work in a responsible way.
- Students handle materials responsibly.
- Students listen respectfully to the thinking of others and share their own.

Day 1

Word Study
Guided Spelling

Materials

- Wipe-off board, dry-erase marker, and tissue or cloth for each student
- (Optional) *Word Study Notebooks*

Spelling Support

Spelling this week continues to focus on high-frequency words. To support the students' spelling, you might have them refer to the word list in their *Word Study Notebooks* or to the word wall.

In this lesson, the students:

- Spell high-frequency words
- Handle materials responsibly

1 Get Ready to Spell

Have the students stay in their seats. Explain that today the students will spell words with unusual spellings.

2 Guide the Students' Spelling

Remind the students that they will spell words with unusual spellings—words or parts that cannot be sounded out. Distribute the wipe-off boards, markers, and cloths or tissues. Tell the students that this week they will spell four words that use the *e-r* spelling for /ər/ at the end of a word.

> better   "I like oranges better than apples."

Say *better*. Use *better* in a sentence. Have the students say *better*. Then ask:

Q *How many syllables are in* better? *(two)*

Q *What is the first syllable in* better? *(bet)*

Q *What is the second syllable in* better? *(/ər/)*

Tell the students that there are two *t*s in *better* and that /ər/ is spelled *e-r*. Have the students write *better*.

Write *better* where everyone can see it and have the students check their writing and erase and correct mistakes.

> letter   "My grandmother sent me a letter."

Say *letter*. Use *letter* in a sentence. Tell the students that *letter* rhymes with *better* and most of the word is spelled the same way. Have the students say *letter*. Then ask:

Q *What sound do you hear at the beginning of* letter? *(/l/)*

Have the students write *letter*.

Write *letter* where everyone can see it and have the students check their writing and erase and correct mistakes.

> other   "One book is thick, and the other is thin."

Say *other*. Use *other* in a sentence. Have the students say *other* and write *other*.

Write *other* where everyone can see it and have the students check their work.

> mother   "My mother calls me on the phone on Sunday mornings."

Say *mother*. Use *mother* in a sentence. Tell the students that *mother* rhymes with *other* and is spelled almost the same way. Have the students say *mother*. Ask:

Q *What sound do you hear at the beginning of* mother? *(/m/)*

Have the students write *mother*.

Write *mother* where everyone can see it and have the students check their writing and erase and correct mistakes.

Teacher Note

If you plan to have the students use their Word Banks, have them turn to that section of their *Word Study Notebooks*.

brother   "Johanna walks to school with her brother."

Say *brother*. Use *brother* in a sentence. Tell the students that *brother* rhymes with *other* and *mother* and is spelled almost the same way. Have the students say *brother*. Ask:

Q   *What sounds do you hear at the beginning of* brother? *(/br/)*

Have the students write *brother*.

Write *brother* where everyone can see it and have the students check their writing and erase and correct mistakes.

because   "You will need to wear a jacket because it is cold."

Say *because*. Use *because* in a sentence. Have the students say *because* and write *because*.

Write *because* where everyone can see it and have the students check their work.

answer   "Sam figured out the answer to the math problem."

color   "My favorite color is blue."

Repeat the above procedure with *answer* and *color*.

3 Wrap Up

Remind the students they will have a spelling test on Friday (or whichever day of the week you will teach the Day 4 lesson). Tell them that when they go to independent word work, they will practice spelling these words before choosing another activity.

Teacher Note
You may wish to post the *Word Study Notebook* page number for the spelling practice in the word work area for the students to refer to during Independent Work.

Day 2

Word Study
Introduce the Suffixes *-ment* and *-ness*

Materials
- "Week 26, Day 2 Words" (WA1)

In this lesson, the students:
- Learn about the suffixes *-ment* and *-ness*
- Read words with the suffixes *-ment* and *-ness*
- Listen respectfully to the thinking of others and share their own

1 Gather and Review Dividing a Word into Syllables

Gather the class with the students sitting, facing you. Review that the students have been learning about dividing words into syllables. Remind the students that when dividing a longer word into syllables, they can look for consonants between vowels. If there are two consonants, they can divide between the consonants. If there is just one consonant, the students can first try dividing the word before the consonant and try a long vowel sound in the first syllable. If they do not recognize the word, they can try dividing after the consonant and try a short vowel sound in the first syllable.

Write *details* where everyone can see it. Ask:

Q *Where can we divide this word into syllables?*

As the students respond, draw a dot between *de* and *tails*. Point out that the first syllable in this word ends with a vowel. Review that when a syllable ends with a vowel, it is called an *open syllable*, and that the vowel sound is usually long. Have the students read *details*, first by syllables and then as a whole word.

Write *explain* where everyone can see it. Draw a dot between *ex* and *plain*. Point out that the first syllable in this word ends with a consonant. Review that when a syllable ends with a consonant, it is called a *closed syllable*, and that the vowel sound in a closed syllable is usually short. Remind the students that in words that begin with *ex*, they will always keep the *x* with the *e* to make the first syllable.

Have the students read *explain* first by syllables and then as a whole word.

2 Review Prefixes and Suffixes

Review that the students have been reading and sorting words with more than one syllable. Review that a syllable may be a prefix or suffix—a letter or group of letters added to the beginning (a *prefix*) or end (a *suffix*) of a base word to make a new word.

Write *replay* where everyone can see it. Draw a dot between *re* and *play*. Ask:

Q *Based on what you know about the word* play *and the prefix* re-, *what do you think* replay *means?*

Repeat the procedure to review other prefixes and suffixes that have meaning, using the words *uncover*, *homeless*, and *smoothly*.

Review that some suffixes, such as *-tion*, *-sion*, and *-ion*, show that a word is a noun, or the name of something.

Write *illustrate* where everyone can see it and read it for the students. Have the students say the word. Tell the students that *illustrate* is a verb, or action word, that means "draw a picture." Erase the final *e* and add *ion* to change *illustrate* to *illustration*, and say the word. Ask and briefly discuss:

Q *If* illustrate *means "draw a picture," what might* illustration *mean?*

Use each word in a sentence. (For example, "I will illustrate the story I wrote. This is my favorite illustration in this book.")

Repeat the procedure with the words *division*, *discussion*, and *prediction* to review the suffixes *-sion* and *-ion*.

3 Introduce the Suffixes *-ment* and *-ness*

Write *agreement* where everyone can see it but do not read it aloud. Draw a dot between *agree* and *ment* and then underline *ment*. Explain that the suffix *-ment* is another ending that shows that a word is a noun, or the name of something.

Cover *ment* with your hand and have the students read the base word. Explain that *agree* means "think the same way about something." Use *agree* in a sentence. (For example, "I agree with you that we should stay inside for recess because it is raining.") Uncover *ment* and read *agreement* with the students, first by syllables and then as a whole word. Explain that an *agreement* is something that two or more people make when they think the same way about something. Use *agreement* in a sentence. (For example, "The agreement we made is to stay inside for recess.") Explain that *agree* is the action word, or verb, and that *agreement* is the noun, or thing, that is what happens because of the action. Agreeing on staying in for recess resulted in an agreement to stay inside. Explain that the noun *agreement* is made by adding the suffix *-ment* to the verb *agree*.

Repeat the procedure with the words *amaze* and *amazement*.

Write *sadness* where everyone can see it. Draw a dot between *sad* and *ness* and then underline *ness*. Explain that the suffix *-ness* is another ending that shows that a word is a noun. Cover *ness* with your hand and have the students read the base word. Use *sad* in a sentence. (For example, "I was sad when I lost my favorite sweater.") Point to *sadness* and read the word with the students. Explain that *sadness* is the feeling we have when we are sad. Use *sadness* in a sentence. (For example, "I felt sadness when I lost my favorite sweater.") Explain that *sad* is a describing word that tells how a person feels. *Sadness* is the noun that names the feeling. Being sad is the same as feeling sadness.

Repeat the procedure with the words *silly* and *silliness*, pointing out how to change the *y* to *i* to add *ness*.

4 Read Words with the Suffixes *-ment* and *-ness*

Remind the students that one way to read longer words is to look for suffixes and prefixes and then, if needed, divide the rest of the word into syllables.

Display the "Week 26, Day 2 Words" activity (◗ WA1), and point to the word *sadness*. Ask:

Q *What is the suffix in this word? What is the base word?*

Teacher Note

If you are teaching the *Making Meaning®* program from Center for the Collaborative Classroom, the suffixes *-ment* and *-ness* are introduced in the *Vocabulary Teaching Guide*. If you have taught the vocabulary lesson, you may want to review *-ment* and *-ness* and simply move on to Step 4.

Teacher Note

For polysyllabic words, if necessary, support the students by framing syllables or drawing dots between them if the students cannot read the base word. For *tidiness* and *happiness*, remind the students that when adding a suffix to a word that ends in *y*, the *y* is changed to *i* before the suffix is added.

Draw a dot between *sad* and *ness*. Have the students read *sadness* by covering the suffix and having them read the base word and then the whole word. Repeat this procedure with the remaining words.

Suggested Vocabulary

tidiness: being tidy, or clean and neat

announcement: important news that is written or said

treatment: giving medicine or care to someone sick or hurt

🌐 ELL Vocabulary

English Language Learners may benefit from hearing additional words defined, including:

amazement: feeling of being very surprised

excitement: feeling of being very happy or interested

improvement: something that makes a person, place, or thing better than it was before

punishment: what someone might have to do if they are in trouble or did something wrong

soreness: pain

WA1

sadness	appointment	improvement	gladness
happiness	amazement	softness	treatment
agreement	darkness	tidiness	punishment
brightness	excitement	announcement	soreness

5 Reflect on Reading Together

Have the students reflect on how they participated today. Ask and briefly discuss:

Q *How did you do with reading the words today?*

Tell the students that discussing and reading words together as a class gives everyone a chance to practice.

Day 3

Word Study
Pair Sort (Open)

Materials

- "Week 26, Day 3 Sort" (WA2)
- Copy of "Week 26, Day 3 Sort" (BLM1) for each pair
- Scissors for each pair
- *Word Study Notebooks* (in student toolboxes)
- Pencils
- "Word Sort Steps" chart
- "Class Assessment Record" sheet (CA1)

In this lesson, the students:

- Read and sort words with the suffixes *-ment* and *-ness*
- Work responsibly with a partner
- Handle materials responsibly

1 Gather and Review the Suffixes *-ment* and *-ness*

Have the students bring their pencils, pick up their independent work toolboxes and gather with partners sitting together, facing you. Have them put their toolboxes on the floor next to them. Review that in the last lesson the students read words with the suffixes *-ment* and *-ness* and that these suffixes usually show that the word is a noun.

Write *excitement* and *enjoyment* where everyone can see them and, in each, have the students first identify the base word and then read the whole word. Use each word in a sentence. (For example, "The crowd felt excitement as they watched the game." and "I listen to music for my own enjoyment.") Then write *smoothness*, *cleverness*, and *gentleness* and have the students read each word, first by syllables and then as a whole word. Use each word in a sentence. (For example, "I felt the smoothness of the rock as I turned it in my hand." "The student's cleverness helped her solve a tricky problem." "Visitors to the farm noticed the gentleness of the cows.")

2 Introduce the Sort

Display the "Week 26, Day 3 Sort" activity (WA2) and explain that pairs will do an open sort with the words they read yesterday. Read the words with the students.

sadness	appointment	improvement	gladness
happiness	amazement	softness	treatment
agreement	darkness	tidiness	punishment
brightness	excitement	announcement	soreness

Ask:

Q *Which words in this sort can you group together? Turn to your partner.*

After a few moments, signal for the students' attention and have a few pairs share their thinking with the class.

Students might say:

"We can group words with the suffix -*ness* in one group and words with -*ment* in another."

"We can sort by number of syllables."

"We can put all the words that show feelings in one group."

3 Sort in Pairs

Distribute a copy of "Week 26, Day 3 Sort" (BLM1) and scissors to each pair. Have each pair use the steps on the "Word Sort Steps" chart to cut apart and sort the words and then record their sort in their *Word Study Notebooks*.

Teacher Note

Pair sorting allows you to observe and identify students who may need additional support. If the students need more support, you might use the "Week 26, Day 3 Sort" activity (WA2) to sort a few words as a class.

 CLASS ASSESSMENT NOTE

Ask yourself:

- Are the students able to analyze the words?
- Can they create categories for sorting?
- Are partners able to work together to sort the words?

Record your observations on the "Class Assessment Record" sheet (CA1); see page 100 of the *Assessment Resource Book*.

Have pairs who finish early find another way to sort the words. They need not record the second sort.

4 Reflect on Partner Work

Ask and briefly discuss:

Q *What did you and your partner do to work responsibly today?*

Tell the students that next week they will work with partners again to sort words.

 Facilitation Tip

We invite you to **ask the question once**, and then **use wait-time** to give the students time to think before calling on anyone to respond. If the students are confused by a question or need to hear it again, encourage them to ask you to repeat or rephrase the question. This builds student responsibility for focusing on the discussion and helps the students develop the habit of listening the first time. To see this Facilitation Tip in action, view "Asking Questions Once and Using Wait-time" (AV11).

Materials

- "Week 26, Day 4 Spelling Words" (WA3)
- Lined paper and a pencil for each student

In this lesson, the students:

- Spell high-frequency words
- Handle materials responsibly

1 Get Ready to Spell

Have the students stay in their seats. Ask and briefly discuss:

Q *How did you do with your spelling practice this week?*

2 Spelling Test

Distribute paper and pencils to the students. Have them write their names at the top and number the first eight lines 1 to 8.

Begin the test. Say "Number one: better." Use *better* in a sentence. Say *better* again. Have the students write *better*. Allow enough time for all the students to finish before moving on to the next word.

Repeat this procedure for the remaining spelling words.

1.	better	"I like yellow better than blue."
2.	letter	"We wrote a letter to Davon after he moved away."
3.	other	"One pencil is blue, and the other is black."
4.	mother	"My mother reads to me at bedtime."
5.	brother	"My brother Alex likes to skateboard."
6.	because	"We are staying inside because it is raining."
7.	answer	"Miriam gave the answer to the question."
8.	color	"Which color is your favorite?"

3 Check and Correct the Words

After the students are finished writing the last word, display the "Week 26, Day 4 Spelling Words" activity (◖ WA3). Have the students check their work and correct mistakes.

4 Wrap Up

Tell the students they will have more opportunities to practice spelling in the coming weeks.

EXTENSION

Connect Spelling to Writing

Review that one reason writers spell words correctly is to make sure readers can understand and enjoy their writing. Think aloud about how one of the words reminds you of something that happened to you.

> **You might say:**
>
> "When I read the word *brother*, it reminds me of the time my brother and I went to a basketball game together. It was really exciting. I can write about that."

Ask:

Q *Which of these words reminds you of something that happened to you? What is a story you could write about that? Turn to your partner.*

After a few moments, signal for the students' attention and have a few volunteers share their thinking with the class. Encourage the students to use the spelling words and other words from the week's sort in their writing.

Independent Work Connection

For next week's Independent Work, we suggest the following:

▪ Make additional copies of "Week 26, Day 3 Sort" (BLM1) to place in the word work area.

This week the students continue to rotate to and work in all three independent work areas around the room while you teach Small-group Reading. We suggest continuing any procedures that have worked effectively in previous weeks.

Independent Work Check-in

This week you will continue to teach an Independent Work Check-in lesson on the day of the week you do not teach Small-group Reading. The purpose of these check-in lessons is to ensure that the students are able to maintain successful independent work rotations. The lessons provide the time for you to assess your students, conduct conferences, and introduce new materials and activities. For more information about the check-in lessons, see Appendix B, "Independent Work Resources."

This week we suggest you teach the "Share a Book" check-in lesson in Appendix B, "Independent Work Resources." Depending on the needs of your students, you may decide to teach a different check-in lesson.

Week 27 OVERVIEW

Whole-class Instruction

Word Study

This week the students continue to read polysyllabic words using the three-step procedure: first, look for prefixes and suffixes; second, divide the rest of the word into syllables; and third, say the whole word to see if they recognize it. The spelling words this week are high-frequency irregular words. You may wish to assess your students' understanding of concepts taught in the previous ten weeks using the Word Study Progress Assessment. See the Word Study Progress Assessment Note at the end of the Day 4 lesson.

Independent Work Check-in

This week we suggest you teach the "Share Writing" check-in lesson in Appendix B, "Independent Work Resources." Depending on the needs of your students, you may decide to teach a different check-in lesson.

Small-group Reading Instruction and Independent Work Rotations

Small-group Reading

This week, you will continue to teach Small-group Reading lessons at the small-group reading table while the students work independently in the reading, writing, and word work areas.

Independent Work

The students may have assigned work from Small-group Reading to do during Independent Work. The following are materials you might incorporate into independent work areas this week:

Word Work:

- "Week 26, Day 3 Sort" (see "Independent Work Connection" on page 501)

Week 27

RESOURCES

Assessment Resource Book
- Week 27 assessment
- Word Study Progress Assessment 3

Word Study Notebook
- Word Sorts
- Spelling Practice
- (Optional) Word Bank

 Online Resources

Visit the CCC Learning Hub (ccclearninghub.org) to find your online resources for this week.

Whiteboard Activities
- WA1–WA3

Assessment Forms
- "Class Assessment Record" sheet (CA1)
- "Word Study Progress Assessment 3" recording form (WS3)
- "Word Study Progress Assessment 3 Student Card" (SC3)
- "Word Study Progress Assessment 3 Class Record" sheet (CR3)

Reproducible
- "Week 27, Day 3 Sort" (BLM1)

⏱ DO AHEAD

Word Study

✓ Prior to Day 1, familiarize yourself with the Day 1 Spelling Words.

✓ Prior to Day 2, familiarize yourself with the Day 2 Practice/Day 3 Sort Words.

✓ Prior to Day 3, visit the CCC Learning Hub (ccclearninghub.org) to access and print "Week 27, Day 3 Sort" (BLM1). Make enough copies for each pair of students to have one.

✓ Prior to Day 4, visit the CCC Learning Hub (ccclearninghub.org) to access and print the "Class Assessment Record" sheet (CA1); see page 101 of the *Assessment Resource Book*.

Independent Work Check-in

✓ Familiarize yourself with the "Share Writing" check-in lesson (or another check-in lesson of your choice) in Appendix B, "Independent Work Resources." Collect and prepare any necessary materials. For more information about the check-in lessons, see Appendix B, "Independent Work Resources."

📅 SUGGESTED WEEKLY SCHEDULE

Monday	Tuesday	Wednesday	Thursday	Friday
Word Study (20)	Word Study (20)		Word Study (20)	Word Study (20)
Independent Work Rotations/Small-group Reading (60)	Independent Work Rotations/Small-group Reading (60)	Independent Work Check-in (35)	Independent Work Rotations/Small-group Reading (60)	Independent Work Rotations/Small-group Reading (60)
80 minutes	**80 minutes**	**35 minutes**	**80 minutes**	**80 minutes**

Day 1 Spelling Words		Day 2 Practice/ Day 3 Sort Words	
climb	friend	connection	forgiveness
comb	kind	continue	important
done	mind	discover	introduce
find	one	excitement	introduction
		experiment	invention
		explained	memorize
		fantastic	recognize
		forgetful	unwelcome

Academic Focus

- Students spell high-frequency words with irregular spellings.
- Students read and sort two-, three-, and four-syllable words.

Social Development Focus

- Students work in a responsible way.
- Students handle materials responsibly.
- Students listen respectfully to the thinking of others and share their own.

Day 1

Word Study
Guided Spelling

Materials

- Wipe-off board, dry-erase marker, and tissue or cloth for each student
- (Optional) *Word Study Notebooks*

Spelling Support

Continue to support the students by allowing them to refer to the Word Bank at the end of their *Word Study Notebooks* or to the word wall.

In this lesson, the students:

- Spell high-frequency words with irregular spellings
- Handle materials responsibly

1 Get Ready to Spell

Have the students stay in their seats today.

2 Guide the Students' Spelling

Distribute the wipe-off boards, markers, and cloths or tissues.

Tell the students that this week some of the words they will spell are rhyming words.

| one | "You may choose one or two books." |

Say *one*. Use *one* in a sentence. Have the students say and write *one*.

Write *one* where everyone can see it and have the students check their writing and erase and correct mistakes.

| done | "When you are done reading, tell me about the book." |

Say *done*. Use *done* in a sentence. Tell the students that *done* rhymes with *one* and that it is spelled almost the same way. Have the students say *done*. Ask:

Q *What sound do you hear at the beginning of* done? *(/d/)*

Have the students write *done*.

Write *done* where everyone can see it and have the students check their writing and erase and correct mistakes.

Use the same procedure to guide the students in spelling the following words:

find	"I hope you find the book you lost."
kind	"The kind woman told me how to get to the park."
mind	"Picture the park in your mind."

Tell the students that the next two words they will spell have a silent letter at the end—a silent *b*. Explain that there are not many words with a silent *b* at the end.

| climb | "I can climb this hill easily." |
| comb | "I brush and comb my hair every morning." |

Write the word *climb* where everyone can see it. Say *climb* and use it in a sentence. Then have the students say *climb* and copy it. Repeat the procedure with *comb*.

| friend | "My best friend visited me yesterday." |

Tell the students that the last word they will spell is *friend*. Use *friend* in a sentence. Then have the students say *friend* and write *friend*.

Write *friend* where everyone can see it and have the students check their writing and erase and correct mistakes.

3 Wrap Up

Remind the students they will have a spelling test on Friday (or whichever day of the week you will teach the Day 4 lesson). Tell them that when they go to independent word work, they will practice spelling these words before choosing another activity.

Teacher Note

You may wish to post the *Word Study Notebook* page number for the spelling practice in the word work area for the students to refer to during Independent Work.

Materials

- "Week 27, Day 2 Words" (WA1)

In this lesson, the students:

- Review and practice strategies for reading longer words
- Read two-, three-, and four-syllable words
- Listen respectfully to the thinking of others and share their own

ABOUT READING POLYSYLLABIC WORDS

Learning to read polysyllabic words is a step toward fluent reading in more complex texts. The intention of these syllabication lessons is to give students tools to read and understand polysyllabic words when they encounter them in their reading. The tools we provide include learning to recognize affixes and base words and understanding basic guidelines for dividing words into syllables. The lessons are not intended to teach syllabication "rules" to apply rigidly.

Students may use a variety of strategies to decode longer words. The process the students learn is: first, look for prefixes and suffixes; second, divide the rest of the word into syllables, if needed; and third, say the whole word to see if they recognize it. Throughout the past several weeks, the students have had guidance for breaking words into syllables; however, the students may divide words into smaller parts in different ways. Keep in mind that the purpose of dividing words into smaller parts is to put the parts together to make a word they recognize. We do not recommend requiring students to identify dictionary syllable breaks at this time.

1 Gather and Review Word-reading Strategies

Gather the class with partners sitting together, facing you. Review that the students have learned strategies for reading longer words.

Review that when the students come to a longer word they do not recognize, it is helpful to always follow the same process: first, look for prefixes and suffixes; second, divide the rest of the word into syllables, if needed; and third, say the whole word to see if they recognize it.

Write *replanted* where everyone can see it. Ask:

 Q *How can we divide this word into parts so that it is easier to read? Turn to your partner.*

After a few moments, signal for the students' attention and have a few volunteers share.

> **Students might say:**
>
> "I see *e-d* at the end of the word."
>
> "I see *r-e* at the beginning of the word. Lots of words start with *r-e*."
>
> "The word *plant* is in the middle."

As the students share, draw dots between the syllables. Have the students read *replanted*, first by syllables and then as a whole word. Review that when *p* and *l* come next to each other, they stay together. Tell the students that there are other pairs of consonants that stay together in syllables. As you say each of the following consonant blends, write it where everyone can see it: *dr, gr, st, sp, sl, cl*.

Repeat the word analysis procedure with the word *important*.

2 Read the Words

Display the "Week 27, Day 2 Words" activity (● WA1). Work with the students to read the words using the same procedure.

Tell the students they can use these strategies when they come to words they are not sure of in their reading.

> ### Suggested Vocabulary
>
> **discover:** see or figure out for the first time
>
> ### 🌐 ELL Vocabulary
>
> English Language Learners may benefit from hearing additional vocabulary defined, including:
>
> **introduction:** words written or said that give information about something new
>
> **experiment:** follow a set of steps to see what happens
>
> **forgiveness:** deciding not to feel upset or angry with someone
>
> **introduce:** tell others about something or someone for the first time
>
> **recognize:** see something and remember seeing it before
>
> **memorize:** learn something so that you remember it perfectly

Teacher Note

There are additional consonant blends that stay in syllables as a unit, but these are the most common. The students are unlikely to remember more than a few of them. This explanation simply introduces the concept to the students.

forgetful	unwelcome	fantastic	introduce
important	continue	experiment	recognize
introduction	discover	explained	invention
connection	excitement	forgiveness	memorize

3 Reflect on Reading

Ask:

 Q *What did you like about reading the words today? Turn to your partner.*

After a few moments, signal for the students' attention and have a few pairs share their thinking with the class. Tell the students that in the next few weeks they will have more opportunities to read long words.

Day 3 | Word Study
Pair Sort (Open)

Materials

- "Week 27, Day 3 Sort" (WA2)
- Copy of "Week 27, Day 3 Sort" (BLM1) for each pair
- Scissors for each pair
- *Word Study Notebooks* (in student toolboxes)
- Pencils
- "Word Sort Steps" chart

In this lesson, the students:

- Read and sort two-, three-, and four-syllable words
- Work responsibly with a partner
- Handle materials responsibly

1 Gather and Review a Word-analysis Strategy

Have the students bring their pencils, pick up their independent work toolboxes, and gather with partners sitting together, facing you. Have them put their toolboxes on the floor next to them. Review that in the last lesson, the students read a list of longer words. Ask:

 Q *What do you remember about reading longer words? Turn to your partner.*

Students might say:

"You look for prefixes."

"Sometimes you see parts of the word you know."

"You can try dividing a word into syllables."

After a few moments, signal for the students' attention, and have a few volunteers share. Review that one strategy for reading longer words is to first look for a prefix or suffix and then divide the rest of the word into syllables, if needed. Review that to divide words into syllables, first look for consonants between vowels. If there are two consonants, try dividing between them. If there is just one consonant, the students can divide the word before the consonant and try saying a long vowel sound in the first syllable. If they do not recognize the word, they can divide after the consonant and try saying a short vowel sound in the first syllable.

2 Sort in Pairs

Explain that today partners will work together to do an open sort with words that have two-, three-, or four-syllables. Ask:

 Q *How does open sorting help you think carefully about words? Turn to your partner.*

After a few moments, signal for the students' attention and have a few pairs share their thinking with the class.

Students might say:

"It makes you look carefully at the word parts."

"It makes you think about the meanings of the words."

"It makes you figure out how the words are the same."

Display the "Week 27, Day 3 Sort" activity (🌓 WA2) and read the words with the students.

forgetful	unwelcome	fantastic	introduce
important	continue	experiment	recognize
introduction	discover	explained	invention
connection	excitement	forgiveness	memorize

 Distribute a copy of "Week 27, Day 3 Sort" (BLM1) and scissors to each pair of students. Have each pair refer to the steps on the "Word Sort Steps" chart to cut apart and sort the words and then record their sort in their *Word Study Notebooks.*

3 Reflect on Sorting

Have the students reflect on sorting. Ask and briefly discuss:

Q *What did you like about sorting with your partner?*

Teacher Note

Pair sorting allows you to observe and identify students who may need additional support. Support students who struggle to read the words by framing the syllables and having the students read each word first by syllables and then as a whole word.

If your students need more support, you might use the "Week 27, Day 3 Sort" activity (WA2) to sort a few words as a class.

Have a few volunteers share their thinking with the class. Tell the students that next week, they will learn more about reading longer words.

Day 4

Word Study
Spelling Test

Materials

- "Week 27, Day 4 Spelling Words" (WA3)
- Lined paper and a pencil for each student
- "Class Assessment Record" sheet (CA1)

In this lesson, the students:

- Spell high-frequency words with irregular spellings
- Handle materials responsibly

1 Get Ready to Spell

Have the students stay in their seats. Ask and briefly discuss:

Q *How did you do with your spelling practice this week?*

2 Spelling Test

Distribute paper and pencils to the students. Have them write their names at the top and number the first eight lines 1 to 8.

Begin the test. Say "Number one: one." Use *one* in a sentence. Say *one* again. Have the students write *one*. Allow enough time for all the students to finish before moving on to the next word.

Repeat this procedure for the remaining spelling words.

1. one "There is one clock on the classroom wall."
2. done "When we are done spelling, we will go to independent work."
3. find "You can find many books in a library."
4. kind "It was kind of her to take time to help."
5. mind "I can make pictures in mind when I read interesting stories."
6. friend "A friend is someone who likes to spend time with you."
7. climb "The worker can climb a ladder to get onto the roof."
8. comb "The students will comb their hair carefully on class picture day."

3 Check and Correct the Words

After the students are finished writing the last word, display the "Week 27, Day 4 Spelling Words" activity (WA3). Have the students check their work and correct mistakes.

✓ CLASS ASSESSMENT NOTE

Ask yourself:

- Are the students able to memorize eight irregular words per week?
- Do they notice when they spell a word incorrectly?

Record your observations on the "Class Assessment Record" sheet (CA1); see page 101 of the *Assessment Resource Book*. If your students are struggling to remember eight words, consider giving them only five or six in the coming weeks.

4 Reflect on Spelling

Have the students reflect on the spelling test. Ask and briefly discuss:

Q *How did you do with spelling the words this week?*

Tell the students they will have more opportunities to practice spelling in the coming weeks.

✓ WORD STUDY ASSESSMENT NOTE

Administer Word Study Progress Assessment 3 after this lesson, using "Word Study Progress Assessment 3" recording form (WS3) and "Word Study Progress Assessment 3 Student Card" (SC3); see pages 113–114 of the *Assessment Resource Book*.

Support any students who struggle to read the words by repeating instruction for concepts that are challenging for them, individually or in a small group. Keep in mind that the best assessment of students' reading is to notice how they use what they have learned when reading connected text.

Teacher Note

You may wish to use "Word Study Progress Assessment 3 Class Record" sheet (CR3) to record the assessment results for the whole class. See page 115 of the *Assessment Resource Book*.

Independent Work Connection

For next week's Independent Work, we suggest the following:

- Make several copies of "Week 27, Day 3 Sort" (BLM1) to place in the word work area.

OVERVIEW Independent Work

This week the students continue to rotate to and work in all three independent work areas around the room while you teach Small-group Reading. We suggest continuing any procedures that have worked effectively in previous weeks.

Independent Work Check-in

This week you will continue to teach an Independent Work Check-in lesson on the day of the week you do not teach Small-group Reading. The purpose of these check-in lessons is to ensure that the students are able to maintain successful independent work rotations. The lessons provide the time for you to assess your students, conduct conferences, and introduce new materials and activities. For more information about the check-in lessons, see Appendix B, "Independent Work Resources."

This week we suggest you continue to teach the "Share Writing" check-in lesson in Appendix B, "Independent Work Resources." Depending on the needs of your students, you may decide to teach a different check-in lesson.

Week 28 OVERVIEW

Whole-class Instruction

Word Study

This week the students continue to use read polysyllabic words using the three-step procedure: first, look for prefixes and suffixes; second, divide the rest of the word into syllables if necessary; and third, say the whole word to see if they recognize it. On Day 3, the students read morphemic transformations. The spelling words this week are again high-frequency irregular words.

Independent Work Check-in

This week we suggest you continue to teach the "Share Writing" check-in lesson in Appendix B, "Independent Work Resources." Depending on the needs of your students, you may decide to teach a different check-in lesson.

Small-group Reading Instruction and Independent Work Rotations

Small-group Reading

This week you will continue to teach Small-group Reading lessons at the small-group reading table while the students work independently in the reading, writing, and word work areas.

Independent Work

The students may have assigned work from Small-group Reading to do during Independent Work. The following are materials you might incorporate into independent work areas this week:

Word Work:

- "Week 27, Day 3 Sort" (see "Independent Work Connection" on page 513)

Week 28

RESOURCES

Assessment Resource Book
- Week 28 assessment

Word Study Notebook
- Spelling Practice
- (Optional) Word Bank

 Online Resources

Visit the CCC Learning Hub (ccclearninghub.org) to find your online resources for this week.

Whiteboard Activities
- WA1–WA2

Assessment Form
- "Class Assessment Record" sheet (CA1)

Reproducible
- "Week 28, Day 2 Sort" (BLM1)

Professional Development Media
- "Asking Questions Once and Using Wait-time" (AV11)

⏱ DO AHEAD

Word Study

✓ Prior to Day 1, familiarize yourself with the Day 1 Spelling Words.

✓ Prior to Day 2, familiarize yourself with the Day 2 Practice Words.

✓ Prior to Day 2, visit the CCC Learning Hub (ccclearninghub.org) to access and print "Week 28, Day 2 Sort" (BLM1). Make several copies to place in the word work area before the lesson.

✓ Prior to Day 3, visit the CCC Learning Hub (ccclearninghub.org) to access and print the "Class Assessment Record" sheet (CA1); see page 102 of the *Assessment Resource Book.*

✓ Prior to Day 3, identify content words from your social studies or science curriculum that you can use for word analysis examples (see Step 1).

✓ Prior to Day 3, familiarize yourself with the Day 3 Practice Words.

✓ (Optional) Prior to Day 3, write down the transformation sequences on a self-stick note or scratch paper to expedite the lesson (see Step 3).

Independent Work Check-in

✓ Familiarize yourself with the "Share Writing" check-in lesson (or another check-in lesson of your choice) in Appendix B, "Independent Work Resources." Collect and prepare any necessary materials. For more information about the check-in lessons, see Appendix B, "Independent Work Resources."

📅 SUGGESTED WEEKLY SCHEDULE

Monday	Tuesday	Wednesday	Thursday	Friday
Word Study (20)	Word Study (20)		Word Study (20)	Word Study (20)
Independent Work Rotations/Small-group Reading (60)	Independent Work Rotations/Small-group Reading (60)	Independent Work Check-in (35)	Independent Work Rotations/Small-group Reading (60)	Independent Work Rotations/Small-group Reading (60)
80 minutes	80 minutes	35 minutes	80 minutes	80 minutes

Day 1 Spelling Words		Day 2 Practice Words		Day 3 Practice Words	
become	some	adorable	impossible	believable	reuse
both	someone	agreeable	invisible	believe	rewash
come	something	believable	moveable	break	unbelievable
does	sometimes	bendable	payable	breakable	unbreakable
		breakable	possible	comfort	uncomfortable
		changeable	terrible	comfortable	use
		comfortable	understandable	impossible	visible
		edible	useable	invisible	wash
		excitable	visible	possible	washable
		horrible		reusable	

Academic Focus

- Students spell high-frequency words with irregular spellings.
- Students learn the suffixes *-able* and *-ible*.
- Student read polysyllabic words.

Social Development Focus

- Students work in a responsible way.
- Students handle materials responsibly.
- Students listen respectfully to the thinking of others and share their own.

Day 1

Word Study
Guided Spelling

Materials

- Wipe-off board, dry-erase marker, and tissue or cloth for each student
- (Optional) *Word Study Notebooks*

In this lesson, the students:

- Spell high-frequency words with irregular spellings
- Handle materials responsibly

1 Get Ready to Spell

Have the students stay in their seats today.

2 Guide the Students' Spelling

Remind the students that they will spell words with unusual spellings—words or parts that cannot be sounded out. Distribute the wipe-off boards, markers, and cloths or tissues.

some	"We will write some words now."

Say *some* and use it in a sentence. Have the students say *some* and write *some*.

Write *some* where everyone can see it and have the students check their writing and erase and correct mistakes.

Remind the students that a *compound word* is made up of two smaller words put together to make a longer word. Tell the students that the next three words they will spell are compound words that have *some* as the first small word.

something	"I found something at the library that you will like."
sometimes	"I sometimes like to read mystery books."
someone	"Someone told me about a new mystery book."

Say *something*. Use *something* in a sentence. Then have the students say *something* and write *something*.

Write *something* where everyone can see it and have the students check their writing and erase and correct mistakes.

Repeat the procedure with *sometimes* and *someone*.

In the same way, guide the students in the spelling of each of the following words by saying the word, using it in a sentence, and then having the students say, write, and check it.

come	"Alberto will come to the library with me."
become	"If you practice, you will become an excellent swimmer."
does	"Kaly does her homework every afternoon."
both	"Both Alberto and Kaly love to swim."

3 Wrap Up

Remind the students that they will have a spelling test on Friday (or whichever day of the week you will teach the Day 4 lesson). Tell them that when they go to independent word work, they will practice spelling these words before choosing another activity.

Spelling Support

Continue to support the students by allowing them to refer to the Word Bank at the end of their *Word Study Notebooks* or to the word wall.

Teacher Note

You may wish to post the *Word Study Notebook* page number for the spelling practice in the word work area for the students to refer to during Independent Work.

Materials

- "Week 28, Day 2 Words" (WA1)
- Copies of "Week 28, Day 2 Sort" (BLM1) in the word work area

Teacher Note

If you are teaching the *Making Meaning®* program from Center for the Collaborative Classroom, the suffixes *-able* and *-ible* are introduced in the *Vocabulary Teaching Guide*. If you have taught the vocabulary lesson, you may want to review *-able* and *-ible* and simply move on to Step 3.

In this lesson, the students:

- Learn about the suffixes *-able* and *-ible*
- Read words with the suffixes *-able* and *-ible*
- Listen respectfully to the thinking of others and share their own

1 Gather and Review Prefixes and Suffixes

Gather the class with the students sitting, facing you. Review that the students have been reading words with more than one syllable. Review that a syllable may be a prefix or a suffix—a letter or group of letters that is added to the beginning (a *prefix*) or end (a *suffix*) of a base word to make a new word. Prefixes and suffixes often have their own meanings, and suffixes can show that a word is a *noun* (the name of something) or an *adjective* (a describing word).

Write *rewash* where everyone can see it. Have the students read *rewash*; then ask:

Q *What do you think* rewash *might mean?*

Use the same procedure with the words *helpful*, *sadness*, and *unkind* to review the suffixes *-ful* and *-ness* and the prefix *un-*.

2 Introduce the Suffixes *-able* and *-ible*

Display the "Week 28, Day 2 Words" activity (◖ WA1) and read the displayed words aloud.

moveable

bendable

visible

edible

> ### Suggested Vocabulary
>
> **visible:** able to be seen

Ask:

Q *What do you notice about these words?*

Have a few volunteers share their thinking with the class.

Point to the word *moveable*. Read the word for the students. Underline *able*, and tell the students this is the suffix *-able*. Explain that in *moveable*, *move* is the base word and *able* is the suffix.

Use *move* in a sentence. (For example, "We can move the shelves under the window; they are not fastened to the wall.")

Explain that if something is moveable, it can be moved. Use *moveable* in your example. (For example, "We can move the shelves; the shelves are moveable.")

Tell the students that adding the suffix *-able* usually shows that a word is an adjective, or a describing word. *Moveable* is an adjective; it describes or tells about the shelves.

Point to the word *bendable*. Read the word for the students. Underline *able* and ask:

Q   *What is the base word in* bendable? *(bend)*

Use *bend* in a sentence. (For example, "The ruler will bend; it is made of soft plastic.")

Explain that if something is bendable, it can be bent. Use *bendable* in your example. (For example, "The ruler will bend; it is bendable.")

Review that adding the suffix *-able* usually shows that a word is an adjective, or a describing word. *Bendable* is an adjective; it describes or tells about the ruler.

Point to the words *visible* and *edible* and read them for the students. Underline *ible* and use each word in an example.

Explain that some words that end with *-ible*, such as *visible* and *edible*, may not have base words the student can recognize, but the suffix still shows that the word is an adjective, or a describing word.

3 Read Words with the Suffixes *-able* and *-ible*

Explain that now the students will read words with the suffixes *-able* and *-ible*.

Direct the students' attention to the "Week 28, Day 2 Words" activity (◖ WA1). Click to reveal the remaining words.

Point to *breakable*. Draw a dot between *break* and *able*. Have the students read the word, first the base word and suffix and then the whole word.

Repeat this procedure for the remaining words.

> ### Suggested Vocabulary
>
> **excitable:** able to get excited easily
> **agreeable:** nice or pleasant
> **payable:** able to be paid
>
> ### 🌐 ELL Vocabulary
>
> English Language Learners may benefit from hearing additional vocabulary defined, including:
> **visible:** easy to see
> **edible:** safe to eat
> **invisible:** impossible to see
> **adorable:** able to be loved; very cute

move**able**	● break·able	understand·able
bend**able**	comfort·able	invis·ible
vis**ible**	horr·ible	change·able
ed**ible**	us·able	agree·able
	excit·able	ador·able
	poss·ible	pay·able
	believ·able	imposs·ible
	terr·ible	

4 Wrap Up

Tell the students that they will sort these words when they go to independent word work and that you have put copies of the sort in the word work area. They can sort with a partner or individually.

Teacher Note

For *horrible, usable, excitable, terrible, believable,* and *adorable,* identify the base words for the students (*horror, excite, believe, terror,* and *adore*).

Teacher Note

If the students need additional support, frame the base words by syllable as the students read the words.

In this lesson, the students:

- Review morphemic transformations
- Read words with morphemic transformations
- Listen respectfully to the thinking of others and share their own

Materials

- "Class Assessment Record" sheet (CA1)
- (Optional) Transformation sequence on scratch paper or a self-stick note, prepared ahead

1 Gather and Review a Word-analysis Strategy

Gather the class with partners sitting together, facing you. Remind the students that they have learned a few strategies for reading and understanding longer words. Ask and briefly discuss:

Q *What can you try when you come to a word you don't know in your reading?*

> **Students might say:**
>
> "I can see if I know what the base word is. That will help me understand the word."
>
> "I can look for prefixes like *re-* and *un-*."
>
> "I can look for ending parts I know, like *-ful* and *-ment*."
>
> "If it is a longer word, I can try reading the syllables and putting them together to make the word."

Review that when the students come to a word they do not know, they can first try looking for prefixes and suffixes and then read the rest of the word by syllables. Then they can reread the whole sentence or look at the illustrations to see whether the word makes sense in what they are reading.

Model using these strategies to analyze and read words from your social studies or science curriculum. For example, you might write the word *erosion* where everyone can see it. Draw a dot or dots between the base word and any affixes, and then divide the base word into syllables, if needed. Point out and pronounce any unusual spellings. Then have the students read the word, first by syllables then as a whole word. Ask:

Q *Is [erosion] a word you recognize?*

Use the word in a sentence to clarify its meaning. Repeat the procedure for two or three more words you selected.

2 Review Morphemic Transformations

Tell the students they will now read more words with prefixes and suffixes. Explain that they will start by reading a base word. You will

Facilitation Tip

We invite you to **practice asking questions once and then waiting.** This means not repeating the question or asking it again in a different way; it means just asking the question once, and then using wait-time to give the students time to think before calling on anyone to respond. If the students are confused by a question or need to hear it again, encourage them to ask you to repeat or rephrase the question. This builds student responsibility for focusing on the discussion and helps them develop the habit of listening the first time. To see this Facilitation Tip in action, view "Asking Questions Once and Using Wait-time" (AV11).

Teacher Note

If necessary, have the students read by syllables before reading the whole word.

---

make new words by adding and changing prefixes and suffixes, and they will read the prefixes, base words, and suffixes and then the new words. Ask:

 Q *Why is it fair to wait for the signal to read? Turn to your partner.*

After a few moments, signal for the students' attention and have a few volunteers share their thinking with the class.

Remind the students that when they wait for your signal and read together, everyone has a chance to think carefully about what they are reading.

3 Read Morphemic Transformations

Tell the students that they will read a series of words that can be made from a base word. Write the word *use* where everyone can see it. Have the students read it aloud.

Add *re* to the beginning of *use*. Draw a dot between *re* and *use*, just below the word. Have the students read *reuse*.

Use *reuse* in a sentence. (For example, "We like to reuse our shopping bags.")

Erase *e* and add *able*. Draw a dot between *s* and *able*, just below the word. Have the students read *reusable*.

Use *reusable* in a sentence. (For example, "I bring my snack to school in a reusable container.")

Follow the same procedure for the following words, erasing word parts as needed to make changes:

- *comfort, comfortable, uncomfortable*
- *believe, believable, unbelievable*
- *break, breakable, unbreakable*
- *visible, invisible*
- *possible, impossible*
- *wash, rewash, washable*

 CLASS ASSESSMENT NOTE

After this lesson, ask yourself:

- Are the students able to easily recognize prefixes and suffixes?
- Do they use the affixes to understand word meanings?

Record your observations on the "Class Assessment Record" sheet (CA1); see page 102 of the *Assessment Resource Book*.

4 Reflect on Reading

Ask:

 Q *What did you like about reading words today? Turn to your partner.*

After a few moments, signal for the students' attention and have a few pairs share their thinking with the class. Tell the students that in the next few weeks, they will have more opportunities to read long words.

Word Study
Spelling Test

Day 4

In this lesson, the students:
- Spell high-frequency words with irregular spellings
- Handle materials responsibly

Materials
- "Week 28, Day 4 Spelling Words" (WA2)
- Lined paper and a pencil for each student

1 Get Ready to Spell

Have the students stay in their seats today.

2 Spelling Test

Distribute paper and pencils to the students. Have them write their names at the top and number the first eight lines 1 to 8.

Begin the test. Say "Number one: some." Use *some* in a sentence. Say *some* again. Have the students write *some*. Allow enough time for all the students to finish before moving on to the next word.

Repeat this procedure for the remaining spelling words.

1. some — "We chose some new books when we went to the library."

2. something — "I bought something at the grocery store last week."

3. sometimes — "When it is raining, we sometimes go to the cafeteria for recess."

4. someone — "Someone knocked at the door and Scottie went to open it."

5. come — "I come to school on time."

6. become   "A caterpillar can become a butterfly."

7. does   "Does anyone have a purple marker?"

8. both   "Both Angelica and Sean have purple markers."

3 Check and Correct the Words

After the students are finished writing the last word, display the "Week 28, Day 4 Spelling Words" activity (◖ WA2). Have the students check their work and correct mistakes.

4 Reflect on Spelling

Have the students reflect on the spelling test. Ask and briefly discuss:

Q   *How does spelling practice help you in your writing?*

Tell the students they will have more opportunities to practice spelling in the coming weeks.

Independent Work Connection

For next week's Independent Work, we suggest the following:

- Make additional copies of "Week 28, Day 2 Sort" (BLM1) to place in the word work area.

Independent Work  OVERVIEW

This week the students continue to rotate to and work in all three independent work areas around the room while you teach Small-group Reading. We suggest continuing any procedures that have worked effectively in previous weeks.

Independent Work Check-in

This week you will continue to teach an Independent Work Check-in lesson on the day of the week you do not teach Small-group Reading. The purpose of these check-in lessons is to ensure that the students are able to maintain successful independent work rotations. The lessons provide the time for you to assess your students, conduct conferences, and introduce new materials and activities. For more information about the check-in lessons, see Appendix B, "Independent Work Resources."

This week we suggest you continue to teach the "Share Writing" check-in lesson in Appendix B, "Independent Work Resources." Depending on the needs of your students, you may decide to teach a different check-in lesson.

Week 29 OVERVIEW

Whole-class Instruction

Word Study

This week the students review prefixes and suffixes and use what they know about affixes and syllabication to read and understand longer words. On Day 3, they do an open sort using several common base words and a variety of affixes. The spelling words this week are again high-frequency irregular words.

Independent Work Check-in

This week we suggest you continue to teach the "Share Writing" check-in lesson in Appendix B, "Independent Work Resources." Depending on the needs of your students, you may decide to teach a different check-in lesson.

Small-group Reading Instruction and Independent Work Rotations

Small-group Reading

This week you will continue to teach Small-group Reading lessons at the small-group reading table while the students work independently in the reading, writing, and word work areas.

Independent Work

The students may have assigned work from Small-group Reading to do during Independent Work. The following are materials you might incorporate into independent work areas this week:

Word Work:

- "Week 28, Day 2 Sort" (see "Independent Work Connection" on page 526)

Week 29

RESOURCES

Assessment Resource Book
- Week 29 assessment
- Social skills assessment

Word Study Notebook
- Word Sorts
- Spelling Practice
- (Optional) Word Bank

 Online Resources

Visit the CCC Learning Hub (ccclearninghub.org) to find your online resources for this week.

Whiteboard Activities
- WA1-WA3

Assessment Forms
- "Class Assessment Record" sheet (CA1)
- "Social Skills Assessment Record" sheet (SS1)

Reproducible
- "Week 29, Day 3 Sort" (BLM1)

⏱ DO AHEAD

Word Study

✓ Prior to Day 1, familiarize yourself with the Day 1 Spelling Words.

✓ Prior to Day 2, familiarize yourself with the Day 2 Practice/Day 3 Sort Words.

✓ Prior to Day 3, visit the CCC Learning Hub (ccclearninghub.org) to access and print "Week 29, Day 3 Sort" (BLM1). Make enough copies for each pair of students to have one.

✓ Prior to Day 3, visit the CCC Learning Hub (ccclearninghub.org) to access and print the "Class Assessment Record" sheet (CA1); see page 103 of the *Assessment Resource Book*.

Independent Work Check-in

✓ Familiarize yourself with the "Share Writing" check-in lesson (or another check-in lesson of your choice) in Appendix B, "Independent Work Resources." Collect and prepare any necessary materials. For more information about the check-in lessons, see Appendix B, "Independent Work Resources."

📅 SUGGESTED WEEKLY SCHEDULE

Monday	Tuesday	Wednesday	Thursday	Friday
Word Study (20)	Word Study (20)		Word Study (20)	Word Study (20)
Independent Work Rotations/Small-group Reading (60)	Independent Work Rotations/Small-group Reading (60)	Independent Work Check-in (35)	Independent Work Rotations/Small-group Reading (60)	Independent Work Rotations/Small-group Reading (60)
80 minutes	**80 minutes**	**35 minutes**	**80 minutes**	**80 minutes**

Word Study

Day 1 Spelling Words		Day 2 Practice/ Day 3 Sort Words	
can't	I'm	enjoyable	predict
doesn't	isn't	forget	predictable
don't	we'll	forgetful	successful
I'll	won't	forgetfully	successfully
		hopefully	unenjoyable
		hopefulness	unpredictable
		hopelessness	unsuccessfully
		importantly	

Academic Focus

- Students spell high-frequency words with irregular spellings.
- Students read polysyllabic words.
- Students sort polysyllabic words.

Social Development Focus

- Students work in a responsible way.
- Students handle materials responsibly.
- Students listen respectfully to the thinking of others and share their own.

Day 1

Word Study
Guided Spelling

Materials

- Wipe-off board, dry-erase marker, and tissue or cloth for each student
- (Optional) *Word Study Notebooks*

Spelling Support

Continue to support the students by allowing them to refer to the Word Bank at the end of their *Word Study Notebooks* or to the word wall.

In this lesson, the students:

- Spell high-frequency words with irregular spellings
- Handle materials responsibly

1 Get Ready to Spell

Have the students stay in their seats today.

2 Guide the Students' Spelling

Remind the students that they have been spelling words with unusual spellings—words or parts that cannot be sounded out. Distribute the wipe-off boards, markers, and cloths or tissues.

One at a time, say each word that follows, use it in a sentence, and point out the two words that form the contraction. Then have the students say and write the word.

I'm	"I'm standing in front of you right now."
I'll	"I'll sit at my desk later."
we'll	"We'll go to lunch in a little while."
can't	"I can't reach the top shelf without standing on something."
won't	"We won't go outside if it rains."
don't	"Most four-year-olds don't know how to read."
isn't	"It isn't raining yet, so we may go outside."
doesn't	"The singer doesn't know the words to the song yet."

3 Wrap Up

Remind the students that they will have a spelling test on Friday (or whichever day of the week you will teach the Day 4 lesson). Tell them that when they go to independent word work, they will practice spelling these words before choosing another activity.

 SOCIAL SKILLS ASSESSMENT

Over the course of this week, assess the students' social skill development using the "Social Skills Assessment Record" sheet (SS1). Access and print a record sheet from the CCC Learning Hub (ccclearninghub.org) or make a copy from pages 118–119 of the *Assessment Resource Book*. For more information, see "Social Skills Assessment" in the Assessment Overview of the *Assessment Resource Book*.

Teacher Note

You may wish to post the *Word Study Notebook* page number for the spelling practice in the word work area for the students to refer to during Independent Work.

Materials

- "Week 29, Day 2 Words" (WA1)

In this lesson, the students:

- Review reading words with affixes
- Read words with multiple affixes
- Listen respectfully to the thinking of others and share their own

1 Gather and Review Prefixes and Suffixes

Gather the class with partners sitting together, facing you. Remind the students that this year they have learned many prefixes and suffixes. Ask and briefly discuss:

Q *What do you know about prefixes and suffixes?*

Q *Why is it important to know about prefixes and suffixes?*

2 Review the Affixes -*able*, -*ible*, and -*un*

Review that last week the students learned the suffixes -*able* and -*ible*, which mean "able to be." Write *readable* where everyone can see it and read it aloud. Ask and briefly discuss:

Q *Based on what you know about the suffix* -able, *what do you think* readable *means?*

If necessary, explain that if something is readable, they can read and understand it. Write *unreadable* below *readable*. Ask:

 Q *What do you think* unreadable *means? Turn to your partner.*

After a few moments, signal for the students' attention and have a few volunteers share. Explain that today the students will read words with different prefixes and suffixes.

3 Read the Words

Display the "Week 29, Day 2 Words" activity (WA1). Point to *successful* and read it aloud. Ask:

 Q *What is the base word in* successful? *What is the suffix? Turn to your partner.*

After a few moments, signal for the students' attention and have a few volunteers share. Explain that to be successful means to do or finish something you wanted to do. Use the word in a sentence. (For example, "We were successful in taking care of our class guinea pig all year.") Click to reveal *successfully* and have the students read the word. Use the word in a sentence. (For example, "We took care of the guinea pig successfully.") Click to reveal *unsuccessfully* and have the students read the word. Use it in a sentence. (For example, "I tried unsuccessfully to teach the guinea pig a trick. I couldn't do it.")

Use the same procedure for each group of words on the list.

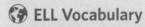 **ELL Vocabulary**

English Language Learners may benefit from hearing additional vocabulary defined, including:

enjoyable: fun to do

predict: say what you think will happen

successful	unenjoyable	important	unpredictable
successfully	forget	importantly	hopefully
unsuccessfully	forgetful	predict	hopefulness
enjoyable	forgetfully	predictable	hopelessness

4 Wrap Up

Tell the students that in the next lesson they will sort the words they read today.

Word Study
Pair Sort (Open)
Day 3

In this lesson, the students:

- Sort words with multiple affixes
- Listen respectfully to the thinking of others and share their own

1 Gather and Review Words

Have the students bring their pencils, pick up their independent work toolboxes, and gather with partners sitting together, facing you. Have them put their toolboxes on the floor next to them. Remind the students that in the last lesson they read words with prefixes and suffixes. Tell the students that today partners will work together to sort these same words.

Materials:

- "Week 29, Day 3 Sort" (WA2)
- Copy of "Week 29, Day 3 Sort" (BLM1) for each pair
- Scissors for each pair
- *Word Study Notebooks* (in student toolboxes)
- Pencils
- "Class Assessment Record" sheet (CA1)

2 Review the Words

Display the "Week 29, Day 3 Sort" activity (WA2) and read the words with the students, first the base word and affixes and then the whole word.

successful	enjoyable	importantly	forgetful
forgetfully	hopefulness	predict	successfully
hopefully	unenjoyable	unpredictable	hopelessness
unsuccessfully	forget	predictable	

Explain that one way they could sort the words is by base word. Ask:

 Q *What is another way to sort these words? Which words can you group together? Turn to your partner.*

After a few moments, signal for the students' attention and have a few volunteers share.

3 Sort in Pairs

Distribute a copy of "Week 29, Day 3 Sort" (BLM1) and scissors to each pair of students. Have each pair refer to the steps on the "Word Sort Steps" chart to cut apart and sort the words and then record their sort in their *Word Study Notebooks*. Circulate and observe as the students work.

> ☑ **CLASS ASSESSMENT NOTE**
>
> Ask yourself:
>
> - Are the students able to read the words?
> - Are the pairs able to come to agreement on how they will sort?
> - Are they able to sort the words into established categories?
>
> Record your observations on the "Class Assessment Record" sheet (CA1); see page 103 of the *Assessment Resource Book*.

4 Reflect on Partner Work

Ask:

 Q *What did you do to work well with your partner today? Turn to your partner.*

After a few moments, signal for the students' attention and have a few volunteers share their thinking.

Tell the students that next week they will talk about how Word Study has helped them learn to read longer words this year.

In this lesson, the students:

- Spell contractions
- Handle materials responsibly

1 Get Ready to Spell

Have the students stay in their seats today.

2 Spelling Test

Distribute paper and pencils to the students. Have them write their names at the top and number the first eight lines 1 to 8.

Begin the test. Say "Number one: I'm." Use *I'm* in a sentence. Say *I'm* again. Have the students write *I'm*. Allow enough time for all the students to finish before moving on to the next word.

Repeat this procedure for the remaining spelling words.

1.	I'm	"I'm going to ring the chimes when it is cleanup time."
2.	I'll	"I'll wait for you to put away your pencils and scissors."
3.	we'll	"We'll talk more about reading longer words next week."
4.	can't	"Celine can't open the door. It is locked."
5.	won't	"We won't come to school on Saturday."
6.	don't	"You don't stay inside on sunny days."
7.	isn't	"It isn't time for lunch yet."
8.	doesn't	"Ramon doesn't like to play football."

3 Check and Correct the Words

After the students are finished writing the last word, display the "Week 29, Day 4 Spelling Words" activity (WA3).

Have the students check their work and correct mistakes.

Materials

- "Week 29, Day 4 Spelling Words" (WA3)
- Lined paper and a pencil for each student

4 Reflect on Spelling

Have the students reflect on spelling. Ask:

Q *What is challenging about spelling contractions?*

Have a few volunteers share their thinking with the class. Tell the students that this is the last week of spelling tests this year.

Independent Work Connection

For next week's Independent Work, we suggest the following:

- Make several copies of "Week 29, Day 3 Sort" (BLM1) to place in the word work area.

Independent Work OVERVIEW

This week the students continue to rotate to and work in all three independent work areas around the room while you teach Small-group Reading. We suggest continuing any procedures that have worked effectively in previous weeks.

Independent Work Check-in

This week you will continue to teach an Independent Work Check-in lesson on the day of the week you do not teach Small-group Reading. The purpose of these check-in lessons is to ensure that the students are able to maintain successful independent work rotations. The lessons provide the time for you to assess your students, conduct conferences, and introduce new materials and activities. For more information about the check-in lessons, see Appendix B, "Independent Work Resources."

This week we suggest you continue to teach the "Share Writing" check-in lesson in Appendix B, "Independent Work Resources." Depending on the needs of your students, you may decide to teach a different check-in lesson.

Week 30 OVERVIEW

Whole-class Instruction

Word Study

This week, the students hear and discuss the book *Max's Words*, analyze words from the story, and identify word categories the character Max uses in making his own word collection. On Day 3, the students create word collections by searching their *Word Study Notebooks* for words that belong in categories from the story. They end the year by making calligrams for words they like.

Independent Work Check-in

Because this is the last week of the program, we suggest that on the day of the week you do not teach Small-group Reading you observe how the students use the independent work routines, procedures, and work habits, and record your observations on the "Independent Work Observation Class Assessment Record" sheet. Then facilitate a class discussion about what has gone well and what the students have enjoyed about working independently this year.

Small-group Reading Instruction and Independent Work Rotations

Small-group Reading

This week, you will continue to teach Small-group Reading lessons at the small-group reading table while the students work independently in the reading, writing, and word work areas.

Independent Work

The students may have assigned work from Small-group Reading to do during Independent Work. The following are materials you might incorporate into independent work areas this week:

Word Work:

- "Week 29, Day 3 Sort" (see "Independent Work Connection" on page 538)
- Magazines and newspapers (see "Independent Work Connection" on page 554)

Week 30

RESOURCES

Read-aloud
- *Max's Words*

Assessment Resource Book
- Week 30 assessments

Word Study Notebook
- Word Sorts

 Online Resources

Visit the CCC Learning Hub (ccclearninghub.org) to find your online resources for this week.

Whiteboard Activities
- WA1–WA4

Assessment Forms
- "Class Assessment Record" sheet (CA1)
- "Independent Work Observation Class Assessment Record" sheet (CA1)

Reproducibles
- "Word Collection" (BLM1)
- "Calligrams" (BLM2)

⏱ DO AHEAD

Word Study

✓ Prior to Day 2, visit the CCC Learning Hub (ccclearninghub.org) to access and print "Word Collection" (BLM1). Make enough copies for each pair of students to have one.

✓ Prior to Day 3, familiarize yourself with the Day 3 Practice Words.

✓ Prior to Day 3, visit the CCC Learning Hub (ccclearninghub.org) to access and print the "Class Assessment Record" sheet (CA1); see page 104 of the *Assessment Resource Book*.

✓ Prior to Day 4, visit the CCC Learning Hub (ccclearninghub.org) to access and print "Calligrams" (BLM2). Make enough copies for each student to have one.

✓ Prior to Day 4, you may want to practice drawing a calligram (see Step 2).

Independent Work Check-in

✓ Visit the CCC Learning Hub (ccclearninghub.org) to access and print the "Independent Work Observation Class Assessment Record" sheet (CA1); see page 122 of the *Assessment Resource Book*.

📅 SUGGESTED WEEKLY SCHEDULE

Monday	Tuesday	Wednesday	Thursday	Friday
Word Study (20)	Word Study (20)		Word Study (20)	Word Study (20)
Independent Work Rotations/Small-group Reading (60)	Independent Work Rotations/Small-group Reading (60)	Independent Work Check-in (35)	Independent Work Rotations/Small-group Reading (60)	Independent Work Rotations/Small-group Reading (60)
80 minutes	**80 minutes**	**35 minutes**	**80 minutes**	**80 minutes**

OVERVIEW Word Study

Max's Words

by Kate Banks,
illustrated by Boris Kulikov

Max wants to start a collection like his brothers' stamps and coins, and he hits upon the idea of collecting words.

**Day 3
Practice Words**

collection	newspapers
continued	quicker
crocodile	reminded
different	reminded
different	scrambled
hundred	slithered

Academic Focus

- Students categorize Word Study words.
- Students apply what they have learned to read polysyllabic words.
- Students review Word Study words.
- Students listen to and discuss a story.
- Students create calligrams.

Social Development Focus

- Students listen respectfully to the thinking of others and share their own.
- Students handle materials responsibly.

Day 1 Word Study
Read-aloud

Materials

- *Max's Words*
- "Max's Word Collection" (WA1)

In this lesson, the students:

- Listen to and discuss a story
- Participate responsibly

1 Gather and Get Ready to Read

Gather the class with partners sitting together, facing you. Explain that this is the last week of Word Study lessons this year. This week the students will talk and think about what they have learned about words and about words they like.

Explain that the students will hear a story read aloud. They will talk about the story and think about the words in it. Ask and briefly discuss:

Q *What will you do to listen respectfully to the story?*

2 Read *Max's Words* Aloud and Discuss

Show the cover of *Max's Words* and read the title and the author's name aloud. Ask and briefly discuss:

Q *What do you think this story might be about?*

Read pages 1–9 aloud slowly and clearly, showing the illustrations as you read, and stopping as described below. Clarify vocabulary as you encounter it in the text by reading the word, briefly defining it, rereading the sentence, and continuing. (For example, "'Everyone admired it'— *admired* means 'looked at with enjoyment'—'Everyone admired it.'")

Suggested Vocabulary

admired: looked at with enjoyment (p. 4)
arranging: putting in order (p. 20)
scrambled for: hurried to get (p. 26)

🌐 ELL Vocabulary

English Language Learners may benefit from hearing additional vocabulary defined, including:
collected: gathered together (p. 4)

Stop after:

p. 9 "And he spread them across his desk."

Ask:

Q *Why does Max want to collect words?*

> **Students might say:**
>
> "He wants to collect words because he wants to have a collection like his brothers."
>
> "His brothers won't share their coins and stamps, so Max has to make his own collection."
>
> "Max's brothers get attention for their collections, and Max wants a collection, too."

Explain that in the story, Max will pick several different categories for his words and that you will keep a list of the kinds of words Max collects. Display the "Max's Word Collection" activity (WA1) and write *small words* on it.

Teacher Note

The words on pages 10 and 11 are written as *calligrams*: the words are drawn in a way that shows their meaning. The students may enjoy looking closely at the illustrations on this page.

Continue reading, stopping after:

> **p. 11**   "Park, baseball, dogs, hugs"

Ask:

Q *First, Max collects small words. What kinds of words does he collect next?*

Add *bigger words* and *words that make him feel good* to the "Max's Word Collection" activity (WA1) as the students share those answers.

Continue reading, stopping after:

> **p. 13**   "Iguana"

Ask:

Q *What other kinds of words does Max collect?*

Add *words of things he liked to eat, words that were spoken to him, his favorite colors,* and *words he did not know* as the students share these answers.

WA1

> ## Max's Word Collection
>
> small words
>
> bigger words
>
> words that make him feel good
>
> words of things he liked to eat
>
> words that were spoken to him
>
> his favorite colors
>
> words he did not know

Continue reading, stopping after:

> **p. 19**   " 'Let's see,' said Max."

Ask:

Q *What has happened in the story so far? Turn to your partner.*

After a few moments, signal for the students' attention and have a few volunteers share their thinking with the class.

Continue reading to the end of the story. Then ask:

Q *What happens in the rest of the story? Turn to your partner.*

After a few moments, signal for the students' attention and have a few volunteers share their thinking with the class.

Teacher's Note

Your students may not know how to interpret pages 30–31. You may choose to point out the smiles on the boys' faces to support comprehension.

Then ask and briefly discuss:

Q *Do you think* Max's Words *has a happy ending? Why do you think that?*

> **Students might say:**
>
> "The book has a happy ending because Max and his brothers have fun writing stories together."
>
> "The book has a happy ending because Max gets a coin and a stamp like he wanted."

If the students struggle to answer this question, ask additional questions, such as:

Q *Did Max create a collection?*

Q *How do you think he feels about his collection? What in the story makes you think that?*

Q *Did he get the coins and stamps he wanted?*

Q *What makes Max's collection different from the others?*

3 Reflect on *Max's Words*

Ask and briefly discuss:

Q *What did you like about* Max's Words?

Tell the students that in the next lesson they will think more about *Max's Words* and about words they have studied this year.

Word Study
Review Word Study
Day 2

In this lesson, the students:

- Review Word Study words
- Categorize Word Study words
- Listen respectfully to the thinking of others and share their own

1 Review *Max's Words*

Have the students bring their pencils, pick up their independent work toolboxes, and sit at tables with partners together. Show the cover of *Max's Words* and review that in the last lesson, the students heard this story and talked about the book. Ask and briefly discuss:

Q *What do you remember about the story* Max's Words?

Materials

- "Max's Word Collection" (WA1) from Day 1
- "Word Collection" (WA2)
- *Word Study Notebooks* (in student toolboxes)
- Pencils
- Copy of "Word Collection" (BLM1) for each pair

Explain that partners will work together today to sort words. Ask and briefly discuss:

Q *What can you and your partner do to work well together today?*

2 Sort Words

Display the saved "Max's Word Collection" activity (◖ WA1) from Day 1 and review the categories Max used to collect words by reading the entries aloud.

Explain that partners will work together today to create their own word collections. Then display the "Word Collection" activity (◖ WA2). Explain that the chart shows the categories from the book and two more categories: "words for things you find outside" and "words that are fun to say." Explain that you will sort some of the words the class studied this year by writing them under the appropriate category headings on the chart.

> **You might say:**
>
> "We have studied hundreds of words this year in Word Study. We've sorted these words in different ways. Today we will sort some of the same words into different categories, starting with the categories Max uses in the book."

WA2

small	bigger	feel good
eat	spoken	colors
did not know	find outside	fun to say

Explain that you will begin by looking for words that fit into Max's first category "small words." Borrow a student's *Word Study Notebook* and page through the book. As you come to small words (such as *my, cry, see, zip*), write them under the category heading "small."

Ask the students to take their *Word Study Notebooks* from their toolboxes and look for small words that can be added to the chart. After a moment, ask:

Q *What words did you find that we can add to the "small words" category?*

Have two or three students share their thinking with the class; add the words the students suggest to the chart.

Tell the students that you will work on one more category as a class, and then partners will look for words together. Explain that this time the students will look for words that belong in the "words that make you feel good" category. Ask:

Q *What words in your notebook belong in the "words that make you feel good" category?*

Give the students a few moments to look through their notebooks, and then have a few volunteers share. Add the words they suggest to the chart.

Explain that the students will now work in pairs to look for words that belong in Max's categories.

Distribute a copy of "Word Collection" (BLM1) to each pair of students. Read the category headings with the students. Have each pair choose words from their *Word Study Notebooks* and record them under the appropriate category heading. Tell the students that it is fine if they do not agree on every word they collect. What is important is that they explain their thinking to each other. Explain that they will record all the words either partner can explain.

3 Reflect on Words

Refer to the "Word Collection" activity (WA2) and ask:

Q *What is a word you wrote under the category name "feel good"?*

Have several students share their ideas, and record the words on the chart. Then ask:

Q *What is a word you wrote under the category name "fun to say"?*

Have several students share their ideas, and record the words on the chart. Ask:

Q *What do you notice about the words in the two categories we just talked about?*

Tell the students that in the next lesson they will talk more about words in the book *Max's Words* and about ways to read longer words.

Materials

- "Words from *Max's Words*" (WA3)
- "Class Assessment Record" sheet (CA1)

In this lesson, the students:

- Read words from *Max's Words*
- Apply what they have learned to read polysyllabic words
- Listen respectfully to the thinking of others and share their own

1 Gather and Get Ready to Read

Gather the class with partners sitting together, facing you. Remind the students that in the last lesson they talked about collecting different kinds of words and partners looked in their *Word Study Notebooks* for words that fit in different categories. Explain that today the students will use what they have learned about reading longer words to read words from *Max's Words*. Point out that it would not have been possible for you to read the book aloud to the class if you had not been able to read these longer words.

2 Read the Words

Display the "Words from *Max's Words*" activity (◑ WA3). Point to *quicker*. Without reading it aloud, ask:

Q *Think of the spellings, prefixes, and suffixes we have studied this year. What have you learned this year that helps you read this word? What is the word?*

> **You might say:**
>
> "In this first word, I see *e-r* at the end, and we learned that *e-r* stands for /ər/. I will cover the ending and read the base word, *quick*. The word is *quicker*. I know that *e-r* can mean 'more' or it can mean 'a person who.' 'I'm pretty sure the *-er* in quicker means 'more' and that the word *quicker* means 'more quick,' so I'm going to try it in a sentence. 'A car is quicker than a bicycle.' That definitely sounds right, so *quicker* must mean 'more quick' or 'faster.'"

Click to reveal the next word, and repeat the process. Have the students analyze and read each word as you reveal it.

quicker	• collection
• hundred	• different
• scrambled	• slithered
• newspapers	• crocodile
• reminded	• continued

 CLASS ASSESSMENT NOTE

After the lesson, ask yourself:

- Are the students able to read the words?
- Are they able to use strategies they have learned to analyze the words?

Record your observations on the "Class Assessment Record" sheet (CA1); see page 104 of the *Assessment Resource Book*.

3 Reflect on Words

Ask:

 Q *If you wanted to help a younger student read the word [collection], what might you say to help him? Turn to your partner.*

After a few moments, signal for the students' attention and have a few students share their thinking.

Tell the students that in the next lesson they will think and talk more about the words in *Max's Words*.

Materials

- *Max's Words*
- "Calligrams" (WA4)
- Copy of "Calligrams" (BLM2) for each student
- Crayons, markers, or colored pencils

In this lesson, the students:

- Explore words
- Create calligrams
- Handle materials responsibly

1 Introduce Calligrams

Have the students stay at their desks. Display the "Calligrams" activity (🌑 WA4) and ask:

Q *What do you notice about these words?*

Have a few volunteers share their thinking with the class. Explain that words written this way are called *calligrams*. Ask:

Q *What do you think a calligram might be?*

Have a few volunteers share their thinking with the class.

WA4

Explain that a *calligram* is a word that is drawn in a way that shows its meaning. Refer to each illustration and ask:

Q *Why do you think this is a calligram?*

> **Students might say:**
>
> "It's a calligram because the word is *baseball* and it's written like a baseball bat."
>
> "That's a calligram because the word is *hug* and the *h* and *g* have arms that are hugging each other."
>
> "The word is *hungry* and it looks like there is a bite taken out of it, like somebody got hungry."

2 Model How to Draw Calligrams

Tell the students that today they will draw their own calligrams. Explain that it is easiest to make a calligram from a word that makes a picture in their minds.

Ask the students to picture what comes to mind when they hear the word *birthday*. Write the word *birthday* and a few student responses where everyone can see them.

Ask the students to share other words that make pictures in their minds. For each word, record a few student suggestions for images. After generating a list of 7-10 words, model drawing the word *birthday* as a calligram.

3 Draw Calligrams

Explain that students can select one of the words from the list of ideas the class generated, or they may select their own words. Explain that each student will get a sheet to draw their calligrams. Distribute "Calligrams" (BLM2) to each student. Discuss the two examples and point out the four spaces. Tell the students that they will use these spaces to experiment with drawing calligrams.

When students have created a draft they like, they can turn the paper over and draw their favorite calligram in color on the other side of the paper.

4 Reflect on Word Study

Explain that this is the final Word Study lesson for the year. Ask:

Q *What have you liked most about reading words this year? Turn to someone sitting next to you.*

Teacher Note

You might choose to display the students' final calligrams on a bulletin board or bind them together in a class book.

After a few moments, signal for the students' attention and have a few volunteers share their thinking with the class.

Independent Work Connection

For this week's Independent Work, we suggest the following:

- Provide magazines and newspapers in the word work area. Have the students choose and cut out words they like and glue them to sheets of paper to make collections. You may wish to have the students share their collections and explain why they chose these words.

Independent Work

This is the last week in the *Being a Reader* program. The students continue to rotate to and work in all three independent work areas around the room while you teach Small-group Reading. We suggest continuing any procedures that have worked effectively in previous weeks.

Independent Work Check-in

Because this is the last week of the program, we suggest that on the day of the week you do not teach Small-group Reading, you observe how the students use the independent work routines, procedures, and work habits, and record your observations on the "Independent Work Observation Class Assessment Record" sheet (CA1); see page 122 of the *Assessment Resource Book*. Then facilitate a class discussion about what has gone well and what the students have enjoyed about working independently this year.

Appendices

Teaching a Procedure for Gathering

⏱ DO AHEAD

✓ Plan a space in the classroom, such as a rug area, for the whole class to gather. If a rug area is not available, plan how the students will sit in their chairs facing you. Keep in mind that the space should allow for students to easily turn to their partners and talk. The students should sit close enough to see the lesson materials.

In this lesson, the students:

- Learn and practice the procedure for gathering
- Gather in a responsible way

1 Learn and Practice the Procedure for Gathering

Explain that at the beginning of many lessons, the students will gather together. Direct their attention to the gathering area. Model where you will sit and explain where you would like the students to sit. Before asking the students to move, state your expectations for how to gather in an orderly way.

> **You might say:**
>
> "I expect you to walk quietly and quickly to the gathering area without bumping into one another, and I expect you to sit down and wait quietly until everyone else is seated."

Have the students practice gathering. As they practice, comment on what you observe without mentioning any of the students' names.

> **You might say:**
>
> "I notice people are sitting toward the front of the rug so that others can sit behind them."

If necessary, have the students return to their seats and practice the procedure until they are able to gather in an orderly way.

2 Reflect on Gathering

Tell the students that when they work *responsibly*, they act in ways that help them learn and work well with their classmates. Tell the students that one way to work responsibly is to gather in a calm and orderly way. Without mentioning any of the students' names, offer your own observations.

> **You might say:**
>
> "I noticed students taking seats in the gathering area and waiting there quietly until everyone else was seated."

Ask and discuss:

Q *What might we want to work on doing better the next time we gather?*

Tell the students that this is the way you expect them to gather for lessons. Then explain how you expect them to return to their seats or transition to the next activity. If necessary, practice the procedure until the students are able to return to their seats or transition to the next activity in an orderly way.

Teacher Note

When you focus on describing appropriate behavior, the students learn what it means to work responsibly, and they develop the intrinsic motivation to do so.

Mini-lesson 2 | Teaching a Procedure for "Turn to Your Partner"

⏱ DO AHEAD

✓ Decide how you will randomly assign partners to work together for Word Study and Independent Work. For suggestions about assigning partners, see "Random Pairing" and "Cooperative Structures" in the Introduction. For more information, view "Cooperative Structures Overview" (AV1).

In this lesson, the students:

- Learn and practice the procedure for "Turn to Your Partner"
- Listen respectfully to the thinking of others and share their own
- Work in a responsible way

1 Pair Students and Practice the Procedure for Gathering with Partners

Tell the students that they will often work with partners during lessons. Explain that working with partners gives everyone a chance to talk

Teacher Note

The cooperative structures "Turn to Your Partner" and "Think, Pair, Share" are used in whole-class and small-group instruction to increase students' engagement and accountability for participation. The students may have different partners when they work in small groups than they do in whole-class lessons.

about what they are thinking and learning before sharing their ideas with the class.

Randomly assign partners and make sure they know each other's names. Explain and model how you would like pairs to gather, sitting together and facing you, and then have them gather. If pairs have difficulty gathering in an orderly way, ask them to return to their seats and practice the procedure.

2 Introduce "Turn to Your Partner"

Explain the "Turn to Your Partner" procedure.

> **You might say:**
>
> "Sometimes I will ask a question and say, 'Turn to your partner.' When you hear this, you will turn to face your partner and take turns talking about the question. When I raise my hand, you will finish what you're saying, raise your own hand so others can see the signal, and turn back to face me."

3 Model and Practice "Turn to Your Partner"

Have a student act as your partner, and model turning to face each other and introducing yourselves by your full names. Turn back to the class. Point out that you and your partner looked at each other as you talked, and explain that looking at your partner is important because it is one way to show that you are listening. Also point out that you and your partner took turns talking and listening. Explain that it is important for the students to take turns so that each partner gets a chance to talk.

Have partners turn and introduce themselves. After a moment, raise your hand and have them turn back to face you. Practice again by asking:

Q *What is an animal that you like? Turn to your partner.*

Have partners take turns talking about their thinking. After a moment, signal for their attention and have a few volunteers briefly share what they discussed with the class.

If the students need further practice with "Turn to Your Partner," have partners practice again by asking:

Q *What is a food you like to eat? Turn to your partner.*

Q *What is something you like to do after school? Turn to your partner.*

Teacher Note

To see an example, view "Using 'Turn to Your Partner'" (AV2).

Teacher Note

Using a signal that the students will notice but that does not interrupt their discussion, such as a raised hand, allows them to finish what they are saying before turning back to face you.

ELL Note

A cooperative structure like "Turn to Your Partner" supports students' language development by providing frequent opportunities for them to talk about their thinking and listen to the thinking of others.

Teacher Note

Notice that you ask the question *before* saying, "Turn to your partner." This gives all the students a chance to hear and consider the question before moving to face their partners.

4 Reflect on "Turn to Your Partner"

Tell the students that when they work *responsibly*, they act in ways that help them learn and work well with their classmates. Ask and briefly discuss:

Q *What did you and your partner do to act responsibly during "Turn to Your Partner"?*

Q *In what ways did "Turn to Your Partner" go well?*

Q *What might you do differently next time?*

Have the students return to their seats or transition to the next activity.

Mini-lesson 3 | Teaching a Procedure for "Think, Pair, Share"

ⓙ DO AHEAD

✓ Before teaching this lesson, teach the procedure for "Turn to Your Partner" using Mini-lesson 2, "Teaching a Procedure for 'Turn to Your Partner.'" For more information, view "Cooperative Structures Overview" (AV1).

In this lesson, the students:

- Learn and practice the procedure for "Think, Pair, Share"
- Listen respectfully to the thinking of others and share their own
- Work in a responsible way

1 Practice the Procedure for Gathering with Partners

Tell the students that today they will practice gathering with their partners. Remind them that working with partners gives everyone a chance to talk about what they are thinking and learning before sharing their ideas with the class.

Have the students practice gathering with their partners. If necessary, ask them to return to their seats, and then practice the procedure until they are able to gather in an orderly way.

Teacher Note

The cooperative structures "Turn to Your Partner" and "Think, Pair, Share" are used in whole-class and small-group instruction to increase students' engagement and accountability for participation. The students may have different partners when they work in small groups than they do in whole-class lessons.

---

2 Introduce "Think, Pair, Share"

Remind the students that they have used "Turn to Your Partner" to talk in pairs. Explain that today they will learn a new way to talk with their partners called "Think, Pair, Share."

Tell the students that "Think, Pair, Share" is like "Turn to Your Partner." The difference is that the students think by themselves before they talk in pairs. Explain the procedure for "Think, Pair, Share."

> **You might say:**
>
> "Sometimes I will ask a question and then you will think about it quietly for a moment. When I say, 'Turn to your partner,' you will turn to face your partner and take turns talking about the question. When I raise my hand, you will finish what you're saying, raise your own hand so others can see the signal, and turn back to face me."

Teacher Note

To see an example, view "Using 'Think, Pair, Share'" (AV3).

🌐 **ELL Note**

A cooperative structure like "Think, Pair, Share" supports students' language development by providing frequent opportunities for them to talk about their thinking and listen to the thinking of others.

3 Model and Practice "Think, Pair, Share"

Have a student act as your partner to help you model "Think, Pair, Share." Model "Think, Pair, Share" with the student volunteer by asking:

Q *What is something you do in the morning to get ready for school?*

Model pausing for 5-10 seconds to think about the question. Then, with your partner, model turning to face each other and taking turns answering the question, listening to each other, and speaking clearly. Turn back to the class and point out that you paused to think about the question before taking turns talking and listening.

Have the students practice "Think, Pair, Share" by asking:

Q *What is something you like to do in school?* [pause] *Turn to your partner.*

Have partners take turns talking about their thinking. After a moment, signal for their attention and have a few volunteers briefly share what they discussed with the class.

If the students need further practice with "Think, Pair, Share," have partners practice again by asking:

Q *What do you like to do in your free time?* [pause] *Turn to your partner.*

Q *What can you do to be a good partner?* [pause] *Turn to your partner.*

4 Reflect on "Think, Pair, Share"

Tell the students that when they work *responsibly*, they act in ways that help them learn and work well with their classmates. Ask:

Q *What did you do to be a good partner today?*

Q *What can you do to be a better partner next time?*

Teacher Note

By listening to your observations, the students will become more thoughtful about their social interactions over time.

If the students have difficulty answering the questions, share some of your observations without mentioning any of their names.

> **You might say:**
>
> "I noticed that partners let each other think quietly before starting to talk. I also noticed that partners looked at each other as they talked, and they didn't interrupt each other. This is important because it shows that you think what your partner is saying is important."

Use "Think, Pair, Share" to have partners first think about and then discuss:

 Q *How does having time to think before you talk with your partner help you?* [pause] *Turn to your partner.*

Have the students return to their seats or transition to the next activity.

Appendix B

INDEPENDENT WORK RESOURCES

Introduction

The Independent Work component in the *Being a Reader* program provides students with constructive opportunities to learn to work independently and cooperatively without much teacher support or intervention. A key feature is teacher instruction and modeling during the first four weeks or the "foundation-setting" period. You model using different strategies, handling and sharing materials, and making choices. You then guide the students as they practice these skills and build their capacity to work independently and solve problems on their own. Each week, the work becomes increasingly student driven. By the end of Week 4, the students are able to rotate to and use their independent work skills and habits in three work areas around the room for 60 minutes. You can then use this time to work with small groups of students in differentiated reading groups.

The benefits of Independent Work are:

- The teacher has designated time to work on reading with individual students and small groups at their differentiated reading levels.

- The students learn to take responsibility for their own learning.

- The students have time for extensive practice on concepts and skills that are taught in a whole-class setting across the language arts block.

- The students develop confidence to take initiative and make choices.

- The students build stamina to read, write, and explore word-review and word-building activities on their own for 20 minutes at a time.

WHAT DOES INDEPENDENT WORK LOOK LIKE?

The first few weeks of Independent Work are devoted to laying the foundation for success in the classroom. The students are introduced to all three types of independent work (reading, writing, and word work), and they build stamina for working on their own at their seats with teacher support and guidance.

One of the most important goals of Independent Work is to help the students identify and practice work habits that allow them to work effectively and independently for longer periods of time. The early foundation-setting weeks are focused on helping the students develop these important work habits, which are charted and referred to throughout the year.

Beginning in Week 3, the students begin to work independently in reading, writing, and word work areas around the room, and they begin to rotate to these work areas each day. After

Week 4, the students work in these areas with little teacher support, while you use this time to work with differentiated small groups of students.

Daily Lessons During Weeks 1–4

Independent Work lessons are held with the whole class. These lessons include short blocks of time for the students to explore independent reading, writing, and word work activities—first at their seats and then in work areas around the room. There is an explicit focus on developing effective work habits and on building the students' stamina to work on their own. Student work time builds from 5 to 10 to 20 minutes over these first weeks.

Developing Effective Work Habits

A significant focus during Weeks 1–4 is helping the students identify and practice work habits so they can work effectively and build stamina for independent work.

Work Habits

- Using a quiet voice
- Getting started right away
- Working for the whole time
- Handling materials responsibly
- Sharing materials fairly
- Putting materials away upon hearing the cleanup signal

One or two habits are focused on each week, and the students are given opportunities to discuss how they will use the work habits and why they are important. Each work habit is discussed, charted, and then revisited several times during this period. The students have multiple opportunities to talk about how they will use each work habit, what this looks like, and why it is important. The lessons provide support for modeling these work habits, reflecting on how the students are doing with using the work habits, and discussing possible solutions for any challenges that arise. In addition, the lessons guide you to ask reflective questions about how the students are using each work habit and how they might improve. We suggest that during the reflection at the end of each lesson you help the students brainstorm possible solutions for any challenges they are having using work habits.

Building Stamina and Independence

Students build their stamina for working independently during the foundation-setting weeks. At first the students read, write, and do word work independently for only 5 minutes at a time while you circulate around the room supporting those who need help. Over 3–4 weeks, this time is increased by amounts in step with what the students can manage, building up to 20 minutes of work time for each area: reading, writing, and word work. You first begin to stand aside, and then sit aside at the small-group reading table, while the students work on their own. By taking these gradual steps and intervening less over time, you signal to the students that they can work with greater independence and manage challenges that arise.

Independent Work in Week 5 and Beyond

After you have formed groups for Small-group Reading, you begin to bring the students in each small group to a table for differentiated instruction. During this time, the remainder of the students in the class rotate in groups to the three independent work areas around the room (reading, writing, and word work). They work for 20 minutes in each area, attempting to solve problems on their own.

To maintain Independent Work throughout the year after the foundation-setting weeks, the *Teacher's Manual* suggests a short check-in lesson each week, provided in this appendix. Additionally, we recommend returning to the process of modeling work habits, reflecting on how things are going, and brainstorming any necessary solutions throughout the year.

GETTING READY FOR INDEPENDENT WORK

During the foundation-setting weeks, the students work from bins at table groups (groups of students who sit at the same table or group of desks). Later, the students begin rotating through the work areas. In order to prepare your classroom, your students, and yourself for Independent Work—both the foundation-setting lessons as well the ongoing independent work rotations—we offer the following suggestions.

Setting Up Your Classroom

At the start of the school year, your classroom will need to be arranged in a way to best support learning during the foundation-setting lessons and then as independent work rotations during small-group reading instruction begin (as early as Week 5). You will need a space for the whole class to gather and three independent work areas for groups of students to gather, in addition to a small-group reading table, where you provide reading instruction. You will also need to dedicate space for the students to keep their independent work "toolboxes" (boxes in which to store their small-group reading books and other independent work materials).

Gathering

Plan a space in the classroom, such as a rug area, for the class to gather. If a rug area is not available, plan how the students will sit in their chairs facing you. Your setup should allow for partners to easily turn and talk to each other. For more information, see Mini-lesson 1, "Teaching a Procedure for Gathering," in Appendix A.

Independent Work Areas

During the foundation-setting weeks of independent work instruction, the students will work in their table groups using bins of materials that you prepare. Later, they transition from using these bins at their seats to working at specific independent work areas. For the foundation-setting weeks of instruction, you will need to fill these bins with appropriate materials. (For information about setting up your bins, including suggestions for materials, see "Preparing and Using Independent Work Bins, Areas, and Toolboxes" on page 569.) Later, as you transition to having the students work in the areas around the classroom, you will integrate the materials from these bins into those areas.

You will need to set up areas for reading, writing, and word work in your classroom. Suggestions are provided below.

Setting Up the Reading Area (Classroom Library)

The classroom library is one key to helping your students become better readers and lovers of reading. It also is integral to supporting students' ability to read independently. Beginning in Week 3, the students start to use the classroom library ("reading area"), where they choose and exchange books to keep in their toolboxes for their independent reading. Later, as the students become more established in their work habits, you may also offer the classroom library as a place for students to read during independent work rotations.

In the first few weeks, when the students are reading from bins in their table groups, you can use books from your classroom library to fill the bins. Later, as the students begin exchanging books in the library and then also reading in this area, you will need to have your library set up for them to do so.

Your library should have a wide range of fiction and nonfiction texts at various levels. For easy browsing, you might display books in boxes or baskets labeled with the name of the book category and/or a picture cue. Categories can include:

- Genres (such as mystery, science fiction, folktale, poetry, biography)
- Subjects or topics (animals, weather, school, sports)
- Themes (faraway places, friendship, growing up)
- Favorite authors or illustrators
- Popular series
- Student favorites
- Recent read-aloud texts
- Student-made books

A classroom library will ideally consist of at least 300–600 titles, although many teachers start with a smaller collection and add to it over time. The library should include a balance of fiction and nonfiction books. Consider also having a place to display charts and poems and to store big books in your library area.

Consider arrangements that could make your library an inviting place to read. You might add a beanbag chair, pillows, a rug, or other comfortable places to sit. You also might add some items that bring novelty to the library, such as old glasses with the lenses popped out for students to wear when they read or a collection of pointers for the students to use as they read big books and charts.

Discuss your expectations for the classroom library with your students. You might address the following:

- What are the rules and procedures for using the library?

- How many students can be in the library at any one time?

- What are the expectations for behavior in the library?

- What are the procedures for taking out and returning books?

- What are the cleanup procedures?

You will introduce the procedures for using the classroom library when the students begin to rotate to the independent work areas, and you may follow up during subsequent check-in lessons.

Setting Up the Writing Area

Ideally, the writing area in your classroom is a place to store bins that contain a variety of materials for writing and also a place where the students can work. Post the "Writing Ideas" chart that the students create in the whole-class sessions to the wall in or near the writing area. For suggestions about writing materials to incorporate into the bins and the writing area, see "Writing Notebooks and Writing Bins" on the next page.

Setting Up the Word Work Area

Ideally, the word work area in your classroom is a place to both store materials for word work and a place for the students to work during independent work rotations. The students can choose from a variety of materials in word work bins to engage in word-building, letter games, and more. For suggestions about word work materials, see "Word Work Bins" on the next page.

Preparing and Using Independent Work Bins, Areas, and Toolboxes

During the foundation-setting weeks of Independent Work, you will need bins to store reading, writing, and word work materials for the students to use. These bins rotate each day to give students opportunities to interact with a variety of different books (reading bins) and materials (word work and writing bins). You might choose to use plastic dish tubs, milk crates, or similar sized storage containers for your bins.

In addition to the suggestions on the following pages, an Independent Work Connections feature at the end of many Word Study lessons alerts you to additional suggestions for materials to incorporate into the bins or the independent work areas.

Reading Bins (Foundation-setting Weeks)

The reading bins used during the foundation-setting weeks of independent work instruction can easily be created using books from your classroom library. Collect as many bins as you have table groups (or sets of desks). Fill each bin with a selection of fiction and nonfiction books in a variety of reading levels. You should have enough books in a bin so that each student in a table group is able to select five books from the bin. Label each bin so that you can keep track of the bin each table group uses, as you will rotate the reading bins among the table groups for the first weeks until you establish procedures for exchanging books in the reading area.

Writing Notebooks and Writing Bins

Students in grade 2 use a notebook for their independent writing. You will need to provide a writing notebook for each student, plus one for yourself to use in modeling. If you do not have access to premade composition or spiral notebooks, you can create notebooks using construction paper and plain paper. Write your name on the cover of your notebook and decide where you will keep the notebooks for the first week of foundation-setting instruction. After Week 1, the students will keep their writing notebooks in their toolboxes.

In Week 4, when the students transition to working in the writing area, you will want to add writing bins with supplies to this area. We suggest creating bins containing a variety of writing materials, such as:

- Pencils and erasers

- Colored pencils, markers, and crayons

- Paper—both lined and unlined in a variety of sizes

- Card-making materials

- Staplers

Word Work Bins

In grade 2, the goal of independent word work is to engage the students in language exploration through enjoyable activities and games and also to reinforce spelling, vocabulary, and word usage. The students begin word work in Week 2 with two types of activities: word work card games and word work activity sheets. In subsequent weeks, the students will have word sorts and other activities to do during independent word work. In Weeks 2-3, you will set up and create the materials for three bins: "Word Work Card Games," "Word Work Activity Sheets," and "Word Work Sorts."

The word work card games, activity sheets, and the word sort materials can be found as reproducibles on the CCC Learning Hub (ccclearninghub.org). Each week, the Do Ahead section in the Week Overview will alert you to any new materials to access and print. Additional Word Scramble reproducible activities can be found in General Resources on the CCC Learning Hub (ccclearninghub.org). When copies need additional preparation, such as cutting word or letter tiles apart and placing them into bags, you may choose to do so yourself or have the students prepare the materials as part of their work at the word work area.

In Week 4, when the students transition from working at their seats to working in the word work area, you will add additional materials to this area for the students to choose from after they complete their weekly sorts. The following are some suggested materials for the word work area:

- Paper, pencils, markers, letter stamps, ink pads, and stencils
- Wipe-off boards and dry-erase markers
- Developmentally appropriate board games
- Tablet devices preloaded with appropriate apps (see the "Introduce a Tablet App" check-in lesson on page 606)

Independent Work Folders

The students are responsible for maintaining word work folders for papers they generate while working independently. Label these folders with the students' names, and encourage the students to be responsible for maintaining these in good shape in their toolboxes. The students will be generating work during word work that they will put in their folder at the end of the independent work rotation. As the students' work accumulates in their folders, you will need to determine and introduce a procedure for managing the papers. We suggest having the students take home or turn in any work they have finished or no longer want to work on. We suggest revisiting this procedure weekly or as the folders fill up.

Toolboxes

Beginning in Week 2, the students keep and manage their own independent work toolboxes. These toolboxes store the students' small-group reading books, word work folders, and other materials. You will need to provide each student with a box or an alternative, such as a book bin, magazine file, cereal box with the top and part of narrow side cut away, or resealable plastic bag (large enough to hold books). Label the toolboxes with the students' names, and encourage them to be responsible for maintaining these in good shape throughout the year.

Managing and Grouping Students for Independent Work Rotations

Independent work groups, unlike small-group reading groups, should include students at a variety of reading levels. Heterogeneous groups will allow for students to engage with and learn from one another as the students explore materials and activities in each of the independent work areas in ways that homogenous groups might not.

The students begin working in groups for independent work rotations in Week 3. Prior to Day 1 of that week, divide the class into three heterogeneous groups. Consider creating an "Independent Work Groups" chart that lists the students in each group. Choose easy-to-remember group names, such as colors, and consider color-coding the chart and placing a colored dot sticker on each student's toolbox.

Beginning as early as Week 5, you will begin pulling small groups of students for differentiated small-group reading instruction. The students in the rest of the class will rotate through the three independent work areas on the four days each week that you teach the Small-group Reading lessons. For management, you may additionally want to create a chart that shows the group rotations for each day.

Later in the year, if you feel your students are successfully rotating through the independent work areas and are staying engaged with their work during each rotation period, you may wish to move to a model in which students self-select their work areas. In this model, the students would self-manage their independent work choices, completing any assigned work and keeping track of their independent work choices over the course of the day or week. If you choose to move toward self-selection of work areas, we suggest you transition to this model slowly and with ample support for your students. Prior to the transition, share your expectations for self-selected independent work rotations with your students. Consider questions such as:

- Are there limits to the number of students who can be at one area at one time? How will decisions about who can work in each area be made?

- May a student work at one area for more than one rotation period in a day?

- Are there requirements as to how much time must be spent in each area daily? Weekly? Whose responsibility is it to track time spent and areas chosen? How will those choices be tracked and how will the information be shared?

As with all instruction surrounding students' independent work, we suggest you allow ample time for discussing, modeling, practicing, and reflecting upon the students' behavior during independent work rotations, whether you are using a rotation management chart or allowing the students to self-select their work areas. A "Self-selecting Work Areas" check-in lesson is provided (see page 602).

ABOUT THE CHECK-IN LESSONS

To maintain the students' ability to successfully work independently after the foundation-setting instruction is complete, continue to remind the students about the importance of independent work and the work habits by teaching a check-in lesson each week. Specific lessons are suggested in each week's instruction over the course of the year and are provided in this appendix. Although we do suggest a check-in lesson, you may choose to teach another lesson during any given week depending on the needs of your class. A series of three lessons on introducing blogging to your class is included for teachers who want to introduce technology into the writing area. A single lesson that supports you in introducing new apps to your students is also included, should you have tablet devices for the students to use, but it is not suggested in the weekly instruction.

Familiarize yourself with these lessons so that you can easily choose a lesson for your class each week. To choose a lesson, consider how the students have been working independently and ask yourself questions such as:

- Might you need to introduce new materials to one of the work areas?

- Is the noise level in the classroom creeping up day by day?

- Would the students benefit from reviewing the "Independent Work Habits" chart?

- Will having the students share their writing increase motivation for the writing area?

Once you have selected a lesson, review the materials and any preparation needed for the lesson. Read the lesson and consider how you might adapt it for your particular needs.

⏱ DO AHEAD

✓ Select a picture book to use for modeling (see Step 1).

✓ Write the following prompts where everyone can see them:
My book is _____, written by _____. The book is about _____. I like this book because _____. I think you'll like this book if _____.

Materials

- Student toolboxes
- Written prompts, prepared ahead
- Picture book to use for modeling

In this lesson, the students:

- Share independent reading books in pairs
- Speak clearly
- Listen carefully

ABOUT THE SHARE A BOOK CHECK-IN LESSON

In this lesson, each student chooses an independent reading book to share with a partner. Sharing about books requires the students to think more deeply about their reading, and hearing about others' books allows them to get ideas for things they would like to read in the future.

1 Gather and Model Sharing a Book

Have the students pick up their toolboxes and gather with partners sitting together, facing you. Ask them to put their toolboxes on the floor in front of them. Review that the students have been reading books during independent reading and that today they will each choose one to share with a partner.

Direct the students' attention to the prompts you have written and read them aloud. Tell the students that they will use these prompts to help them share about their books, and that they can also share other things about their books.

Show the cover of the book you selected and ask the students to listen as you share the book with them.

> **You might say:**
>
> "My book is *Sheila Rae, the Brave* by Kevin Henkes. The book is about a mouse named Sheila Rae who isn't afraid of things like stepping on cracks in the sidewalk. I like this book because the story ends differently than how you'd expect. I think you'll like this book if you have ever felt brave or scared."

Then ask and briefly discuss:

Q *What did you learn about my book?*

Q *Is [Sheila Rae, the Brave] a book you might want to read? Why or why not?*

Point out that you used the prompts to help you share your book. Tell the students that if they would like to share more about their books than the prompts suggest, they may do so.

2 Choose Books and Prepare to Share

Explain that now the students will each choose a book from their toolboxes to share with a partner. Have them look at the books in their toolboxes, each choose one to share, and hold the books in their laps.

When all of the students have books to share, ask:

Q *What can you do to make sure you and your partner both have a chance to share?*

Have a few volunteers share their thinking with the class. Explain that the students should be ready to share what their partners talked about.

Direct the students' attention to the prompts and read them aloud again. Ask the students to use the prompts to think quietly for a moment about what they will say about the books they chose.

3 Share Books in Pairs

 Have partners turn to face each other and take turns sharing their books. As they share, walk around and observe, assisting as needed. After a few minutes, remind partners to change roles, if necessary.

After 5-10 minutes, signal for the students' attention; then ask:

Q *What book did your partner share with you? What did you learn about the book?*

Q *Would you like to read your partner's book? Why or why not?*

Have a few volunteers share with the class.

4 Reflect on Sharing Books

Ask and briefly discuss:

Q *What did you like about sharing books today?*

Follow-up Tip

Over the next few days, have any students who want to share their books with the whole class do so at the beginning and end of independent work time. After each student shares, ask and discuss:

Q *What did you find out about [Zane's] book?*

Q *What questions do you have for [Zane] about his book?*

Teacher Note

Repeat this check-in lesson at other times during the year or whenever the students have independent reading books they want to share.

⏱ DO AHEAD

✓ Visit the CCC Learning Hub (ccclearninghub.org) to access and print "Blogging Permission Slip" (BLM1). Make enough copies to send one home with each student. Collect a signed permission slip from each student before teaching this lesson.

✓ Visit the CCC Learning Hub (ccclearninghub.org) to access "Primary Class Blog Resources" (BLM2), and choose one to share with your students as an example. Decide which features of the blog you will share and discuss with the students (see Step 2).

✓ Create your own class blog and create a page for yourself and each student, linked from the home page. For information about creating a class blog with student links, view the "Preparing a Class Blog" tutorial (AV25) and the "Preparing Student Blogs" tutorial (AV26). After selecting a blogging platform, familiarize yourself with the procedures so that you can introduce them to the students in Step 3.

AV25   AV26

✓ Bookmark the blog to display on the whiteboard in Step 3.

✓ Prepare the computers so that the students can easily access the class blog when they are ready to post. Set the privacy settings on the blog so that only you and the students can access it. For more information, view the "Setting Up Student Blog Access" tutorial (AV27).

✓ Prepare a chart titled "Our Class Blogging Rules" (see Step 4).

✓ Find out if your school has an acceptable use policy that the students and their families need to sign before the students can use the computers. Be prepared to review it with the students in Step 4.

✓ Select a piece of your own writing and practice posting it to the blog to prepare for the modeling you will do in Step 5.

In this lesson, the students:

- Learn about blogs and explore a sample class blog
- Reflect on class blogging rules
- Learn how to create a blog post
- Discuss sharing computers fairly

ABOUT THE BLOGGING CHECK-IN LESSONS

In the blogging check-in lessons, the students learn about and explore class blogs. They learn how to post their writing, how to comment on others' posts, and how to add other blog features such as header images, photographs, video clips, and styled text using computers in the independent writing area. They discuss the class blogging rules and reflect on what it means to blog safely and respectfully.

This lesson can be adapted for any blogging platform you have selected.

1 Gather the Students and Introduce Blogging

Have the students pick up their toolboxes and gather with partners sitting together, facing the whiteboard.

Remind the students that the Internet is a worldwide resource that millions of people use every day. Using the Internet, or going online, can connect the students to the world and allow them to find interesting facts and information. Tell the students that today you will show them a type of website on the Internet called a *blog*. Explain that a *blog* is a website on which people share information about themselves and show what they are doing and learning.

Ask and briefly discuss:

Q *Have you ever read a blog on the Internet? If so, what was it about?*

2 Explore and Discuss a Class Blog

Tell the students that some teachers and students create blogs to share what they are learning in school. Point out that a blog is like a bulletin board in the classroom, but that it is on the Internet so it can be viewed by people close-by and far away.

Direct the students' attention to the sample class blog displayed on the whiteboard, and point to and read aloud the title of the blog. Next, point out several features of the blog, such as recent posts by the teacher, recent posts by the students, and other useful links or menus.

Ask and briefly discuss:

Q *What do you see on this class's blog? What do you like about it?*

Materials

- Student toolboxes
- Whiteboard with a sample class blog displayed, prepared ahead
- Bookmarked class blog, prepared ahead for projection onto the whiteboard
- "Our Class Blogging Rules" chart, prepared ahead, and a marker
- Self-stick notes

Teacher Note

This lesson will take 40–45 minutes.

Point out that class blogs help you learn information about the teacher and the students. Ask:

Q *What is something you learned about the students or the teacher from their class blog?*

Have a few students share their thinking with the class.

3° Introduce Your Class Blog

Tell the students that you have created a class blog. Explain that it is a place where you will share what is happening in the class, what the students are learning, and tell about any special events. Point out that for now, only you and the students will be able to read the blog. Later, you will give the students' families access so that they can also read the blog.

Display the class blog, log in, and point to and read the title of the blog aloud. Read aloud the information you have already posted; then have partners discuss:

Q *What do you see on our class blog? Turn to your partner.*

Signal for the students' attention and have one or two pairs share with the class. Explain that the students will have the chance to post, or share their learning, on the blog using computers during independent writing time. Point to the links with the students' names and explain that each link leads to a student's own page on the blog. Then log out and close the blog page.

4 Discuss the Class Blogging Rules

Explain that you will show the students how to post their writing on the blog, but that first you will discuss some rules they need to follow to stay safe when they go online and post to the blog.

Tell the students that before they post something, they each need to log in to the blog by typing a username as well as a password that you will give them ahead of time. Explain that passwords are private and that the students will not share their passwords with anyone. Also, they will use only their first names when they use the site, and they will not share other any contact information such as phone numbers and e-mail addresses. Point out that whenever they use a computer in school, they need to follow the school's computer rules.

Post the "Our Class Blogging Rules" chart and read aloud each rule to the class.

Teacher Note

Because you will demonstrate how to access the blog and log in in Step 5, you will need to close the page after this step.

Teacher Note

If your school has an acceptable use policy that the students and their families need to sign before they students can use the computers, review it with the students and confirm that the search engine settings are set to "Strict," Safe," or a comparable mode.

> # Our Class Blogging Rules
>
> We follow all school computer rules.
>
> We keep contact information private.
>
> We keep passwords private.

Use "Think, Pair, Share" to discuss why each rule is important. Ask:

Q *Why is it important to [keep your passwords private] when blogging?* *[pause] Turn to your partner.*

After a moment, have a few volunteers share their thinking with the class.

> **Students might say:**
>
> "If other people know our passwords, they can change our posts."
>
> "The blog will share what we are learning in class, and people don't need to know how to e-mail us."
>
> "We are not allowed to use the computers if we don't follow the school's rules."

Explain that you would like the students to commit to following these rules before posting on the blog.

5 Model How to Create a Post

Direct the students' attention to the whiteboard and tell them that now you will show them how to create a post on the blog. Demonstrate how to find the blog and then how to log in using a username and password. Review that you will give each of the students individual passwords and that you will always know the passwords if they forget them. Review that they will post on their own page of the blog, and point to the menu with the students' names. Explain that when a student clicks her name, her own page will appear.

Ask the students to watch and listen as you model and describe each step for adding a post.

Teacher Note

If the students will use tablets in the independent writing area, model creating a post with a tablet rather than with a computer.

Teacher Note

For information about choosing and managing student passwords, view the "Blogging Tips and Tricks" tutorial (AV28).

You might say:

"When I click **New Post**, a window appears for me to add my writing. I want to post a poem I wrote last week titled 'Golden Fields.' I see a box for the title, so I will type it there. [Type in the title.] I will type my poem in the large box below. [Type in the poem.] Before I save it, I will read it again to make sure it is correct and that I am happy with what I wrote. When I am ready, I need to choose **Draft**, **Review**, or **Publish**. I am going to click **Draft** to save my writing so that I can work on it later. When you post your writing, if you want to save it and work on it later, you will click **Draft**. If you are finished, you will click **Review**, then I will review your post before it appears on the blog. [Click **Draft**.] When I am ready, I can post it by clicking **Publish**. After I am finished, I will log out so that my blog page doesn't appear when the next person uses this computer." [Show the students how to log out.]

Tell the students that if they do not finish a post during independent writing time, they can finish it the next time they are in the writing area. Remind them that you will always review their posts before they appear on the blog. Ask and briefly discuss:

Q *What questions do you have about creating a post?*

6 Choose Writing to Post on the Blog

Explain that now the students will each choose a piece of writing from their independent writing notebooks to post on the blog when they work in the independent writing area this week.

Give the students a few minutes to review their writing and choose one piece each to post on the blog. Distribute a self-stick note to each student and have him use it to mark the piece of writing he chose; then signal for the students' attention.

Ask:

Q *What piece of writing did you choose to post on the blog? Why did you choose that piece?*

Have one or two volunteers share with the class; then have the students return their notebooks to their toolboxes.

7 Discuss Sharing the Computers

Review that the students will use computers to create the blog posts, and explain that it is important that they use them responsibly and fairly. Ask:

Q *What can you do if there are not enough computers for everyone to use?*

Q *What is important to remember if you are posting on the blog and other students are waiting to post?*

Q *What can you do if it is time to move to another independent work area and you did not get a chance to post on the blog?*

Have a few students share their thinking with the class.

> **Students might say:**
>
> "If there isn't a computer available, I'll work in my writing notebook and wait my turn."
>
> "We can each work for only part of the time, like 10 minutes each."
>
> "I can wait to post on another day."
>
> "I will remember that I don't get to post my writing every time I'm in the writing area."

Add the following rule to the "Our Class Blogging Rules" chart: *We use the computers in fair and responsible ways.*

Add the following rule to the "Our Class Blogging Rules" chart: *We use the computers in fair and responsible ways.*

Our Class Blogging Rules

We follow all school computer rules.

We keep contact information private.

We keep passwords private.

We use the computers in fair and responsible ways.

---

8 Wrap Up

Review that the next time the students work in the independent writing area, they may post their writing to the class blog. Tell the students that you will review and discuss the blog posts with the class throughout the year. Ask and briefly discuss:

Q *What do you think you will like about posting on the blog? What might be challenging?*

Q *Why is it important to follow the class blogging rules?*

Tell the students that in the next blogging lesson they will learn how to comment on each other's posts.

Teacher Note

If the students have difficulty answering these questions, offer some examples such as those in the "Students might say" note.

Teacher Note

Post the "Our Class Blogging Rules" chart near the independent writing area. You will use it again in the "Blogging 2" check-in lesson.

Teacher Note

Before the next independent work time, prepare the computers your students will use for blogging and make them available in the independent writing area. If you have not already done so, set up the computers so that the students can easily access the blog on the desktop.

Follow-up Tip

Follow up by asking questions such as the following at the beginning of independent work time this week, and provide any necessary support:

Q *What questions do you have about posting to the blog?*

Q *What will you do to use the computers responsibly and fairly?*

Q *What can you do if you need help with your post?*

Q *What can you do if you forget your password?*

Q *What can you do to help yourself remember the class blogging rules?*

Throughout the week, review the students' posts to assess what is going well and what kind of additional support or instruction is needed. Be prepared to share your observations with the class in the next check-in lesson. Address any challenges the students are facing by reviewing and discussing the blog posts as a class, and by assisting individual students whenever possible.

Check-in | Blogging 2

⏰ DO AHEAD

✓ Review the students' blog posts from the previous week and think about what is going well and what kind of support the students need. Prepare to share your observations and review any procedures in Step 1.

✓ Select a few of the students' blog posts from the previous week to share and discuss with the class in Step 2.

✓ Visit the CCC Learning Hub (ccclearninghub.org) to access "Primary Class Blog Resources" (BLM2). Choose a blog with examples of respectful student comments to share with the class in Step 3.

✓ Add the rules about using respectful language to the "Our Class Blogging Rules" chart (see Step 4). Cover the new rules with another sheet of paper until you introduce them in Step 4.

✓ Familiarize yourself with the comment feature on the class blog and practice adding comments to prepare for the modeling you will do in Step 5.

In this lesson, the students:

- Reflect on how they are doing with blogging
- Learn how to comment on blogs
- Reflect on using respectful language on blogs

Materials

- Whiteboard with class blog login page displayed, prepared ahead
- Bookmarked sample class blog, prepared ahead for projection onto the whiteboard
- "Our Class Blogging Rules" chart from Blogging 1 check-in lesson

1 Gather and Review the Class Blog

Gather the students with partners sitting together, facing the whiteboard. Remind the students that they have been posting writing to their own page of the class blog during independent writing. Ask and briefly discuss:

Q *What went well with posting to the blog this week? What was challenging?*

If necessary, show the students how to access the blog and again model how to log in using a username and password. Share some of your own observations about how the students did with posting to the blog this week and briefly review any procedures for which the students need support.

Teacher Note

This lesson will take 40–45 minutes.

2 Discuss the Students' Posts

Explain that now the class will look at some of the posts the students added this week. Direct the students' attention to the displayed class blog, click on a student's name and read aloud the post. Ask:

Q *What do you like about [Annabelle's] post?*

Q *What else would you like to say to or ask [Annabelle] about her post?*

Have a few students share their thinking with the class.

> **Students might say:**
>
> "I liked how she described the dog in her story."
>
> "The end of the story surprised me!"
>
> "I want to ask her where she got the idea for the story."

Repeat this procedure with another student's post. Then log out and close the blog.

Teacher Note

If necessary, remind the students that it is important to be positive and respectful when commenting on another student's writing.

3 Introduce Commenting and Discuss a Blog from Another Class

Tell the students that today they will learn how to leave a comment about each other's writing on the blog. Explain that before you show them how to leave a comment, they will discuss the posts and comments on another class's blog.

Display the sample class blog, click one of the student's posts, and read the post aloud. Next, point out the comments following the post and read them aloud. Ask the students to think about the comments for the post; then have partners discuss:

 Q *Are the comments for this post respectful? Why or why not? Turn to your partner.*

After a few moments, signal for the students' attention and have one or two pairs share their thinking with the class.

> **Students might say:**
>
> "I think they are respectful because most of them tell what they like about the post."
>
> "The second comment asks a question about the writing. It helps the writer think more about his writing."

Then ask and briefly discuss:

Q *How do you think you would feel if you saw comments like this on your post?*

4 Discuss Showing Respect When Commenting on Blogs

Point out that just as the students are expected to be respectful when they talk to someone face-to-face, they are expected to be respectful when they post comments on a blog.

Direct the students' attention to the "Our Class Blogging Rules" chart and uncover the rules you added to it. Read each new rule to the class:

Our Class Blogging Rules

We always use respectful language in our writing.

We think about others' feelings before we post a comment.

We reread what we write before posting to the blog or commenting.

Teacher Note

Post the revised "Our Class Blogging Rules" chart near the independent writing area after the lesson.

Use "Think, Pair, Share" to have partners discuss why each rule is important. Ask:

 Q *Why is it important to [think about others' feelings before posting a comment]? [pause] Turn to your partner.*

After a few moments, signal for the students' attention and have a few volunteers share their thinking with the class.

> **Students might say:**
>
> "You can't see the person's face when commenting on a blog, so it is hard to tell how he feels."
>
> "We always need to be respectful, and it's no different when we post comments."
>
> "Rereading what you wrote helps you think about how it might sound to the other person."

Explain that the students need to follow these rules when posting writing or comments on blogs.

5 Model How to Post a Comment

Direct the students' attention to the whiteboard and tell the students that now you will demonstrate how to post a comment on your own class blog. Review how to open the blog and how to log in. Remind the students that they need to use a password whenever they want to access the class blog.

Ask the students to watch and listen as you model and describe each step for commenting on a post.

> **You might say:**
>
> "When I click another student's post [click on a student's post], a window appears below the post that says, **Leave a comment**. I can see my name above the comment box. First I will read the post and then think about what I want to say to Carlos about his writing. [Read the post aloud.] I really like Carlos's post about the baseball game he played in over the weekend. I can tell how much he loves playing baseball, so I am going to tell him that in my comment. I also want to know what the name of his team is, so I will ask that question. [Type your thinking into the comment box.] Now I will reread my writing to make sure it is respectful and helpful. [Read your writing aloud.] When I am ready, I need to click the **Comment** button to post my comment. [Click **Comment**.] After I am finished, I will log out." [Show the students how to log out.]

Ask and briefly discuss:

Q *What questions do you have about posting a comment on the blog?*

Teacher Note

If the students use tablets in the independent writing area, model creating a post with a tablet rather than with a computer.

Teacher Note

For information about choosing and managing student passwords, view the "Blogging Tips and Tricks" tutorial (AV28).

6 | Wrap Up

Tell the students that the next time they work in the independent writing area, they can choose to post writing to the blog or to comment on another student's post. Remind them to always use respectful language in their posts and comments, and review that you will always read their posts and comments before they appear on the blog.

Explain that in the next blogging lesson, the students will learn how to use more features on the blog, such as adding pictures or video clips and styling text.

Follow-up Tip

Follow up by asking questions such as the following at the beginning of independent work time over the next few days, and provide any necessary support:

Q *What questions do you have about [posting a comment]?*

Q *What will you do to use the computers responsibly and fairly?*

Q *What can you do if you need help with your post?*

Q *What can you do if you forget your password?*

Q *What can you do to help yourself remember the class blogging rules?*

Review the students' posts and any comments they make on other students' posts to assess what is going well and what kind of additional support or instruction is needed. Be prepared to share your observations with the class in the next check-in lesson. Address any challenges the students are facing by reviewing and discussing the blog posts as a class and by assisting individual students whenever possible.

⏱ DO AHEAD

✓ Review the students' blog posts and comments from the previous week, and think about what is going well and what kind of support the students need. Prepare to share your observations and review any procedures in Step 1.

✓ Visit the CCC Learning Hub (ccclearninghub.org) to access "Primary Class Blog Resources" (BLM2). Choose a blog that incorporates features that the students have not yet learned (such as header images, pictures, video clips, or styled text). Bookmark the blog to discuss with the class in Step 2.

✓ Familiarize yourself with the various blog features available to the students and practice adding them to a post to prepare for the modeling you will do in Step 3.

✓ Change the privacy settings on the class blog to give the students' families access to the blog. You will discuss the new blog audience with the students in Step 4. For information, view the "Expanding the Blog Audience" tutorial (AV29).

In this lesson, the students:

- Reflect on how things are going with blogging
- Learn how to add new blogging features to their posts
- Discuss the blog audience

1 Gather and Review Posting and Commenting on the Class Blog

Gather the students with partners sitting together, facing the whiteboard. Remind the students that they have been posting writing to their own pages of the class blog and also commenting on other students' posts during independent writing. Ask and briefly discuss:

Q *What went well with posting or commenting on the blog this week? What was challenging?*

Share some of your own observations about how the students did with posting or commenting on the blog this week. Briefly review any

Materials

- Whiteboard with class blog displayed, prepared ahead
- Bookmarked sample class blog, prepared ahead for projection on the whiteboard

Teacher Note

This lesson will take 40–45 minutes.

procedures for which the students need support, and remind them to follow the class blogging rules whenever they post to the blog.

2 Explore New Blog Features

Tell the students that today they will learn how to add new features to their posts, such as pictures, video clips, or styled text. Explain that you will show them another class's blog and that you would like them to pay attention to any features in the blog that they might want to use in their own posts. Display the sample class blog, click one of the students' posts, and read the post aloud. Ask:

Q *What do you like about this blog? Why do you like it?*

Q *What is a feature on this blog that you would like to use in your own posts?*

Have a few students share their thinking with the class. If necessary, point out any features they do not mention.

> **Students might say:**
>
> "I like how she added a picture of a dog. It's like an illustration for her story."
>
> "I like the fancy font she used for her story. It makes the whole page look more interesting."
>
> "I want to learn how to add a video."

Teacher Note

If the students use tablets in the independent writing area, model creating a post with a tablet rather than with a computer.

3 Model How to Add New Blog Features

Explain that now you will show the students how to add some of these new features on the blog. Display your class's blog.

Ask the students to watch and listen as you model and describe how to add a new feature.

> **You might say:**
>
> "I want to add a picture in the *header*, or top section, of my last post. I will click my last post to open it up [click on your most recent post] and when I do, I see an **Edit** button. I need to click this button before I can make any changes to the post. [Click the **Edit** button.] Now I can add an image at the top by clicking **Add Header Image**. [Click **Add Header Image**.] When I click that button, a menu appears. I can use a picture on my computer, take a new picture, or choose another available image. When I click **Headers**, I see the headers that are available to me. [Click **Headers**.] When I move my cursor over an image, it gives me the option to **Add**, which would add the header to my post. [Choose a header and click **Add**.] Now the header appears in my post. Since I made changes to this post, I have to save it by clicking **Update**. [Click **Update**.] After I am finished, I will log out." [Show the students how to log out.]

Ask and briefly discuss:

Q *What questions do you have about [adding a header image] to the blog?*

Repeat this procedure for at least one other blog feature. Explain that when the students go to the independent writing area this week, they can choose to add a new feature to their posts, post writing, or post a comment.

4 Discuss the Blog Audience

Explain that up to this point, the audience for the class blog—the people who can see the blog—has been just you and the students. Tell the students that you will invite their parents, guardians, and other family members to read the blog to help them know what is happening in the class.

Use "Think, Pair, Share" to have partners discuss:

 Q *How does it feel knowing that your families will be able to read our classroom blog?* [pause] *Turn to your partner.*

After a few moments, signal for the students' attention and have a few volunteers share their thinking with the class.

> **Students might say:**
>
> "I am glad because I have been telling my grandma all about our class blog!"
>
> "I think it will be a good way for families to see what we are doing in school."
>
> "I am a little nervous knowing other people will be able to see my writing."

5 Wrap Up

Tell the students that the next time they work in the independent writing area, they can add a new feature to their posts, post new writing, or comment on another student's post. Remind them that you will always review their posts before they appear on the blog.

> **Follow-up Tip**
>
> Follow up by asking questions such as the following at the beginning of independent work time this week, and provide any necessary support:
>
> **Q** *What questions do you have about [posting a comment]?*
>
> **Q** *What will you do to use the computers responsibly and fairly?*
>
> **Q** *What can you do if you need help with your post?*
>
> **Q** *What can you do if you forget your password?*
>
> **Q** *What can you do to help yourself remember the class blogging rules?*
>
> Throughout the year, review the students' posts and comments to assess what is going well and what kind of additional support or instruction is needed. Review the "Our Class Blogging Rules" chart periodically during the year, and address any challenges the students are facing by reviewing and discussing the blog posts as a class and by assisting individual students whenever possible.

Teacher Note

You will not have time during this lesson to show the students how to use every available blog feature. Depending on the students' interests, take time on another day or at the beginning of independent work time to model how to add additional features. In many classrooms, the students discover a range of features on their own as they blog.

⏱ DO AHEAD

✓ Preview this lesson and consider the new material you plan to introduce. Do any necessary preparations. For example, if you are introducing new word work or writing material, prepare and label a bin with enough new materials for the number of students who will visit the area at any one time. If you are introducing a game, familiarize yourself with the game's directions and consider any modifications you might want to make.

✓ Consider how you will describe the new material to the students and any procedures you want them to follow when working with the new material (see Step 1).

Materials

- New material, prepared ahead
- Student toolboxes

In this lesson, the students:

- Learn about using new material in the word work, writing, or reading area
- Handle materials responsibly
- Share materials fairly

ABOUT THE INTRODUCE NEW MATERIALS CHECK-IN LESSON

In this lesson, the students are introduced to a new material in one of the independent work areas. Introducing new materials from time to time will help maintain the students' interest in independent work activities and will give them opportunities to apply and practice what they have learned in reading, writing, and word work.

1 Gather and Introduce Using a New Material

Have the students pick up their toolboxes and gather with partners sitting together, facing you. Explain that today you will introduce a new material for the students to use in an independent work area.

Show the students the new material and tell them in which independent work area they will use it. Ask them to listen as you describe how to use the material and specify the procedures you would like them to follow when working with the material.

You might say:

> "These materials are for 'Sight Word Bingo,' which you will use in the word work area. There are cards with sight words, bingo mats with a sight word in each square, and playing chips. Players take turns turning over a card and reading the word aloud. Then the players each look to see if they have the word on their mats. If they do, they cover the word with a chip. The game ends when one player has covered all the squares in a straight line: up-and-down, side-to-side, or diagonally."

Model how to use the material and, if necessary, have a volunteer help you model. When you are finished, facilitate a discussion about the new material by asking and discussing questions such as:

Q *What questions do you have about [playing "Sight Word Bingo"]?*

Q *What else might you do with ["Sight Word Bingo"] in the [word work] area?*

2 Discuss Using the New Material

Remind the students that it is important they use the materials in the independent work areas responsibly. Have partners discuss:

 Q *What can you do to share ["Sight Word Bingo"] fairly? Turn to your partner.*

After a few moments, signal for the students' attention and have a few volunteers share their thinking with the class.

Then ask and briefly discuss:

Q *What is important to remember when cleaning up ["Sight Word Bingo"]?*

Q *What can you do or say if you think your partner needs some help [reading the word on the card]?*

Explain that the students who go to the area with the new material today may choose to use the new material, and that students who do not go to the area with the new material will have the chance to use it another day.

3 Work Independently: Two Rotations (about 20 minutes)

Have the students take their toolboxes and line up, one independent work group at a time. Send one group at a time to the appropriate independent work area to begin working. Observe the students who are working with the new material, offering support as needed.

ELL Note

You might provide the prompt "We can share ['Sight Word Bingo'] fairly by . . ." to your English Language Learners to help them verbalize their answers to the question.

Teacher Note

You may want to have the students do one long independent work rotation rather than two shorter ones today.

After about 10 minutes, signal for cleanup. Then have the students stand with their toolboxes and move to the next work area. Continue to observe the students who work with the new material, offering support as needed.

After about 10 minutes, signal to let the students know that independent work time is over. Have them clean up, return their toolboxes, and gather sitting, facing you.

4 Reflect on Working with the New Material

Ask and briefly discuss:

Q *If you used the new material today, how did it go?*

Q *What did you like about [playing "Sight Word Bingo"]? What was challenging about it?*

Remind the students that if they did not have the chance to work with the new material today, they will get to work with it on another day.

Follow-up Tip

Follow up by asking questions such as the following at the beginning of independent work time over the next few days:

Q *What can you do to share ["Sight Word Bingo"] fairly?*

Q *What can you do to play ["Sight Word Bingo"] fairly?*

Q *What is important to remember when cleaning up ["Sight Word Bingo"]?*

Throughout the year, repeat this lesson whenever you want to introduce a new material into an independent work area.

Work Habits | Check-in

In this lesson, the students:

- Reflect on how they are doing during independent work time
- Discuss ways to improve on a specific work habit
- Work responsibly

ABOUT THE WORK HABITS CHECK-IN LESSON

In this lesson, the students reflect on what is going well during Independent Work and what is challenging about it. They discuss how they might improve on a specific work habit, and they have the opportunity to practice the work habit during independent work rotations as you observe and support them as needed. Providing time for the students to reflect on and improve their work habits throughout the year will help them maintain successful independent work rotations throughout the year.

1 Gather and Discuss Independent Work

Have the students pick up their toolboxes and gather sitting, facing you. Ask them to put their toolboxes on the floor in front of them. Explain that today the students will discuss how they are working independently.

Direct the students' attention to the "Ways We Work on Our Own" chart and review that these are the work habits the students use during independent work rotations. Read each work habit aloud; then ask and discuss:

Q *What work habits are going well?*

Q *What habits do you still need to work on?*

> **Students might say:**
>
> "We usually use quiet voices."
>
> "I think we get started on our work right away."
>
> "Materials get lost when we don't take care of them."
>
> "Sometimes we don't work for the whole time."

Choose a work habit that the students mention they need to work on; then ask and discuss:

Q *Why do you think it's important to [work for the whole time]?*

Q *What can you do to [work for the whole time]?*

Q *What can you do or say to remind someone else to [work for the whole time]?*

Materials

- Student toolboxes
- "Ways We Work on Our Own" chart

Teacher Note

Choosing just one work habit to focus on today will increase the likelihood that the students will effectively use the work habit during independent work time.

Explain that the students will have an opportunity to practice this work habit during their independent work today and that you will observe and support them as they work. Tell them that you will check in at the end of the lesson to see how they did.

2 Work Independently: One Rotation (about 15 minutes)

Have the students line up, one independent work group at a time. Send one group at a time to the appropriate independent work area to begin working. Walk around and observe, assisting the students as needed. Note your observations to share with the class at the end of the lesson.

After about 15 minutes, signal for cleanup. Have the students return their toolboxes and gather sitting, facing you.

3 Reflect on the Work Habit

Ask and briefly discuss:

Q *What did you do to [work for the whole time] today?*

Q *What did you do or say to remind someone else to [work for the whole time]?*

Without mentioning any names, share some of your own observations with the class.

Follow-up Tip

Follow up by asking questions such as the following as the students begin independent work over the next few days:

Q *What can you do to [work for the whole time]?*

Q *What can you do or say to remind someone else to [work for the whole time]?*

Q *Why is it important to [work for the whole time]?*

Teacher Note

If necessary, remind the students to practice the focus work habit, and support them in doing so.

Teacher Note

Have the students focus on improving other work habits by repeating this lesson at other times during the year.

⏲ DO AHEAD

✓ Visit the CCC Learning Hub (ccclearninghub.org) to access and print the "Independent Work Observation Class Assessment Record" sheet (CA1); see page 122 of the *Assessment Resource Book*.

In this lesson, the students:

- Reflect on ways to improve how they work independently
- Work responsibly

ABOUT THE INDEPENDENT WORK OBSERVATION CHECK-IN LESSON

In this lesson, the students work independently while you observe how they use the independent work routines, procedures, and work habits. Afterward, you share your observations with the students and they reflect on what they can do to improve in their independent work. Taking the time to support the students in using the independent work routines, procedures, and work habits will help them maintain successful independent work rotations throughout the year.

Materials

- Student toolboxes
- "Ways We Work on Our Own" chart
- "Independent Work Observation Class Assessment Record" sheet (CA1)

1 Gather and Get Ready to Work

Have the students pick up their toolboxes and gather sitting, facing you. Ask them to put their toolboxes on the floor in front of them. Tell the students that today they will work in the independent work areas while you walk around the room and observe. Direct the students' attention to the "Ways We Work on Our Own" chart and read it aloud. Explain that you will observe how the students use these work habits as well as other independent work procedures and routines. Tell the students that you will share your observations with the class at the end of independent work time.

2 Work Independently:
Two Rotations (about 20 minutes)

Have the students pick up their toolboxes and line up, one independent work group at a time. Send one group at a time to the appropriate independent work area to begin working. As the students work, walk around and observe.

CLASS ASSESSMENT NOTE

Observe the students and ask yourself:

- Do the students get started right away?
- Do they use quiet voices?
- Do the students handle materials responsibly and share them fairly?
- Do they play games fairly?
- Are the students able to work the whole time?
- Are the students able to rotate between independent work areas calmly and quietly?

Be ready to share your observations with the class during the reflection at the end of the lesson. Record your observations on the "Independent Work Observation Class Assessment Record" sheet (CA1); see page 122 of the *Assessment Resource Book*.

After about 10 minutes, signal for cleanup and have the groups move to the next independent work area. Continue to walk around, observe, and record your observations.

After about 10 minutes, signal for cleanup. Have the students bring their toolboxes and gather sitting, facing you.

3 Discuss Observations

Ask the students to listen as you share your observations of what went well during independent work time.

> **You might say:**
>
> "I noticed you started working right away, which helped you use your time to learn and become better readers and writers. I also noticed that you shared the materials so that all the students in your area could use them. You also used quiet voices, which helped everyone focus on their work."

Then ask and briefly discuss:

Q *What else do you think went well?*

Next, ask the students to listen as you share one thing you would like them to improve on.

> **You might say:**
>
> "I noticed that some students didn't stop and clean up after hearing the signal. After I signaled, they kept playing a game or reading books."

Teacher Note

Focus on just one routine, procedure, or work habit for the students to improve upon today. Choosing one, rather than several, will allow the students to better incorporate the behavior in their independent work.

Ask and discuss:

Q *Why is it important to [stop and clean up when you hear the signal] during independent work time?*

4 Discuss and Model the Routine, Procedure, or Work Habit

Tell the students that now you will ask a volunteer to help you model the routine, procedure, or work habit that the students need to improve on. Explain that you would like the rest of the class to watch and think about what it looks like and sounds like to use the routine, procedure, or work habit.

Ask a volunteer to help you model using the routine, procedure, or work habit. Then ask and briefly discuss:

Q *What does [stopping and cleaning up when you hear the signal] look like? What does it sound like?*

> **Students might say:**
>
> "As soon as you heard the signal, you put the materials away."
>
> "You were quiet when you cleaned up."
>
> "You looked ready to move to the next area."

Explain that now the students will have an opportunity to practice this during independent work time. Tell them that you will check in at the end of the lesson to see how they did.

5 Work Independently: Third Rotation (about 10 minutes)

Have the students in each group line up quietly with their toolboxes. Send one group at a time to the appropriate independent work area to begin working. As the students work, walk around and observe, noting your observations.

After about 10 minutes, signal for cleanup. Have the students return their toolboxes and gather sitting, facing you.

6 Reflect on the Routine, Procedure, or Work Habit

Ask and briefly discuss:

Q *How did you do with [stopping and cleaning up when hearing the signal] during independent work time today?*

Q *What did you do or say to remind someone else to [stop and clean up when hearing the signal]?*

Teacher Note

If necessary, remind the students to practice the routine, procedure, or work habit, and support them in doing so.

Without mentioning any names, share some of your observations about how the students did with the routine, procedure, or work habit during the last independent work rotation.

Follow-up Tip

Follow up by asking questions such as the following when the students begin independent work over the next few days:

Q *What does [stopping and cleaning up when hearing the signal] look like? What does it sound like?*

Q *What can you do or say to remind someone else to [stop and clean up when hearing the signal]?*

Q *Why is it important to [stop and clean up when hearing the signal] during independent work time?*

Teacher Note

Have the students focus on other routines, procedures, and work habits by repeating this lesson at other times during the year.

Check-in | Share Writing

⏱ DO AHEAD

✓ Write and illustrate a short piece to use for modeling (see Step 1).

Materials

- Student toolboxes
- Writing piece to use for modeling, prepared ahead
- Self-stick note for each student

In this lesson, the students:

- Share independent writing in pairs
- Speak clearly
- Listen carefully

ABOUT THE SHARE WRITING CHECK-IN LESSON

In this lesson, the students each choose a piece of writing from their independent writing to share in pairs. Sharing their writing and hearing from others about their writing provides an important purpose for independent writing as well as a way to get future writing ideas.

1 Gather and Model Sharing Writing

Have the students pick up their toolboxes and gather with partners sitting together, facing you. Ask them to put their toolboxes on the floor in front of them. Explain that today each student will choose one piece of independent writing to share with a partner.

Tell the students that first you will share a piece of your writing with the class and that, as you share, you would like them to pay attention to the way you read your writing.

Read your writing aloud, showing any illustrations; then ask and briefly discuss:

Q   *What did you notice about the way I read my writing?*

If necessary, point out that you spoke clearly and that you held the paper in front of you in a way that did not cover your face.

2 Choose a Piece of Writing and Prepare to Share

Explain that the students will look through their independent writing and each choose a piece of writing to share. Encourage the students to choose pieces they are proud of or that they really enjoyed writing and drawing. Distribute a self-stick note to each student and tell the students to place the self-stick note on the piece of writing they choose.

Give the students a few minutes to review their writing, choose a piece to share, and mark it with a self-stick note; then call for their attention. Ask and briefly discuss:

Q   *What can you do to be a good listener when your partner shares?*

Explain that the students should be ready to tell the class what their partners wrote about.

3 Share Writing in Pairs

 Have partners turn to face each other and take turns sharing their writing with one another. Remind the students to speak clearly, if needed. As partners share, walk around and observe, assisting as needed. After a few minutes, remind partners to change roles if they have not done so already.

After 5–10 minutes, signal for the students' attention; then ask:

Q   *What did your partner write about?*

Q   *What did you like about your partner's writing?*

Have a few volunteers share with the class.

> **Students might say:**
>
> "[Van] wrote down all the things he knows about volcanoes."
>
> "I liked the part in my partner's story where the unicorn was flying."
>
> "I liked [Rachel's] story about her family."

4 Reflect on Sharing Writing

Ask and briefly discuss:

Q   *What did you like about sharing your writing today?*

Without mentioning any names, share your observations about how the students did with listening to one another today.

Teacher Note

Repeat this check-in lesson periodically throughout the year as the students produce more pieces of independent writing.

Follow up by having any students who want to share their writing with the whole class do so at the beginning or at the end of independent work time over the next few days. After each student shares, facilitate a class discussion by asking questions, such as:

Q *What do you like about [Cooper's] writing?*

Q *What questions do you have for [Cooper] about his writing?*

Check-in | Conferring

⏱ DO AHEAD

✓ Visit the CCC Learning Hub (ccclearninghub.org) to access and print the "Independent Work Conference Notes" record sheet (CN1); see page 123 of the *Assessment Resource Book*. Make a class set of copies.

Materials

- Student toolboxes
- Class set of the "Independent Work Conference Notes" record sheet (CN1), prepared ahead

In this lesson, the students:

- Share and discuss in individual conferences with the teacher what is going well and what challenges they are having working independently
- Work responsibly

ABOUT THE CONFERRING CHECK-IN LESSON

In this lesson, you will confer with individual students about their independent work. You will discuss what each student is doing during independent work rotations, what is going well, and what challenges may need to be addressed. These conferences provide an opportunity for the students to share their work with you and for you to note areas in which the students need more support. Each student conference should take about 5 minutes; you will need to devote the check-in lessons over the next few weeks to conferring in order to meet with all the students.

1 Gather and Introduce Conferring

Teacher Note

You may want to explain that you will be able to confer with only some of the students today, but that you will make time to confer with the rest of the students in the coming weeks.

Have the students pick up their toolboxes and gather sitting, facing you. Ask them to put their toolboxes on the floor in front to them. Tell the students that today you will meet, or *confer*, with individual students to talk about what they have been working on, what has been going well, and what has been challenging. Explain that when you confer with individual students, the rest of the class will work in the independent work areas.

2 Confer and Work Independently: One Rotation (about 30 minutes)

Have the students pick up their toolboxes and line up, one independent work group at a time. Send one group at a time to the appropriate independent work area to begin working. Ask one student to bring her toolbox to the small-group reading table for a conference.

 CONFERENCE NOTE

Over the next few weeks, confer individually for a few minutes with each student to learn more about the student's independent work. Ask each student to show you what she is working on, and talk about what is going well and what challenges she is experiencing. As you listen, ask yourself:

- Is this student able to share what she is working on?
- Does this student share things that are going well?
- Does this student share things she is struggling with?

You might support the student by asking questions, such as:

Q *Which area do you enjoy working at? What do you like to do there?*

Q *What is going well for you during independent work time?*

Q *What is hard for you during independent work time? What can I do to help you?*

Q *Which work habits do you use during independent work time?*

Q *What else would you like to be able to do in the [reading/writing/ word work] area?*

Document your observations for each student on an "Independent Work Conference Notes" record sheet (CN1); see page 123 of the *Assessment Resource Book*.

After about 5 minutes, bring the conference to a close and ask the student to join her independent work group. Then ask another student to bring his toolbox to the small-group reading table for a conference.

Confer with as many students as time permits. Then signal to let the students know when independent work time is over. Have the students clean up, return their toolboxes, and return to their seats.

3 Wrap Up

Tell the students that you will continue to confer with them about their independent work in the coming weeks.

Teacher Note

We recommend having the students work at only one independent work area for a longer period today rather than doing two rotations. However, if you think your students are able to rotate successfully during this period, you may choose to do two rotations.

Teacher Note

Over the next few weeks, continue to teach this check-in lesson until you have conferred with all of your students about their independent work.

⏱ DO AHEAD

✓ Consider whether or not the students are ready to start self-selecting independent work areas. Ask yourself: *Are the students able to work responsibly on their own? Are they able to solve most problems that arise on their own? Are they able to stay focused on their work?* If you answer "yes" to these questions, the students are likely ready to select independent work areas themselves.

✓ Consider some of the challenges that might arise when the students self-select independent work areas, and decide on expectations for how you would like the students to work during this time. Title a sheet of chart paper "Choosing Independent Work Areas," and list the guidelines under the title. We suggest making the guidelines simple and clear, and keeping the list relatively short (see examples of guidelines in Step 1).

Materials

- Student toolboxes
- "Choosing Independent Work Areas" chart, prepared ahead
- "Ways We Work on Our Own" chart

In this lesson, the students:

- Discuss what they might enjoy and find challenging about selecting independent work areas
- Select independent work areas
- Work responsibly

ABOUT THE SELF-SELECTING WORK AREAS CHECK-IN LESSON

In this lesson, the students learn the procedures and expectations for self-selecting independent work areas, and they discuss how to do so responsibly and fairly. They think ahead about the challenges that may arise and consider ways to solve potential problems. With time and practice, the students will be able to successfully choose and rotate to independent work areas without your direction. Consider whether you want the students to select their independent work areas every day, a few days a week, or only occasionally.

1 Gather and Introduce Self-selecting Work Areas

Have the students pick up their toolboxes and gather sitting, facing you. Ask them to put their toolboxes on the floor in front of them. Tell the students that during independent work time today, they will choose the areas in which they will work rather than you telling them where to work. Explain that you think they are ready to do this because they have consistently been able to do independent work responsibly, solve problems on their own, and stay focused on their work.

Ask and discuss:

Q   *What might you enjoy about choosing your independent work area?*

Q   *What might be challenging about it?*

Point out that it is important that the students make responsible choices when choosing independent work areas. Ask the students to listen as you share your expectations for choosing independent work areas. Direct the students' attention to the "Choosing Independent Work Areas" chart and read it aloud.

Teacher Note

The guidelines shown are simply suggestions. We suggest you share expectations that work best for you, your students, and your classroom setup.

Choosing Independent Work Areas

Up to eight students can be in one work area at a time.

If you want to read and the reading area is too crowded, you may read a book somewhere else in the classroom.

If you want to write and the writing area is too crowded, you may write in your notebook somewhere else in the classroom.

If the word work area is full, you can do independent reading or writing.

You may stay in a work area for as long as you would like.

You may clean up and move to a different work area at any time if there is room.

---

2 Discuss Self-selecting Work Areas

Facilitate a discussion about self-selecting independent work areas by asking questions, such as:

Q   *What can you do to choose a work area in a responsible way?*

Q   *How can you make choosing work areas fair for everyone?*

Q *What else do you think is important to do or remember when choosing independent work areas?*

Have a few volunteers share their thinking with the class.

> **Students might say:**
>
> "I can think about where I went yesterday and go to a different area today."
>
> "I think my friend and I shouldn't go to the same place. We might talk too much."
>
> "If I want to work in more than one area, I need to remember to move before work time is over."
>
> "I think everyone should remember to walk."

3 Work Independently (20–25 minutes)

Direct the students' attention to the "Ways We Work on Our Own" chart, read it aloud, and remind the students to use these work habits when they are working in the independent work areas today.

Have the students line up, one independent work group at a time; then have each student in the first group choose an independent work area, move to it, and begin working. Repeat with the other two work groups. If necessary, remind the students that if an area is full, they may read a book or write in their notebooks somewhere else in the room.

Have the students work independently for about 20–25 minutes. As they work, walk around and observe, assisting as needed. Remind the students that they can move from one work area to another during the session if they would like and if there is room. Note your observations to share with the class at the end of the lesson.

After 20–25 minutes, signal for the students' attention. Have them clean up, return their toolboxes, and gather sitting, facing you.

4 Reflect on Self-selecting Work Areas

Ask and briefly discuss:

Q *What went well with choosing your own independent work areas today? What would you like to do differently next time?*

Without mentioning any names, share some of your observations about how the students did with choosing and working in the independent work areas today.

> **You might say:**
>
> "I noticed that many of you chose to start with independent reading today. The reading area was too crowded for everyone to read there, so some of you read at your seats. Also, I noticed that when you moved to a different area, you remembered to clean up before you moved."

Point out that the students will use what they learned today to help make the next time they choose independent work areas go smoothly.

Follow-up Tip

Follow up by asking questions such as the following before having the students self-select independent work areas over the next few weeks:

Q *What can you do to choose a work area in a responsible way?*

Q *How can you make choosing work areas fair for everyone?*

Q *What can you do if you would like to work in an area that is already full or too crowded?*

(J) DO AHEAD

✓ Find out if your school has an acceptable use policy that the students and their families need to sign before the students can use tablets in the classroom.

✓ Visit the CCC Learning Hub (ccclearninghub.org) to access "Recommended Primary Apps" (BLM3). Choose an app from the list and familiarize yourself with it.

✓ Load the app onto your classroom tablets and prepare them as needed. Place the classroom tablets in the appropriate independent work area for the app you have chosen.

✓ Collect and prepare any other materials that are necessary for modeling how to use the app (for example, you might ask the students to use headphones when using the tablets).

✓ Set up the necessary equipment so that you can display the app from your tablet onto the whiteboard or project it in another way.

In this lesson, the students:

- Learn how to use a new app
- Discuss sharing the tablets fairly

ABOUT THE INTRODUCE A TABLET APP LESSON

In this lesson, the students are introduced to a tablet app, and they review how to share the tablets fairly.

Materials

- Educational app, chosen ahead from "Recommended Primary Apps" (BLM3)
- Tablet device loaded with the app, prepared ahead for display on the whiteboard
- Classroom tablet devices in an independent work area
- Any other necessary materials, prepared ahead

1 Introduce the App

Have the students gather with partners sitting together, facing the whiteboard. Tell them that today you will introduce them to a new app that they may use during independent work time.

Display the app and ask the students to listen as you introduce the app and tell them what they can do on it. As you demonstrate, you may wish to make a few mistakes so that the students can learn the functionality of the app.

You might say:

"This app is called [app name]. It lets you [write a blog post, draw a
  picture, etc.]. You can open the app and then select . . . ."

"You can use this tool to . . . ."

"You can draw using this tool."

"What might this tool do?"

"How do you think you can save your project?"

"This icon allows you to add sound. You may want to wear your
  headphones when using this feature."

Then ask and discuss:

Q *What questions do you have about using this app?*

Q *What can you do if you need help?*

Tell the students that if they are not using the tablets, they will use the
other materials at the independent work area.

2 Discuss Sharing the Tablets

Tell the students that since there are more students in each independent
work group than there are tablets, they will need to share the tablets
fairly. Ask:

 Q *What can you do to share the tablets fairly? Turn to your partner.*

Have a few volunteers share their thinking with the class.

Teacher Note

If you have enough tablets for every
student in an independent work group to
have one, then you may skip to Step 3.

Students might say:

"We can take turns using them."

"You shouldn't get to use the tablet first every time."

"If all the tablets are being used, I can write and wait for someone
  to finish."

"I'll only use a tablet for part of the time, so another person has time to
  use it."

3 Work Independently:
One Rotation (about 15 minutes)

Have the students pick up their toolboxes and line up, one independent
work group at a time. Send one group at a time to the appropriate
independent work area to begin working.

Observe the students who are working in the area with the tablet
devices, and assist them with the app as needed. Note your observations
to share with the class at the end of the lesson.

After about 15 minutes, signal for cleanup. Have the students return
their toolboxes and gather sitting, facing you.

Reflect on Using the App

Ask and briefly discuss:

Q *For those students who used the app today, what went well?*

Q *What was challenging?*

Q *What questions do you have about using the app?*

Without mentioning any names, share some of your own observations with the class.

Follow-up Tip

Follow up by asking questions such as the following at the beginning of independent work time over the next few days:

Q *What questions do you have about using the app?*

Q *What can you do to share the tablets fairly?*

Q *What can you do if you need help?*

Address any challenges the students are having by providing additional support or instruction.

Appendix C

TEXTS IN THE PROGRAM

WHOLE-CLASS INSTRUCTION

Kindergarten

Week	Title	Author(s)
1	Chicka Chicka Boom Boom	Bill Martin Jr. and John Archambault
2	the alphabet	Monique Felix
3	"The Itsy Bitsy Spider"	traditional
4	I Went Walking	Sue Williams
5	"The More We Get Together"	traditional
6	Hands Can	Cheryl Willis Hudson
7	What Is Round?	Rebecca Kai Dotlich
8	Gossie	Olivier Dunrea
9	"Ten Galloping Horses"	traditional
9	"Five Little Monsters"	Eve Merriam
12	Barnyard Banter	Denise Fleming
13	"Windshield Wipers"	Mary Ann Hoberman
14	"Just Watch"	Myra Cohn Livingston
15	red sled	Lita Judge
16	"It Fell in the City"	Eve Merriam
17	Millions of Snowflakes	Mary McKenna Siddals
18	Walking Through The Jungle	Julie Lacome
19	"One, Two, Buckle My Shoe"	traditional
22	Fish Eyes	Lois Ehlert
23	"Way Down Deep"	Mary Ann Hoberman

(continues)

Kindergarten *(continued)*

Week	Title	Author(s)
24	"I'm a Yellow-bill Duck"	Jack Prelutsky
25	*Five Little Ducks*	illustrated by Penny Ives
26	*Here Are My Hands*	Bill Martin Jr. and John Archambault
27	*I Love Bugs!*	Philemon Sturges
28	*My Favorite Bear*	Andrea Gabriel

Grade 1

Week	Title	Author(s)
1	*This Is the Way We Go to School*	Edith Baer
2	"Willaby Wallaby Woo"	adapted from Dennis Lee
3	*Flower Garden*	Eve Bunting
4	"Hippopotamus Stew"	Joan Horton
5	*Over in the Meadow: A Counting Rhyme*	Louise Voce
6	"Bippity Boppity Bumblebee"	traditional
6	"Kitty Caught a Caterpillar"	Jack Prelutsky
7	*This Little Chick*	John Lawrence
8	*The Busy Little Squirrel*	Nancy Tafuri
11	"Listen"	Margaret Hillert
12	*When Winter Comes*	Nancy Van Laan
13	"In a Winter Meadow"	Jack Prelutsky
14	*Up, Down, and Around*	Katherine Ayres
15	*beetle bop*	Denise Fleming
16	"Kick a Little Stone"	Dorothy Aldis
17	*no two alike*	Keith Baker
18	"The Little Turtle"	Vachel Lindsay
21	*I Love Our Earth*	Bill Martin Jr. and Michael Sampson

(continues)

Grade 1 (continued)

Week	Title	Author(s)
22	"Mice"	Rose Fyleman
22	"Caterpillars"	Aileen Fisher
23	*Listen to the Rain*	Bill Martin Jr. and John Archambault
24	"The Secret Song"	Margaret Wise Brown
25	*The Napping House*	Audrey Wood
26	*Bugs for Lunch*	Margery Facklam
27	*A Pig Is Big*	Douglas Florian
28	*One Duck Stuck*	Phyllis Root

Grade 2

Week	Title	Author
1	*There's an Ant in Anthony*	Bernard Most
11	*Alpha Oops! The Day Z Went First*	Alethea Kontis
30	*Max's Words*	Kate Banks

Set 1

Week	Title	Author	Genre
1	*We Can Read*	Amy Bauman	fiction
2	*We Can't See!*	Amy Bauman	fiction
3	*Nan and Sam*	Kenni Alden	fiction
4	*It Can Sit!*	Amy Helfer	expository nonfiction
Review	*Nat the Rat*	Elizabeth Johnson	fiction
5	*Go Down, Fat Fish*	Corinn Kintz	fiction
7	*Where Is My Hat?*	Valerie Fraser	fiction
Review	*Can You See My Fish?*	Corinn Kintz	fiction
7	*My Cat Dot*	Elizabeth Johnson	fiction
8	*The Kick*	Elizabeth Johnson	fiction
Review	*Kat and Rick Get a Rock*	Elizabeth Johnson	fiction

Set 2

Week	Title	Author	Genre
1	*Rub-a-dub-dub*	Erica J. Green	fiction
2	*Pat and Pam*	Valerie Fraser	fiction
Review	*The Pet*	Elizabeth Johnson	fiction
3	*Gus*	Amy Helfer	fiction
4	*We Have Homes*	Amy Helfer	expository nonfiction
Review	*Wag*	Amy Helfer	fiction

(continues)

Set 2 *(continued)*

Week	Title	Author	Genre
5	*Sled Dogs*	Valerie Fraser	narrative nonfiction
6	*What Vets Do*	Lucy Bledsoe	narrative nonfiction
Review	*We Have Fish*	Valerie Fraser	fiction
7	*Fish for Max*	Amy Helfer	fiction
8	*On the Job*	Amy Helfer	narrative nonfiction
Review	*A Bad Fox*	Amy Helfer	fiction

Set 3

Week	Title	Author	Genre
1	*Buzz, Hum, Tap, Whap, Whiz, Ding-a-ling*	Corinn Kintz	expository nonfiction
2	*The Good Little Ducks, Part 1*	Corinn Kintz	fiction
Review	*The Good Little Ducks, Part 2*	Corinn Kintz	fiction
3	*The Jug of Water*	Rob Arego	fiction
4	*Where Is Mom?*	Rob Arego	fiction
Review	*The Skunk*	Kenni Alden	narrative nonfiction
5	*Drip Drop*	Erica J. Green	fiction
6	*Make Plum Jam*	Erica J. Green	narrative nonfiction
Review	*The Band*	Elizabeth Johnson	fiction
7	*The Spelling Test*	Rob Arego	fiction
8	*Winter Fun*	Rob Arego	narrative nonfiction
Review	*The Clowns*	Rob Arego	fiction

Set 4

Week	Title	Author(s)	Genre
1	*A Hike by the Lake*	Corinn Kintz	fiction
2	*Life in a Plains Tribe, Part 1*	Corinn Kintz	expository nonfiction
Review	*Life in a Plains Tribe, Part 2*	Corinn Kintz	expository nonfiction
3	*Snakes!*	Amy Helfer	expository nonfiction
4	*A Cold Ride*	Amy Helfer	fiction
Review	*Get Out and Get Fit*	Amy Helfer	expository nonfiction
5	*Out My Window*	Amy Bauman	narrative nonfiction
6	*What Little Deer Eat*	Amy Bauman	fiction
Review	*A Good Team*	Kenni Alden and Margaret Goldberg	fiction
7	*Bird School*	Amy Helfer	fiction
8	*Fox Spills the Stars*	retold by Amy Helfer	folktale
Review	*Sharks!*	Amy Helfer	expository nonfiction

Set 5

Week	Title	Author	Genre
1	*Fun Forts*	Lucy Bledsoe	expository nonfiction
2	*Ann's Book Club*	Lucy Bledsoe	fiction
Review	*Ants, Moths, and Wasps*	Lucy Bledsoe	narrative nonfiction
3	*Have You Ever?*	Margaret Goldberg	fiction
4	*Spring on the Farm*	Rob Arego	narrative nonfiction
Review	*Animal Homes*	Rob Arego	expository nonfiction
5	*A Play Day with My Brother Ray*	Lucy Bledsoe	fiction
6	*Cook Food on a Campfire*	Lucy Bledsoe	fiction

(continues)

Set 5 *(continued)*

Week	Title	Author	Genre
Review	*Sailboats*	Lucy Bledsoe	expository nonfiction
7	*Ball Games*	Erica J. Green	expository nonfiction
8	*Dance!*	Valerie Fraser	expository nonfiction
Review	*New School*	Kenni Alden	fiction
9	*Sunny Days, Starry Nights*	Corinn Kintz	expository nonfiction
10	*Scout's Puppies*	Corinn Kintz	fiction
Review	*The Night Skies*	Corinn Kintz	expository nonfiction
11	*The Desert*	Rob Arego	expository nonfiction
12	*The Silver Coins*	Rob Arego	folktale
Review	*The Four Seasons*	Rob Arego	expository nonfiction
13	*Grizzly Bears*	Lucy Bledsoe	expository nonfiction
14	*Glaciers*	Kenni Alden	expository nonfiction
Review	*Glaciers and the Earth*	Kenni Alden	expository nonfiction

Set 6

Title	Author	Genre
Sunny Days, Starry Nights	Corinn Kintz	expository nonfiction
New School	Kenni Alden	fiction
Sailboats	Lucy Bledsoe	expository nonfiction
The Silver Coins	Rob Arego	folktale
Ball Games	Erica J. Green	expository nonfiction

Set 7

Title	Author	Genre
Chameleon!	Joy Cowley	expository nonfiction
Cowgirl Kate and Cocoa: Horse in the House	Erica Silverman	fiction: chapter book
Jellyfish	Ann Herriges	expository nonfiction
Elephant	Wendy Perkins	expository nonfiction
Puffin Peter	Petr Horáček	fiction
Aggie Gets Lost	Lori Ries	fiction: chapter book
Iris and Walter and Cousin Howie	Elissa Haden Guest	fiction: chapter book
What's It Like to Be an Ant?	Jinny Johnson	expository nonfiction
Leon and Bob	Simon James	fiction

Set 8

Title	Author	Genre
The Great Gracie Chase	Cynthia Rylant	fiction
Lightning	Ann Herriges	expository nonfiction
The Polar Bear Son	Lydia Dabcovich	folktale
Ruby Bridges Goes to School	Ruby Bridges	memoir
"Under the Ground"	Rhoda Bacmeister	poetry
"Accidentally"	Maxine W. Kumin	poetry
"I Wouldn't"	John Ciardi	poetry
Koalas	Valerie Bodden	expository nonfiction
Jamaica's Find	Juanita Havill	fiction

Set 9

Title	Author	Genre
Not Norman	Kelly Bennett	fiction
Penguins	Valerie Bodden	expository nonfiction
Happy Like Soccer	Maribeth Boelts	fiction
Golden Gate Bridge	Kate Riggs	expository nonfiction
Gravity	Joy Frisch-Schmoll	expository nonfiction
Earth	Derek Zobel	expository nonfiction
Upstairs Mouse, Downstairs Mole	Wong Herbert Yee	fiction: chapter book
Only One Year	Andrea Cheng	fiction: chapter book

Set 10

Title	Author(s)	Genre
Bink & Gollie	Kate DiCamillo and Alison McGhee	graphic novel
To Be an Artist	Maya Ajmera and John D. Ivanko	nonfiction
"Old Tortoise"	Madeline Comora	poetry
"Every Time I Climb a Tree"	Davis McCord	poetry
I Love Guinea Pigs	Dick King-Smith	narrative nonfiction
The Beckoning Cat	Koko Nishizuka	folktale
Helen Keller	Margaret Davidson	biography

Set 11

Title	Author	Genre
The Tree Lady	H. Joseph Hopkins	biography
My Name Is María Isabel	Alma Flor Ada	fiction: chapter book
Ice Bear	Nicola Davies	narrative nonfiction
"Story"	Eloise Greenfield	poetry
The Key Collection	Andrea Cheng	fiction: chapter book
The Babe & I	David A. Adler	historical fiction

Set 12

Title	Author	Genre
Shark Lady	Ann McGovern	biography
Bee	Kate Riggs	expository nonfiction
Pop's Bridge	Eve Bunting	historical fiction
Fly Away Home	Eve Bunting	fiction
Family Reminders	Julie Danneberg	historical fiction

Appendix D

SCOPE AND SEQUENCE

WHOLE-CLASS INSTRUCTION

SHARED READING	K	1	2
Phonological Awareness/Decoding			
Rhyme	■	■	
Syllables (segmenting, clapping, counting)	■	■	
Letter names and sounds	■		
Word recognition and analysis	■	■	
High-frequency words	■	■	
Recognizing classmates' names	■	■	
Rebuilding sentences	■	■	
Sorting words by concepts, sounds, or syllables	■	■	
Comprehension			
Retelling	■	■	
Making text-to-self connections	■	■	
Making text-to-text connections	■	■	
Making predictions	■	■	
Identifying details and facts in informational text	■	■	
Visualizing	■	■	
Using illustrations to build comprehension	■	■	
Responding to/engaging with text in a variety of modalities	■	■	
Concepts of Print and Book			
Directionality	■	■	
Tracking print	■	■	
Concept of letters and words	■	■	
Front cover, author, illustrator	■	■	
Features of a sentence	■	■	
Different text types: poems, books, stories	■	■	
Recognizing punctuation	■	■	

■ = formally instructed

(continues)

	K	1	2
SHARED READING *(continued)*			
Author's Craft			
Alliteration	■	■	
Rhyme	■	■	
Patterns	■	■	
Onomatopoeia	■	■	
Figurative language	■	■	
Oral Fluency			
Echo reading	■	■	
Choral reading	■	■	
Reading with attention to punctuation	■	■	
Reading with attention to a character's feelings	■	■	
Reading with attention to typography	■	■	
HANDWRITING			
Capital letters	■		
Lowercase letters	■	■	
Punctuation marks	■	■	
Spaces between words		■	
INDEPENDENT WORK			
Handles materials responsibly	■	■	■
Uses a quiet voice	■	■	■
Gets started right away	■	■	■
Works for the whole time	■	■	■
Cleans up	■	■	■
WORD STUDY			
Short vowels			■
Long vowels with final e			■
Complex vowels *ai, ay, oa, ow, igh, y, ee, ea, oo, ew, ou, ow, oi, oy, au, aw*			■
r-controlled vowels *er, ir, ur, ar, or*			■
Inflectional endings *-ed, -ing*			■
Alphabetizing			■
Consonant-*l-e* syllables			■

■ = formally instructed

(continues)

WHOLE-CLASS INSTRUCTION *(continued)*

	K	1	2
WORD STUDY *(continued)*			
Open and closed syllables			■
Syllabication strategies			■
Prefixes *re-, un-*			■
Suffixes *-er, -est, -ly, -or, -ist, -ful, -less, -tion, -ion, -sion, -ment, -ness, -able, -ible*			■
Homophones, synonyms, antonyms			■
Compound words			■

■ = formally instructed

SMALL-GROUP INSTRUCTION

	Small-group Reading for Emerging Readers				
	Set 1	Set 2	Set 3	Set 4	Set 5
Phonological Awareness					
Oral blending	■	■	■	■	■
Oral segmenting	■	■	■	■	■
Identifying beginning sounds	■				
Identifying middle sounds	■	■	■		
Identifying ending sounds	■	■			
Blending onsets and rimes		■	■		
Identifying and producing rhymes			■	■	
Identifying syllables				■	■
Dropping first sound					■
Dropping initial blend					■
Dropping last sound					■
Phonics and Decoding					
Single consonants	■	■	●	●	●
Short vowels/CVC pattern	■	■	●	●	●
th, sh, ch, tch, dge		■	■	●	●
Consonant blends			■	●	●
Inflectional endings *-ed, -ing*			■	■	●
Inflectional endings *-s, -es*			■	■	●
Long vowels/CVCE pattern				■	●
ee, ea				■	●
r-controlled vowels *er, ir, ur, ar, or*				■	●
ai, ay, oa, ow, oo, ew, igh, final *y*					■
all, au, aw					■
wr, kn					■
oi, ow, ou					■
ci, ce, cy					■
Word Analysis					
Reading polysyllabic words			■	■	■
Reading compound words				■	■
Analyzing polysyllabic words					
Recognizing homophones				■	■
High-frequency words	■	■	■	■	■

■ = formally instructed   □ = informally instructed   ● = applied

Small-group Reading for Developing Readers						
Set 6	Set 7	Set 8	Set 9	Set 10	Set 11	Set 12
●	●	●	●	●	●	●
●	●	●	●	●	●	●
●	●	●	●	●	●	●
●	●	●	●	●	●	●
●	●	●	●	●	●	●
●	●	●	●	●	●	●
●	●	●	●	●	●	●
●	●	●	●	●	●	●
●	●	●	●	●	●	●
●	●	●	●	●	●	●
●	●	●	●	●	●	●
●	●	●	●	●	●	●
●	●	●	●	●	●	●
●	●	●	●	●	●	●
■	■	■	●	●	●	●
■	●	■	●	●	●	●
	■	■	●	●	●	●
●	●	●	●	●	●	●
●	●	●	●	●	●	●

(continues)

	Small-group Reading for Emerging Readers				
	Set 1	Set 2	Set 3	Set 4	Set 5
Fluency					
Phrasing (grouping words together)					
Paying attention to punctuation					☐
Paying attention to characters' feelings			■		■
Reading for listeners					
Comprehension					
Exploring text features					☐
Sequencing and retelling			☐	☐	☐
Understanding character (and setting)			☐		☐
Understanding problem and solution					☐
Making text-to-self connections			☐	☐	☐
Making text-to-text connections					☐
Determining topic					
Wondering					
Making and supporting predictions					☐
Determining theme					
Self-monitoring and Self-correcting					
Self-monitoring and Self-correcting					
Generating Independent Thinking					
Sharing and supporting opinions					
Responding to literature					

■ = formally instructed   ☐ = informally instructed   ● = applied

	Set 6	Set 7	Set 8	Set 9	Set 10	Set 11	Set 12
Small-group Reading for Developing Readers							
	■				■		
	■	■	■	■			
	■	■		■	■		
		■	■		■	■	
	■	■	■	■			■
	■	■	■				
		■		■	■	■	
				■		■	
	■	■			■	■	
				■	■	■	■
		■		■		■	
		■	■	■			
		■		■			
					■	■	
			■		■	■	
			■		■		■
			■	■	■	■	■

BIBLIOGRAPHY

Adams, Marilyn J. *ABC Foundations for Young Children: A Classroom Curriculum*. Baltimore: Paul H. Brookes Publishing, 2013.

_____. *Beginning to Read: Thinking and Learning about Print*. Cambridge, MA: MIT Press, 1994.

Afflerbach, Peter. *Essential Readings on Assessment*. Newark, DE: International Reading Association, 2010.

_____. *Understanding and Using Reading Assessment, K-12*. 2nd ed. Newark, DE: International Reading Association, 2012.

Anderson, Richard C., Elfrieda H. Hiebert, Judith A. Scott, and Ian A. Wilkinson. *Becoming a Nation of Readers: The Report of the Commission on Reading*. Washington, DC: The National Institute of Education, 1985.

Ankrum, Julie W., and Rita M. Bean. "Differentiated Reading Instruction: What and How," *Reading Horizons* 48, no.1 (2007): 133-146.

Asher, Asha V. "Handwriting Instruction in Elementary Schools." *American Journal of Occupational Therapy* 60, no. 4 (July/August 2006): 461-471.

Asher, James J. "Children Learning Another Language: A Developmental Hypothesis." *Child Development* 48 (1977): 1040-1048.

_____. "Children's First Language as a Model for Second Language Learning." *The Modern Language Journal* 56 (1972): 133-139.

_____. "The Strategy of Total Physical Response: An Application to Learning Russian." *International Review of Applied Linguistics* 3 (1965): 291-300.

Battistich, Victor, Daniel Solomon, Dong-il Kim, Marilyn Watson, and Eric Schaps. "Schools as Communities, Poverty Levels of Student Populations, and Students' Attitudes, Motives, and Performance: A Multilevel Analysis." *American Educational Research Journal* 32, no. 3 (1995): 627-658.

Bear, Donald R., Marcia Invernizzi, Shane Templeton, and Francine Johnston. *Words Their Way: Word Study for Phonics, Vocabulary, and Spelling Instruction*. 5th ed. Boston: Pearson, 2012.

Beaver, Joetta M. *Developmental Reading Assessment*. Upper Saddle River, NJ: Pearson, 2006.

Beck, Isabel L. *Making Sense of Phonics: The Hows and Whys*. New York: Guilford Press, 2006.

Beck, Isabel L., Margaret G. McKeown, and Linda Kucan. *Bringing Words to Life: Robust Vocabulary Instruction*. New York: Guilford Press, 2002.

Boushey, Gail, and Joan Moser. *The CAFE Book: Engaging All Students in Daily Literacy Assessment & Instruction*. Portland, ME: Stenhouse, 2009.

_____. *The Daily Five*. Portland, ME: Stenhouse, 2006.

Brunn, Peter. *The Lesson Planning Handbook*. New York: Scholastic, 2010.

Burkins, Jan Miller, and Melody M. Croft. *Preventing Misguided Reading: New Strategies for Guided Reading Teachers*. Newark, DE: International Reading Association, 2010.

Calkins, Lucy M. *The Art of Teaching Reading*. New York: Longman, 2001.

Calkins, Lucy, Mary Ehrenworth, and Christopher Lehman. *Pathways to the Common Core: Accelerating Achievement*. Portsmouth, NH: Heinemann, 2012.

Cassidy, Kathy. *Connected from the Start: Global Learning in the Primary Grades*. Virginia Beach, VA: Powerful Learning Press, 2013.

Cummins, James. "The Role of Primary Language Development in Promoting Educational Success for Language Minority Students," in *Schooling and Language Minority Students: A Theoretical Framework*, edited by Charles F. Leyba. Los Angeles: Evaluation, Dissemination, and Assessment Center, California State University, 1981.

Cunningham, Patricia. "Decoding Polysyllabic Words: An Alternative Strategy." *Journal of Reading* 21, no. 7 (1978): 608-614.

daCruz Payne, Carleen. *Shared Reading for Today's Classroom*. New York: Scholastic, 2005.

Dahl, K. L., and P. A. Freppon. *Learning to read and write in inner-city schools: A comparison of children's sense-making in skills-based and whole language classrooms*. (Final Report to the Office of Educational Research and Improvement. U.S. Department of Education, Grant Award No. R117E00134.) Cincinnati, OH: University of Cincinnati, 1992.

Dahl, Karin L, Patricia L. Scharer, Lora L. Lawson, and Patricia. R. Grogan. "Phonics instruction and student achievement in whole language first-grade classrooms." *Reading Research* Quarterly 34, no. 3 (1999): 312-341.

Denton, Paula, and Roxann Kriete. *The First Six Weeks of School*. 2nd ed. Greenfield, MA: Northeast Foundation for Children, 2000.

Developmental Studies Center. *Blueprints for a Collaborative Classroom*. Oakland, CA: Developmental Studies Center, 1997.

——. *Ways We Want Our Class to Be*. Oakland, CA: Developmental Studies Center, 1996.

DeVries, Rheta, and Betty Zan. *Moral Classrooms, Moral Children*. New York: Teachers College Press, 1994.

Dewey, John. *Democracy and Education: An Introduction to the Philosophy of Education*. New York: Macmillan, 1916.

Diller, Debbie. *Literacy Work Stations: Making Centers Work*. Portland, ME: Stenhouse, 2003.

——. *Making the Most of Small Groups: Differentiation for All*. Portland, ME: Stenhouse, 2007.

——. *Practice with Purpose: Literacy Work Stations for Grades 3-6*. Portland, ME: Stenhouse, 2005.

Donohue, Chip, ed. *Technology and Digital Media in the Early Years: Tools for Teaching and Learning*. New York: Routledge, 2015.

Durlak, Joseph A., Roger P. Weissberg, Allison B. Dymnicki, Rebecca D. Taylor, and Kriston B. Schellinger. "The Impact of Enhancing Students' Social and Emotional Learning: A Meta-Analysis of School-Based Universal Interventions." *Child Development* 82, no. 1 (2011): 475-501.

Echevarria, Jana, MaryEllen Vogt, and Deborah J. Short. *Making Content Comprehensible for Elementary English Learners: The SIOP Model*. Boston: Pearson, 2010.

Edge, Nellie. "Guidelines for Teaching Handwriting in Kindergarten: Thoughts on What Works Best," http://www.nellieedge.com/articles_resources/GuidelinesHandwriting.htm (accessed September 28, 2015).

Fisher, Bobbi, and Emily Fisher Medvic. *Perspectives on Shared Reading: Planning and Practice*. Portsmouth, NH: Heinemann, 2000.

Flood, James, Diane Lapp, Douglas Fisher, and Julie M. Jensen, eds. *The Handbook of Research on Teaching the English Language*. Mahwah, NJ: Lawrence Erlbaum Associates, 2002.

Fountas, Irene, and Gay Su Pinnell. *Benchmark Assessment System*. Portsmouth, NH: Heinemann, 2008.

_____. *The Continuum of Literacy Learning, Grades PreK-8: A Guide to Teaching*. 2nd ed. Portsmouth, NH: Heinemann, 2010.

_____. *Guided Reading: Good First Teaching for All Children*. Portsmouth, NH: Heinemann, 1996.

_____. *Teaching for Comprehension and Fluency: Thinking, Talking, and Writing About Reading, K-8*. Portsmouth, NH: Heinemann, 2006.

Fry, Edward B., and Jacqueline E. Kress. *The Reading Teacher's Book of Lists: Grades K-12*. 5th ed. San Francisco: Jossey-Bass, 2006.

Gootman, Marilyn. E. *The Caring Teacher's Guide to Discipline: Helping Young Students Learn Self-control, Responsibility, and Respect*. 2nd ed. Thousand Oaks, CA: Corwin Press, Inc., 2001.

Graham, Steve. "Want to Improve Children's Writing? Don't Neglect Their Handwriting." *American Educator* (Winter 2009-2010): 20-40.

Graves, Michael F., Diane August, and Jeannette Mancilla-Martinez. *Teaching Vocabulary to English Language Learners*. New York: Teachers College Press, 2013.

Hakuta, Kenji, Yuko Goto Butler, and Daria Witt. "How Long Does It Take English Learners to Attain Proficiency?" University of California Linguistic Minority Research Institute Policy Report, 2000.

Harp, Bill. *The Handbook of Literacy Assessment and Evaluation*. Norwood, MA: Christopher-Gordon Publishers, Inc., 1996.

Helman, Lori, Donald Bear, Shane Templeton, Marcia Invernizzi, and Francine Johnston. *Words Their Way with English Learners: Word Study for Phonics, Vocabulary, and Spelling*. 2nd ed. Boston: Pearson, 2012.

Herrell, Adrienne L. *Fifty Strategies for Teaching English Language Learners*. Upper Saddle River, NJ: Merrill, 2000.

Hiebert, Elfrieda H., and Michael L. Kamil, eds. *Teaching and Learning Vocabulary: Bringing Research to Practice*. Mahwah, NJ: Lawrence Erlbaum, 2005.

Hiebert, Elfrieda, and Misty Sailors. *Finding the Right Texts: What Works for Beginning and Struggling Readers*. New York: Guilford Press, 2009.

Hill, Jane D., and Cynthia Bjork. *Classroom Instruction That Works with English Language Learners: Facilitator's Guide*. Denver, CO: Mid-continent Research for Education and Learning, 2008.

Holdaway, Don. *The Foundations of Literacy*. Gosford, Australia: Ashton Scholastic, 1979.

Honig, Bill, Linda Diamond, and Linda Gutlohn. *Teaching Reading Sourcebook for Kindergarten through Eighth Grade*. Novato, CA: Arena Press, 2000.

Johns, Jerry L., and Roberta L. Berglund. *Fluency: Differentiated Interventions and Progress-Monitoring Assessments*. 4th ed. Dubuque, IA: Kendall Hunt, 2010.

Johnson, David W., Roger T. Johnson, and Edythe Johnson Holubec. *The New Circles of Learning: Cooperation in the Classroom and School*. Alexandria, VA: Association for Supervision and Curriculum Development, 1994.

Kagan, Spencer, and Miguel Kagan. *Kagan Cooperative Learning*. San Clemente, CA: Kagan Publishing, 1994.

Kamil, Michael L., P. David Pearson, Elizabeth B. Moje, and Peter P. Afflerbach, eds. *Handbook of Reading Research, Volume IV*. New York: Routledge, 2010.

Keene, Ellin O., and Susan Zimmermann. *Mosaic of Thought: Teaching Comprehension in Reader's Workshop*. 2nd ed. Portsmouth, NH: Heinemann, 2007.

Kindle, Karen J. "Same Book, Different Experience: A Comparison of Shared Reading in Preschool Classrooms." *Journal of Language and Literacy Education* [online] 7, no. 1 (2011): 13-34.

Kingsley, Tara, and Susan Tancock. "Internet Inquiry: Fundamental Competencies for Online Comprehension." *The Reading Teacher* 67, no. 5 (2014): 389-399.

Koenke, Karl. "Handwriting Instruction: What Do We Know? ERIC Digest." *ERIC Digests*, 272923. Urbana, IL: ERIC Clearinghouse on Reading and Communication Skills (1986).

Kohlberg, Lawrence. *The Psychology of Moral Development*. New York: Harper and Row, 1984.

Kohn, Alfie. *Beyond Discipline: From Compliance to Community*. Alexandria, VA: Association for Supervision and Curriculum Development, 1996.

——. *Punished by Rewards: The Trouble with Gold Stars, Incentive Plans, A's, Praise, and Other Bribes*. New York: Houghton Mifflin, 1999.

——. *The Schools Our Children Deserve: Moving Beyond Traditional Classrooms and "Tougher Standards."* Boston: Houghton Mifflin, 1999.

Krashen, Stephen D. *Principles and Practice in Second Language Acquisition*. New York: Prentice Hall, 1982.

——. *Second Language Acquisition and Second Language Learning*. New York: Elsevier, 1981.

——. "TPR: Still a Very Good Idea." *Novelty* 5, no. 4 (1998): 82-85.

Krashen, Stephen D., and Tracy D. Terrell. *The Natural Approach: Language Acquisition in the Classroom*. Englewood Cliffs, NJ: Alemany Press: 1983.

McKay, Rebecca, and William H. Teale. *No More Teaching a Letter a Week*. Portsmouth, NH: Heinemann, 2015.

Moats, Louisa C. *Speech to Print: Language Essentials for Teachers*. 2nd ed. Baltimore: Paul H. Brookes, 2010.

Morrow, Lesley M. *Literacy Development in the Early Years: Helping Children Read and Write*. 7th ed. Boston: Pearson, 2012.

Morrow, Lesley M., and Linda B. Gambrell, eds. *Best Practices in Literacy Instruction*. 4th ed. New York: Guilford Press, 2011.

National Writing Project, with Dànielle Nicole DeVoss, Elyse Eidman-Aadahl, and Troy Hicks. *Because Digital Writing Matters: Improving Student Writing in Online and Multimedia Environments*. San Francisco: Jossey-Bass, 2010.

NCTE/IRA Joint Task Force on Assessment, "Standards for the Assessment of Reading and Writing, Revised Edition (2009)." http://www.ncte.org/standards/assessmentstandards. Also available in print as *Standards for the Assessment of Reading and Writing, Revised Edition*. Newark, DE: The International Reading Association, Inc. and the National Council of Teachers of English, 2010.

Newman, Katherine K., and John Shefelbine. *Guided Spelling: Developing Thoughtful Spellers*. Oakland, CA: Developmental Studies Center, 2008.

Nucci, Larry P., ed. *Moral Development and Character Education: A Dialogue*. Berkeley, CA: McCutchan Publishing Corporation, 1989.

Olsen, Janice Z. *Handwriting Without Tears: 1st Grade Printing Teacher's Guide.* Sixth ed. Gaithersburg, MD: Handwriting Without Tears, 2013.

Optiz, Michael F., ed. *Literacy Instruction for Culturally and Linguistically Diverse Students.* Newark, DE: International Reading Association, 1998.

Opitz, Michael F., and Timothy V. Rasinski. *Goodbye Round Robin.* Portsmouth, NH: Heinemann, 2008.

Osborn, Jean, and Fran Lehr, eds. *Literacy for All: Issues in Teaching and Learning.* New York: Guilford Press, 1998.

Piaget, Jean. *The Child's Conception of the World.* Translated by Joan and Andrew Tomlinson. Lanham, MD: Littlefield Adams, 1969.

_____. *The Moral Judgment of the Child.* Translated by Marjorie Gabain. New York: The Free Press, 1965.

Pinnell, Gay Su, and Irene C. Fountas. *When Readers Struggle: Teaching that Works.* Portsmouth, NH: Heinemann, 2008.

Pressley, Michael. *Reading Instruction that Works: The Case for Balanced Teaching.* 3rd ed. New York: Guilford Press, 2005.

Rasinski, Timothy V. *The Fluent Reader.* 2nd ed. New York: Scholastic, 2010.

Rasinski, Timothy V., ed. *Essential Readings on Fluency.* Newark, DE: International Reading Association, 2009.

Routman, Regie. *Transitions: From Literature to Literacy.* Portsmouth, NH: Heinemann, 1988.

Saperstein Associates. "Handwriting in the 21st Century? Research Shows Why Handwriting Belongs in Today's Classroom: A Summary of Research Presented at Handwriting in the 21st Century? An Educational Summit" (Winter 2012). https://www.hw21summit.com/media/zb/hw21/H2948_HW_Summit_White_Paper_eVersion.pdf.

Schaps, Eric, Victor Battistich, and Daniel Solomon. "Community in School as Key to Student Growth: Findings from the Child Development Project," in *Building Academic Success on Social and Emotional Learning*, ed. Joseph E. Zins, Roger P. Weissberg, Margaret C. Yang, and Herbert J. Walberg. New York: Teachers College Press, 2004.

Schaps, Eric, Catherine Lewis, and Marilyn Watson. "Building Classroom Communities." *Thrust for Educational Leadership* (September 1997).

Schaps, Eric, Esther F. Schaeffer, and Sanford N. McDonnell. "What's Right and Wrong in Character Education Today." *Education Week* 21, no. 2 (2001): 40-44.

Schlagal, Bob. "Classroom Spelling Instruction: History, Research, and Practice." *Reading Research and Instruction* 42, no. 1 (2002): 44-57.

Serravallo, Jennifer. *Teaching Reading in Small Groups: Differentiated Instruction for Building Strategic, Independent Readers.* Portsmouth, NH: Heinemann, 2010.

Shefelbine, John, and Katherine K. Newman. *SIPPS: Systematic Instruction in Phonological Awareness, Phonics, and Sight Words.* Oakland, CA: Developmental Studies Center, 2014.

Snowling, Margaret J., and Charles Hulme, eds. *The Science of Reading: A Handbook.* Oxford: Blackwell Publishers, 2007.

South Australia Department of Education and Children's Services. *Handwriting in the South Australian Curriculum.* Adelaide, Australia: Department of Education and Children's Services, 2007.

Swain, Merrill, and Sharon Lapkin. "Problems in Output and the Cognitive Processes They Generate: A Step Towards Second Language Learning." *Applied Linguistics* 16, no. 3 (1995): 371-91.

Teachers College Reading & Writing Project, "Running Records Assessments," http://readingandwritingproject.org/resources/assessments/running-records (accessed September 29, 2015).

Williams, Joan A. "Classroom Conversations: Opportunities to Learn for ESL Students in Mainstream Classrooms." *The Reading Teacher* 54, no. 8 (2001): 750-57.

Zaner-Bloser Handwriting: Kindergarten Teacher's Edition. Columbus, OH: Zaner-Bloser, 2012.

Zemelman, Steven, Harvey "Smokey" Daniels, and Arthur Hyde. *Best Practice: Bringing Standards to Life in America's Classrooms.* Portsmouth, NH: Heinemann, 2012.

Zeno, Susan M., Stephen H. Ivens, Robert T. Millard, and Raj Duvvuri. *The Educator's Word Frequency Guide.* Brewster, NY: Touchstone Applied Science Associates, 1995.

Zubrzycki, Jaclyn. "Experts Fear Handwriting Will Become a Lost Art." *Education Week* 31, no. 18 (2012): 1-3.